# Canada, Nation Branding and Domestic Politics

After his Liberal Party's surprise victory in the 2015 federal Canadian election, Justin Trudeau declared that "Canada was back" on the world stage. This comprehensive volume highlights issues in the relationship between articulated visions of Canada as a global actor, nation branding and domestic politics, noting the dangers of the politicization of the branding of Canada. It also provides the political context for thinking about 'Brand Canada' in the Trudeau era.

The authors explore the Trudeau government's embrace of political branding and how it plays out in key areas central to the brand, including: Canada's relations with Indigenous peoples; social media and digital diplomacy; and the importance of the Arctic region for Canada's brand, even though it is often ignored by politicians and policymakers. The book asks whether the Trudeau government has lived up to its claim that Canada is back, and highlights the challenges that emerge when governments provide optimistic visions for meaningful transformation, but then do not end up leading meaningful change.

This book will be of great interest to students and scholars of political science, particularly those with a focus on Canada. It was originally published as a special issue of *Canadian Foreign Policy Journal*.

**Richard Nimijean** is Instructor III in the School of Indigenous and Canadian Studies at Carleton University in Ottawa, Canada. His research and publications focus on the politics of branding Canada and the connections between the Canadian national identity and its projection globally, public policy, and domestic politics.

**David Carment** is Professor of International Affairs at Carleton University in Ottawa, Canada, and Editor of *Canadian Foreign Policy Journal*. His most recent books examine state fragility theory and policy and third-party intervention in ethnic conflict. He teaches conflict mediation, bargaining and negotiation, and Canadian foreign policy.

# Canada, Nation Branding and Domestic Politics

*Edited by*
Richard Nimijean and David Carment

LONDON AND NEW YORK

First published 2019
by Routledge
2 Park Square, Milton Park, Abingdon, Oxon, OX14 4RN

and by Routledge
605 Third Avenue, New York, NY 10017

First issued in paperback 2020

*Routledge is an imprint of the Taylor & Francis Group, an informa business*

Chapters 1–2, 5–11 © 2019 The Norman Paterson School of International Affairs
Chapter 3 © 2018 Stephen Brown. Originally published as Open Access.
Chapter 4 © 2019 Rebecca Tiessen and David Black

The right of Rebecca Tiessen and David Black to be identified as authors of this work has been asserted by them in accordance with sections 77 and 78 of the Copyright, Designs and Patents Act 1988.

With the exception of Chapter 3, no part of this book may be reprinted or reproduced or utilised in any form or by any electronic, mechanical, or other means, now known or hereafter invented, including photocopying and recording, or in any information storage or retrieval system, without permission in writing from the publishers. For details on the rights for Chapter 3, please see the chapter's Open Access footnote.

All rights reserved. No part of this book may be reprinted or reproduced or utilised in any form or by any electronic, mechanical, or other means, now known or hereafter invented, including photocopying and recording, or in any information storage or retrieval system, without permission in writing from the publishers.

*Trademark notice*: Product or corporate names may be trademarks or registered trademarks, and are used only for identification and explanation without intent to infringe.

*British Library Cataloguing in Publication Data*
A catalogue record for this book is available from the British Library

Typeset in Myriad Pro
by Newgen Publishing UK

**Publisher's Note**
The publisher accepts responsibility for any inconsistencies that may have arisen during the conversion of this book from journal articles to book chapters, namely the inclusion of journal terminology.

**Disclaimer**
Every effort has been made to contact copyright holders for their permission to reprint material in this book. The publishers would be grateful to hear from any copyright holder who is not here acknowledged and will undertake to rectify any errors or omissions in future editions of this book.

ISBN 13: 978-0-367-73115-1 (pbk)
ISBN 13: 978-0-367-14340-4 (hbk)

# Contents

*Citation Information* vii
*Notes on Contributors* ix

1 Introduction: Is Canada back? Brand Canada in a turbulent world 1
   Richard Nimijean

2 The brand image of Canadian Prime Minister Justin Trudeau in international context 13
   Alex Marland

3 All about that base? Branding and the domestic politics of Canadian foreign aid 19
   Stephen Brown

4 Canada's Feminist International Assistance Policy: to whom is Canada back? 39
   Rebecca Tiessen and David Black

5 Friend or faux? Trudeau, Indigenous issues and Canada's brand 46
   Heather Exner-Pirot

6 Predicting the North: sovereignty and the Canadian brand in the Arctic 63
   Mark Paradis, Richard D. Parker and Patrick James

7 Canada's foreign policy and bureaucratic (un)responsiveness: public diplomacy in the digital domain 83
   Kai Ostwald and Julian Dierkes

8 The evolving complementarity of nation-branding and public diplomacy: projecting the Canada brand through "weibo diplomacy" in China 104
   Evan Potter

9 Où donc le Canada est-il de retour dans le monde? 119
   Jocelyn Coulon

10 "Canada's back" – can the Trudeau government resuscitate Canadian diplomacy?  124
*Daryl Copeland*

11 Conclusion: Don't look back: they might be gaining on you  134
*David Carment and Richard Nimijean*

*Index*  141

# Citation Information

The following chapters were originally published in the *Canadian Foreign Policy Journal*, volume 24, issue 2 (June 2018). When citing this material, please use the original page numbering for each article, as follows:

**Chapter 1**
*Introduction: Is Canada back? Brand Canada in a turbulent world*
Richard Nimijean
This chapter was first published in its original format in the *Canadian Foreign Policy Journal*, volume 24, issue 2 (June 2018) pp. 127–138; a slightly edited version is included in the book.

**Chapter 2**
*The brand image of Canadian Prime Minister Justin Trudeau in international context*
Alex Marland
*Canadian Foreign Policy Journal*, volume 24, issue 2 (June 2018) pp. 139–144

**Chapter 3**
*All about that base? Branding and the domestic politics of Canadian foreign aid*
Stephen Brown
*Canadian Foreign Policy Journal*, volume 24, issue 2 (June 2018) pp. 145–164

**Chapter 5**
*Friend or faux? Trudeau, Indigenous issues and Canada's brand*
Heather Exner-Pirot
*Canadian Foreign Policy Journal*, volume 24, issue 2 (June 2018) pp. 165–181

**Chapter 6**
*Predicting the North: sovereignty and the Canadian brand in the Arctic*
Mark Paradis, Richard D. Parker and Patrick James
*Canadian Foreign Policy Journal*, volume 24, issue 2 (June 2018) pp. 182–201

## Chapter 7
*Canada's foreign policy and bureaucratic (un)responsiveness: public diplomacy in the digital domain*
Kai Ostwald and Julian Dierkes
*Canadian Foreign Policy Journal*, volume 24, issue 2 (June 2018) pp. 202–222

## Chapter 8
*The evolving complementarity of nation-branding and public diplomacy: projecting the Canada brand through "weibo diplomacy" in China*
Evan Potter
*Canadian Foreign Policy Journal*, volume 24, issue 2 (June 2018) pp. 223–237

## Chapter 9
*Où donc le Canada est-il de retour dans le monde?*
Jocelyn Coulon
*Canadian Foreign Policy Journal*, volume 24, issue 2 (June 2018) pp. 238–242

## Chapter 10
*"Canada's back" – can the Trudeau government resuscitate Canadian diplomacy?*
Daryl Copeland
*Canadian Foreign Policy Journal*, volume 24, issue 2 (June 2018) pp. 243–252

For any permission-related enquiries please visit:
www.tandfonline.com/page/help/permissions

# Notes on Contributors

**David Black** is a Professor in and Chair of the Department of Political Sciences at Dalhousie University, Canada. His research interests focus on Canada's role in "development cooperation" and in Sub-Saharan Africa (including human security, diplomacy, and the extractive sector); sport in world politics and development; and disability and global development.

**Stephen Brown** is Professor of Political Science in the Faculty of Social Sciences at the University of Ottawa, Canada. He is the author of numerous publications on foreign aid, especially Canada's. His research focuses mainly on the intersection of the policies and practices of Northern countries and other international actors with politics in Southern countries, especially in sub-Saharan Africa.

**David Carment** is Professor of International Affairs at Carleton University in Ottawa, Canada, and Editor of *Canadian Foreign Policy Journal*. His most recent books examine state fragility theory and policy and third-party intervention in ethnic conflict. He teaches conflict mediation, bargaining and negotiation, and Canadian foreign policy.

**Daryl Copeland** is a Research Fellow at the Canadian Global Affairs Institute (CGAI), a Policy Fellow at the University of Montreal's Centre for International Studies (CERIUM), Canada, and Senior Advisor in Science Diplomacy at the International Institute for Applied Systems Analysis (IIASA) in Laxenburg, Austria. He was formerly a diplomat.

**Jocelyn Coulon** is a Researcher at the Center for International Studies and Research at the University of Montreal (CERIUM), Canada, and a Fellow at the Canadian Global Affairs Institute (CGAI). He was a member of Justin Trudeau's Advisory Board on International Affairs in 2014–2015, and a policy advisor to former Foreign Minister Stéphane Dion in 2016–2017.

**Julian Dierkes** is an Associate Professor and Keidanren Chair in Japanese Research at the University of British Columbia's School of Public Policy and Global Affairs, Canada. In addition to Japan and digital diplomacy, much of his research focuses on mining policy and political development in Mongolia. He was trained as a Sociologist at Princeton University, USA.

**Heather Exner-Pirot** is the Managing Editor of the *Arctic Yearbook* and a Strategist for Outreach and Indigenous Engagement at the University of Saskatchewan, Canada. She is also Chair of the Canadian Northern Studies Trust and a Coordinator at UArctic Northern Nursing Education Network.

**Patrick James** is Dornsife Dean's Professor of International Relations at the University of Southern California, USA. He specializes in comparative and international politics. His interests at the international level include the causes, processes, and consequences of conflict, crisis, and war.

**Alex Marland** is Professor in the Department of Political Science at the Memorial University of Newfoundland, Canada. His book *Brand Command: Canadian Politics and Democracy in the Age of Message Control* (2016) won the Donner Prize for best public policy book by a Canadian. He researches political marketing, public policy, election campaigning, and political elites in Canada.

**Richard Nimijean** is Instructor III in the School of Indigenous and Canadian Studies at Carleton University in Ottawa, Canada. His research and publications focus on the politics of branding Canada and the connections between the Canadian national identity and its projection globally, public policy, and domestic politics.

**Kai Ostwald** is an Assistant Professor in the School of Public Policy & Global Affairs and the Department of Political Science at the University of British Columbia (UBC), Canada. He is also the Director of UBC's Centre for Southeast Asia Research, a Fellow at UBC's Institute of Asian Research, and Associate Editor (Southeast Asia) for *Pacific Affairs*.

**Mark Paradis** is a part-time Professor in the Department of Political Science at Concordia University, Canada, and an Instructor in the Department of Social Sciences (Political Science and Methodology) at Champlain College Saint-Lambert, Canada. His primary research interests are at the intersection of international relations, political psychology, and experimental methods.

**Richard D. Parker** is the former President of the Southern Association for Canadian Studies and a graduate of McGill University, Canada.

**Evan Potter** is a Professor in the Co-operative Education Programs at the University of Ottawa, Canada. His expertise is in public sector communications planning, political communication, public opinion, and international communications. His research has focused on the projection of Canada's image in the international arena and the use of communications technologies in diplomacy.

**Rebecca Tiessen** is Professor, University Chair in Teaching, Associate Director/Undergraduate Coordinator and Co-op Coordinator in the School of International Development and Global Studies at the University of Ottawa, Canada. Her research interests include gender and development, learning/volunteering abroad, and the role of Canada and Canadians in the world.

# 1 Introduction

Is Canada back? Brand Canada in a turbulent world

Richard Nimijean

**ABSTRACT**

The Liberal Party's surprise win in the 2015 federal election was partly due to an articulation of liberal internationalism that contrasted with Prime Minister Harper's foreign policy vision. "Canada's back" and "sunny ways" have been key themes for the Trudeau government's branding of Canada, but rhetoric–reality gaps threaten to tarnish the brand. This article highlights issues in the relationship between articulated visions of Canada as a global actor, nation branding and domestic politics, noting the dangers of the politicization of the branding of Canada. It identifies key issues for evaluating the claim that Canada is back and introduces the articles in the special issue.

**RÉSUMÉ**

La victoire surprise du Parti Libéral lors des élections fédérales de 2015 a été due en partie à une formulation de l'internationalisme libéral qui contredisait la vision politique du Premier Ministre Stephen Harper. « Le Canada est de retour » et « la voie ensoleillée » ont été des thèmes clés de la labellisation du Canada par le gouvernement Trudeau, mais les écarts entre rhétorique et réalité menacent de ternir ce label. Cet article met l'accent sur le rapport entre les visions, telles que formulées, du Canada en tant qu'acteur mondial, la labellisation nationale et la politique domestique, en soulignant les dangers d'une politisation de la labellisation du Canada. Par ailleurs, il identifie les questions clés à aborder dans une évaluation de la revendication selon laquelle le Canada est de retour, et il introduit les autres articles de cette édition spéciale.

Competing visions of Canada as a global actor were on display in the 2015 Canadian federal election. In the lead-up to the election, Prime Minister Stephen Harper portrayed the major opposition parties as soft on terrorists and not able to deal with complex global problems. Conservative Party ads mocked Liberal leader Justin Trudeau as an inexperienced leader, albeit with "nice hair," who was "just not ready."

The Conservatives ensured that foreign policy would be central to the election, emphasizing Prime Minister Stephen Harper's strong leadership in turbulent and unsafe times, with a campaign slogan on their tour bus stating "Proven Leadership. Safer Canada. Stronger Economy" (Furey 2015). They agreed to an historic leaders' debate on foreign policy, presumably believing these differences would be made clear and to their advantage.

However, the evolving Syrian refugee crisis, and notably the Canadian connection with the unfortunate death of a three-year-old child whose family was seeking to come to Canada, disrupted these plans. Instead of Harper's strong stance on security and antiterrorism setting the tone, we witnessed a debate about the values Canada stood for in the world and a questioning of whether Canada in the Harper years lived up to so-called "Canadian values." Earlier that year, Trudeau forcefully outlined his belief in the institutions that promote and protect Canadian liberties, especially the Canadian Charter of Rights and Freedoms, in a speech at McGill University (transcript available from Wherry 2015). Trudeau argued that they required ongoing support and leadership, given attacks on liberties in the Harper years. His argument that "Canadian liberty is all about inclusion" was followed by his July statement that "a Canadian is a Canadian is a Canadian." Interestingly, during the election campaign, the Conservatives leaked audio of Trudeau saying this, seeing it as a weakness (CTV News 2015), yet Trudeau used this line against Harper with success during the foreign policy debate.

Trudeau's articulation of liberal internationalism, carefully developed under the tutorship of Roland Paris (Coulon 2018, pp. 53–56), would inform Canada's behavior as a good international citizen under a Liberal government; this, along with an economic platform seen as left of center, overshadowed Harper's narrative. The Liberals also drew on New Democratic Party supporters who were critical of leader Thomas Mulcair's mainstream economic platform and fearful of vote-splitting that could allow Harper to win again. Thus, the Liberals leapfrogged past the other two parties to become the surprise winners of the election (Nimijean 2015, 2017).

Trudeau, in his election night victory speech, spoke of "sunny ways," suggesting that his government would offer a positive, constructive and even nostalgic vision of Canada. Not surprisingly, Canadians – and indeed much of the world – applauded when Trudeau stated the day after the election that "Many of you have worried that Canada has lost its compassionate and constructive voice in the world over the past 10 years.... Well, I have a simple message for you: on behalf of 35 million Canadians, we're back" (cited in Bronskill 2015).

Trudeau's optimism, idealism and personal style signaled a break with Harper's efforts to transform Canadian foreign policy, hinting at a return to the role of helpful fixer that many Canadians identified with. Initial pronouncements on the environment, diversity and gender generated overwhelmingly positive political and media responses, such as Trudeau's retort, "Because it's 2015," when asked why he had gender parity in his cabinet. His messages also provided an opportunity to revamp Brand Canada. "Canada's back" and "sunny ways" became the markers by which the Trudeau government wanted the world to see Canada. The idea of nation branding took the world by storm two decades ago as a strategy for improving a country's economic prospects. Peter van Ham popularized the concept in foreign policy circles with an influential article in *Foreign Policy*, noting that "Smart states are building their brands around reputations and attitudes in the same way smart companies do" (van Ham 2001b, p. 4). He even suggested (van Ham 2001a) that state branding was a form of "playful" nationalism. The subsequent plethora of national and subnational branding strategies pointed to the concept's salience as places sought to revitalize economically and increase their clout politically in an era of globalization and neoliberalism.

However, critics argued that nation branding was often devoid of policy substance and could deepen voter cynicism by failing to engage citizens in thoughtful deliberation (Rose 2010). Thus, it could be understood in terms of an ongoing privatization of foreign policy (Curry Jansen 2008) and the state (Rose 2010). Far from being a playful manipulation of symbols in a new form of nationalism, an emphasis on restoring the neoliberal national and strengthening it with symbols in an era of growing ethnonationalism has ominous overtones. As Curry Jansen (2008, p. 134) writes, "Nation branding is a monologic, hierarchical, reductive form of communication that is intended to privilege one message, require all voices of authority to speak in unison, and marginalize and silence dissenting voices."

Canada in the Chrétien years implemented branding and public diplomacy strategies, including the well-publicized Team Canada trade missions, though its efforts were uneven, and analyses pointed to challenges and opportunities for enhancing these strategies (Nadeau 2004, Potter 2009). These ideas seemed to disappear during the Harper years, apart from occasional references about transforming Canada into a clean-energy superpower (Hester 2007, Way 2011), though this idea never took hold, given widespread criticism of Harper's positions on the environment. The Harper government terminated one of Canada's major public diplomacy programs, "Understanding Canada," in 2012. However, the Trudeau government, circling back to the Chrétien years, revived the idea of an investment promotion strategy, "Investing in Canada," with the minister even saying that he was "Canada's chief marketing officer" (Blanchfield 2018).[1]

Nimijean (2006) pointed to a connection between nation branding, the external projection of national identity, and domestic politics, arguing that constructions of Canada for external audiences increasingly informed domestic politics and, in the case of the Chrétien government, allowed for the selling of neoliberalism under the guise of "progressive" Canadian values. Other critical examinations of this connection have looked at multiculturalism and immigration (Abu-Laban and Gabriel 2002) and gender (Rankin 2012). Numerous foreign policy scholars (among others, see Nossal 2003, Stairs 2003, Howell 2005, Michaud 2007, Paris 2014) have explored the connection between national identity and/or values on the one hand, and foreign policy on the other. This brings us back to the link between Trudeau's personal brand in the world, the values that underlie Brand Canada, the promotion of Brand Canada, and how Canada engages with the world.

Simon Anholt reminds us that nations must earn a good reputation; they cannot simply say that they have or deserve one. In other words, countries must act first. Anholt (2009, p. 90) offers a particular warning for countries like Canada:

> When we're talking about the middle powers, the issue is very often one of relevance; most people don't care very much about most other countries, especially if they don't possess a great deal of economic, military, political or cultural clout. Rather than asking themselves "what can we say to make ourselves more famous?" the governments of such countries should be asking "what can we do to make ourselves more relevant?"

In other words, relevance, supported by concrete action, is key to enhancing a nation brand, for values emerge out of action (Nimijean 2005b). Therefore, if Canada is to be back, as Trudeau vowed, what will need to be done post-Harper to reach this state? (Toope 2016). Does Trudeau's celebrity and sustained rhetoric of liberal internationalism mean that Canada is back, or is it simply empty political messaging?

The Trudeau government envisions Canada as a country that promotes gender equality and development, migration and diversity, reconciliation with Indigenous peoples, peacekeeping, and solutions to climate change that involve a balance between energy and the environment. The campaign to win a seat on the United Nations (UN) Security Council reinforces a multilateralist vision of Canada, reflecting commonly held external perceptions of Canada as a helpful fixer in foreign affairs.

However, the Trudeau government appears to be perpetuating the "paradoxical nature of the Canadian identity," resorting to articulating national distinctiveness by promoting values that emerged through past action; as public policy becomes less distinct, the exhortation of distinctive values is ratcheted up (Nimijean 2005b). Echoing Curry Jansen's depiction of nation branding as a construct that marginalizes dissenting views, Trudeau's "Canada's back" statement hints at a political Achilles' heel of the Liberals, namely arrogance, in arguing that its values are effectively one and the same as Canadian values, as the *Globe and Mail* (2016) editorialized. How did the millions of Canadians who supported the Conservatives feel when Trudeau declared Canada to be back, this despite his belief in the power of positive politics? As former Conservative cabinet Minister Peter MacKay asked, "Where in God's name does this prime minister think we've been?" (cited in Akin 2016).

MacKay's response points to an important question: beyond declaring that Canada was back, what actions would demonstrate this to be the case? As the value of brands is ultimately determined by audiences and markets, Trudeau's rhetoric reshaped perceptions of Brand Canada. However, when actions or experiences do not live up to the brand promise, brands suffer. This is increasingly true of the Trudeau brand, due to rhetoric–reality gaps in several key files:

- On the environment, little progress has been made on achieving emissions targets, as noted in a major audit conducted by the federal Environment Commissioner, the federal auditor general, and nine provincial auditors general (Rabson 2018), and Trudeau is being challenged to defend his view that pipelines and improved environmental performance can coexist.
- Global Affairs Canada (2017) proclaims that "Promoting respect for human rights is at the heart of Canada's international engagement," and Trudeau speaks eloquently of his feminist foreign policy, yet the Trudeau government continues to defend the sale of military equipment to Saudi Arabia despite allegations of human rights abuses that contravene Canadian regulations and an ongoing crackdown on Saudi feminists (Morris 2018). In a 2016 interview, Trudeau stated, "Now, what goes into the brand of a country? Well, obviously it's not just environmental sustainability and good health care for our workers. It's also human rights and respect for individuals. So it's part of Canada's identity that we stand up for human rights" (cited in Wells 2016). Yet in the same interview, he suggested that Canada would look like a "banana republic" if it canceled the contract and would get a bad name in international circles – in other words, it would hurt the brand.
- Despite a longstanding pledge to return to active peacekeeping, it took the Trudeau government two years to finally decide to support the UN mission in Mali, though it appears to be far less than what was promised, and the government has not yet determined benchmarks for success (Naumetz 2018).

- Perhaps most significantly, Trudeau's welcoming of Syrian refugees – "you are home"– informed the idea that Canada was back, as seen in David Parkin's November 2015 editorial cartoon that graces our cover. This idea created a sharp contrast between Canada and the United States following Donald Trump's election in 2016. After President Trump announced a controversial migration ban in January 2017, Prime Minister Trudeau tweeted, "To those fleeing persecution, terror & war, Canadians will welcome you, regardless of your faith. Diversity is our strength #WelcomeToCanada." While this cemented the fusion of Trudeau's and Canada's brand, the growing number of refugee claimants arriving at non-official border crossings since Trudeau's tweet led to a large increase in inquiries from abroad that the government and diplomats abroad had difficulties addressing (Smith 2018). The influx of refugees since the tweet overwhelmed the system to the point that the government developed a new communications strategy seeking to discourage some people from coming to Canada. Thus, while social media have the *potential* to enhance public diplomacy and branding efforts, as discussed in two of our articles, it remains that once a tweet is made, the messenger can lose control of its meaning and interpretation. Political use of social media can therefore also negatively affect the nation brand.

This is precisely why Anholt warns countries not to exaggerate what they stand for but to demonstrate relevance. As he states, "A reputation can never be constructed through communications, slogans and logos; it needs to be earned" (Anholt 2009, p. 90).

The Trudeau government's penchant for public relations and self-promotion also illustrates the tensions between promoting a nation brand, the execution of domestic brand politics, and the separation of government and state, as forewarned by Curry Jansen above. For example, Global Affairs Canada reportedly considered using "Brand Trudeau" to frame Canada's engagement with peacekeeping (Blanchfield 2016), and the Canadian embassy in the United States purchased cardboard cutouts of Trudeau so that targeted audiences could have their own Trudeau selfies (Levin 2017).

The danger lies in linking political and state/citizen interests, promoting the idea that the country only has one voice. The brand espoused by Trudeau in the election and accepted by voters was quickly superseded by political celebrity and bureaucratic pursuit of the national interest that capitalized on this celebrity. However, successful and valuable brands emerge because they deliver on their brand promise; they fail when they don't. In this case, rhetoric–reality gaps have led to a pushback of the Trudeau brand. Trudeau's standing in the global media is diminishing, as seen in the furor over Trudeau's poorly delivered quip about using "peoplekind" instead of "mankind." The *Daily Mail* even asked if Trudeau was the world's most "politically PC" politician (Leonard 2018). While many New York University students were excited that Trudeau received an honorary degree at their graduation ceremony in May 2018, some students argued that he was not deserving of this award, citing environmental policies that are harmful to Indigenous peoples, and the sale of military equipment to Saudi Arabia that is contributing to fatalities in Yemen (Meskhi 2018). Actress and activist Jane Fonda, noting Trudeau's more forceful advocacy of pipelines since his election, said "I guess the lesson is we shouldn't be fooled by good-looking liberals no matter how well-spoken they are" (cited in Associated Press 2017).

Thus, the Trudeau government's branding strategy has been far from successful, in large part because of a failure to act in support of its vision of Canada as an engaged and constructive global actor. For example, Percival (2018) states that "On global health, Canada is not 'back.'... The Trudeau government's foreign policy engagement has been high on rhetoric. ... While our rhetoric shines, our promises are beginning to sound hollow." Carment et al. (2018) stated,

> For a political party that promised to elevate Canada's position in the world, the Liberal government under Justin Trudeau has achieved remarkably little in international diplomacy. In crucial areas such as climate change and strengthening international institutions, the government has underperformed or stalled.

A mid-mandate review of the Trudeau government's foreign policy record concludes that "The government's actions and rhetoric have been inconsistent, at times contradictory and mostly focused on messaging and advancing the Liberal brand than fixing real problems" (iAffairs 2018). Perhaps Harper's claims of inexperience were not far off the mark – not because Trudeau was not ready – but because of basic challenges in political management and public administration?[2]

Political self-promotion and mismanagement came to the fore during Prime Minister Trudeau's controversial trip to India in February 2018. The trip, officially seeking to strengthen economic ties and promote the empowerment of women and girls, was lampooned because of the constant photographing of Trudeau and his family in traditional Indian clothing, photography that no doubt could be communicated to the important Indian diaspora in advance of the 2019 federal election. Additionally, domestic politics appeared to detract from security concerns when controversy erupted over the presence of Jaspal Atwal, a Canadian convicted of attempted murder of an Indian politician in 1986. It was even suggested that factions of the Indian government might have wished to embarrass Canada. Ultimately, the already strained relations between Canada and India became even more tense. Veteran Ottawa pundit Don Martin, observing that this was the third trip after which countries "have lowered their opinion of Canada as a result of prime ministerial visits," stated "If this is Trudeau putting Canada back on the world stage, we should get off" (Martin 2018).

This points to the need for a critical analysis not only of the Trudeau brand but of its relationship with and impact on Canada's brand globally. How prime ministers communicate visions of Canada to the world matters, not simply for messaging policy priorities to international actors, but also to Canadians who interpret rhetoric in terms of their own political values. Rhetoric–reality gaps can be temporarily overcome through the communication of values, as seen in the Chrétien case (Nimijean 2005a), or by the sheer popularity of a leader, as seen initially with Justin Trudeau both at home and abroad. However, as former Ambassador to China Mulroney (2018) argues, the India trip showed how a focus on personality and concerns over diasporic identities and domestic politics make it more difficult to get the type of foreign policy Canada requires, given the current global repositioning of regional powers.

Looking at domestic brand politics and their connection to Canada's brand in the world therefore sheds light on the myriad challenges facing the evolution of Canadian foreign policy and a quest for more substance. This special issue of *Canadian Foreign Policy Journal* seeks to do just that. Contributors were asked to explore various dimensions of the intersection between domestic politics, national identity, and the challenges facing Canada as a global actor, and their articles and policy commentaries address many of the issues raised here. Three key issues emerge:

- *We need to look at the rhetoric of government communications and how it communicates and politicizes values.* For example, Finance Minister Bill Morneau hyped a large increase in development spending in Budget 2018 ("the largest new investments in international assistance in over a decade"), but the Canadian International Development Platform carefully demonstrated that this hardly addresses needs and that contributions as a share of the economy will actually decline (Bhushan 2018).
- *How different is Trudeau's foreign policy from the Harper foreign policy that he criticized?* While the Trudeau government's rhetoric is certainly different from Harper's, have its actions been all that different? Is Ibbitson (2017) correct in arguing that there is considerable continuity once you go beyond the rhetoric?
- *What would it mean for Canada to be back?* It is not enough to simply declare that Canada is back. If Canada is to return to values that the government considers to be central to Canada's role as a global actor, it needs to act in support of them. Has the government done so? If not, what can it do?

In our opening policy commentary, *Alex Marland* ("The brand image of Canadian Prime Minister Justin Trudeau in international context") provides the political context for thinking about Brand Canada in the Trudeau era. Inevitably, branding Canadian politicians abroad is connected to images of Canada, and these are subject to various interpretations. Significantly, he notes how Trudeau's celebrity not only distinguished him from his predecessor, Stephen Harper; it attracted the attention of global elites. Yet celebrity is fleeting, in part due to political mismanagement and not living up to the brand promise, and in the end, Trudeau must retain the support of Canadians if he wishes to remain in power.

*Stephen Brown* ("All about that base? Branding and the domestic politics of Canadian foreign aid") uses the lens of brand politics to further his analysis of the politics of Canadian development assistance. Brown reinforces the idea of a domestic–international nexus in brand politics by demonstrating that Canadian aid policy is increasingly driven by domestic political considerations, namely satisfying political bases, leading to a continuity in policy despite rhetorical differences. The politicization of aid, he notes, often reduces its effectiveness.

*Rebecca Tiessen and David Black* ("Canada's Feminist International Assistance Policy: to whom is Canada back?") build on Brown's analysis by analyzing the Trudeau government's commitment to gender equality, specifically in relation to its Feminist International Assistance Policy (FIAP). They note that this rhetorical commitment to equality is significant, a signal indeed that Canada is back. However, while the FIAP is central to Brand Canada, an examination of intended audiences and actions point to significant rhetoric–reality gaps that challenge the brand, leading them to ask, "for whom is Canada back?" This questioning can inform debates about the commitments required to live up to the ideals of the brand.

*Heather Exner-Pirot* ("Friend or faux? Trudeau, Indigenous issues and Canada's brand") examines how Canada's relations with Indigenous peoples affect Canada's brand. Canada's generally positive international reputation diminishes when considering these relations, such as when prominent politicians deny or ignore Canada's colonial past. Consequently, tensions in the relationship often play out on the international stage. Like Brown, she detects continuity across governments rather than difference.

*Mark Paradis, Richard Parker and Patrick James* ("Predicting the North: sovereignty and the Canadian brand in the Arctic") provide a critical examination of the rhetoric of "Canada's back" by looking at the Arctic region. They describe the Arctic's importance for Canada's brand in the world, even though it is often ignored by politicians and policy-makers. However, shifting geopolitics has led to a growing salience of Arctic issues for Canadian foreign policy and indeed for how the Canadian brand is perceived.

Nation branding and public diplomacy seek to influence key actors in target countries. In an era of heightened social media activity, how has Canada embraced social media to promote its brand? For example, the Trudeau government has spent approximately CAD $20 million advertising on social media in its first two years in power (Aiello 2017, Meyer 2018). Can these tools advance the brand? Two articles look at different dimensions of social media and digital diplomacy.

*Kai Ostwald and Julian Dierkes* ("Canada's foreign policy and bureaucratic (un)responsiveness: public diplomacy in the digital domain") examine whether the Trudeau government's new orientation in foreign policy, including providing diplomats abroad with more latitude to act, is evidenced in social media activities. A detailed analysis of tweets from Global Affairs Canada Twitter accounts reveals that social media activity has not differed considerably from the Harper era. While there has been a change in atmosphere, there is a need to invest in digital diplomacy to achieve policy goals.

*Evan Potter* ("The evolving complementarity of nation-branding and public diplomacy: projecting the Canada Brand through 'weibo' diplomacy in China") looks at how the Canadian Embassy in China used Weibo to advance its agenda. Potter combines theoretical insights into nation branding and public diplomacy with a changing social media environment, suggesting that new opportunities present themselves for promoting the Canadian brand.

While Alex Marland opened the issue with an overview of the nature of political branding in an international context, hinting at some of the challenges that emerge with Trudeau's celebrity, *Jocelyn Coulon* ("Où donc le Canada est-il de retour dans le monde?") highlights the challenges that emerge when governments do not live up to the hype associated with the celebrity. He notes that the Liberal's optimistic vision, carefully developed by a group of thinkers of which he was part, provided great opportunity for a meaningful transformation of Canada's role in the world. However, Trudeau's celebrity has not led to meaningful change to date.

*Daryl Copeland* ("'Canada's back' – can the Trudeau government resuscitate Canadian diplomacy?") evaluates the claim that Canada is back through a broad sweep of post-World War II Canadian foreign policy. He notes that the Harper years saw a decline in Canada's active engagement in global issues, but that, apart from constructive rhetoric, the Trudeau government has yet to indicate how it would return Canada to greater engagement. However, he argues that Canadians cannot just "look back"; thus, he offers a series of recommendations that would really put Canada "back" on the world stage.

Coulon and Copeland bring together the many themes and issues raised by the contributors, providing considerable insights into the politics of branding Canada. The Trudeau government's rhetoric is distinct from the Harper government's. As he promised in 2015, Trudeau continues to offer a compassionate and constructive voice on behalf of Canada; however, more often than not, deeds do not match the rhetoric. Why? We cannot say for sure, though Coulon offers a few possibilities.

*David Carment and Richard Nimijean* ("Conclusion: Don't look back: they might be gaining on you") observe how, rhetoric aside, the Trudeau government has largely continued the foreign policy trajectory of the Harper government. They note how the politics of branding have become intertwined with Canadian foreign policy. The Trudeau government emphasizes the nostalgic past for political purposes through a strategy of image projection and values articulation. Thus, Canada is avoiding addressing important questions about Canadian responses to turbulent times.

Certainly, the Trudeau government demonstrates that domestic brand politics (Nimijean 2014) are alive and well in Canada. Per Anholt, if the Trudeau government truly wants Canada to be back as a constructive global actor, it should begin with a fundamental re-examination of what it does, what it wishes to do and what it must do. Then, and only then, will the plaudits come. Otherwise, disappointment is sure to follow.

Together, the authors have demonstrated that "Is Canada back?" is no longer the appropriate question; instead, we must ask, "What can Canada do to get back?" Arguably, there is considerable public support for the Trudeau agenda (Paris 2014). The challenge lies in focusing less on the brand and more on the doing. Only then will Canada be back. Otherwise, the Trudeau government, like the government that preceded it, will begin to hear, "Where is Canada?"

## Acknowledgements

I would like to thank David Carment for his generous support and wise counsel in the development of this special issue. I would also like to thank Joe Landry and Sam MacIsaac for their considerable efforts in putting the issue together, the two external reviewers, and, of course, the authors for their thoughtful contributions.

## Disclosure statement

No potential conflict of interest was reported by the author.

## Notes on contributor

*Richard Nimijean* is a political scientist and a member of the School of Indigenous and Canadian Studies at Carleton University. He is a co-editor of the *International Journal of Canadian Studies / Revue internationale d'études canadiennes*. His research focuses on brand politics and the Canadian national identity.

## ORCID

*Richard Nimijean* http://orcid.org/0000-0001-5811-4105

## Notes

1 This initiative is off to a stuttering start, thus unintentionally harming the brand. It took 16 months for the government to unveil the agency following its announcement, and the agency's website, www.investcanada.ca, was "under construction, stay tuned!" at launch in March 2018. Despite promises of a more engaged diplomacy, the Trudeau government has yet to restore "Understanding Canada," and it continued the sale of Canadian embassies undertaken by the Harper government.

2 This is also true domestically, as the government faces ongoing important public administration challenges, notably the Phoenix payroll problem, the management of pipelines and a national

carbon tax, the legalization of marijuana, and the National Inquiry into Missing and Murdered Indigenous Women and Girls.

**References**

Abu-Laban, Y. and Gabriel, C., 2002. *Selling diversity: immigration, multiculturalism, employment equity and globalization*. Peterborough: Broadview Press.

Aiello, R., 2017. Trudeau government spent $13.6M on sponsored social media [online]. *CTV News*, 26 September. Available from: www.ctvnews.ca/politics/trudeau-government-spent-13-6m-on-sponsored-social-media-1.3607104 [Accessed 16 October 2017].

Akin, D., 2016. MacKay: "Where in God's name does this prime minister think we've been?" [online]. *David Akin's On the Hill*, 16 March. Available from: http://blogs.canoe.com/davidakin/politics/ mackay-where-in-gods-name-does-this-prime-minister-think-weve-been/ [Accessed 16 May 2018].

Anholt, S., 2009. Nation "branding": propaganda or statecraft? *Public Diplomacy Magazine*, Summer 2009, 88–90.

Associated Press, 2017. Jane Fonda: don't fall for "good-looking liberals" like Trudeau on environment [online]. *The Guardian*, 12 January. Available from: www.theguardian.com/environment/2017/jan/12/jane-fonda-justin-trudeau-environment-canada-pipeline [Accessed 15 May 2018].

Bhushan, A., 2018. Did Budget 2018 deliver the funds Canada needs to lead? Nice try, but no [online]. *OpenCanada*, 1 March. Available from: www.opencanada.org/features/did-budget-2018-deliver-funds-canada-needs-lead-nice-try-no/ [Accessed 23 March 2018].

Blanchfield, M., 2016. "Brand Trudeau" mulled by top bureaucrats to reboot Canada's return to peace-keeping [online]. *Global News*, 30 December. Available from: https://globalnews.ca/news/3152795/brand-trudeau-mulled-by-top-bureaucrats-to-reboot-canadas-return-to-peacekeeping/ [Accessed 2 January 2017].

Blanchfield, M., 2018. New foreign investment promotion agency has work cut out for it: leaders [online]. *CTV News*, 12 March. Available from: www.ctvnews.ca/business/new-foreign-investment-promotion-agency-has-work-cut-out-for-it-leaders-1.3839083 [Accessed 23 March 2018].

Bronskill, J., 2015. "We're back," Justin Trudeau says in message to allies [online]. *National Post*, 20 October. Available from: http://news.nationalpost.com/news/canada/canadian-politics/were-back-justin-trudeau-says-in-message-to-canadas-allies-abroad [Accessed 27 April 2017].

Carment, D., et al., 2018. Trudeau's Liberals are faltering on foreign policy at the midway point of their mandate [online]. *Ottawa Citizen*, 9 March. Available from: http://ottawacitizen.com/opinion/columnists/opinion-trudeaus-liberals-are-faltering-on-foreign-policy-at-the-midway-point-of-their-mandate [Accessed 9 March 2018].

Coulon, J., 2018. *Un selfie avec Justin Trudeau: regard critique sur la diplomatie du premier ministre*. Montréal: Québec Amérique.

CTV News, 2015. In audio recording, Trudeau says Bill C-24 makes citizenship conditional upon "good behaviour" [online]. 27 September. Available from: www.ctvnews.ca/mobile/politics/in-audio-recording-trudeau-says-bill-c-24-makes-citizenship-conditional-upon-good-behaviour-1.2583849 [Accessed 18 May 2018].

Curry Jansen, S., 2008. Designer nations: neo-liberal nation branding – Brand Estonia. *Social Identities*, 14(1), 121–142.

Furey, A., 2015. Harper slogan sets the issues [online]. *Toronto Sun*, 4 August. Available from: http://torontosun.com/2015/08/04/harper-slogan-sets-the-issues [Accessed 18 March 2016].

Global Affairs Canada, 2017. Voices at risk: Canada's guidelines on supporting human rights defenders [online]. 5 June. Available from: http://international.gc.ca/world-monde/issues_development-enjeux_developpement/human_rights-droits_homme/rights_defenders_guide_defenseurs_droits.aspx?lang=eng [Accessed 18 May 2018].

Globe and Mail, 2016. The Trudeau government thinks it has a monopoly on "Canadian" values. It doesn't [online]. 15 February. Available from: www.theglobeandmail.com/opinion/editorials/the-trudeau-government-thinks-it-has-a-monopoly-on-canadian-values-it-doesnt/article28748918/ [Accessed 18 March 2016].

Hester, A., 2007. *Canada as the "emerging energy superpower": testing the case.* Calgary: Canadian Defence & Foreign Affairs Institute.

Howell, A., 2005. Peaceful, tolerant and orderly? A feminist analysis of discourses of "Canadian values" in Canadian foreign policy. *Canadian Foreign Policy Journal*, 12(1), 49–69.

iAffairs, 2018. 2018 Trudeau Report Card [online]. Available from: www.iaffairscanada.com/wp-content/uploads/TrudeauReportCard2018.pdf [Accessed 23 March 2018].

Ibbitson, J., 2017. Trudeau's foreign policy vs. Harper's: there is little difference [online]. *Globe and Mail*, 8 March. Available from: www.theglobeandmail.com/news/politics/trudeau-taking-foreign-policy-cue-from-tory-playbook/article34241539/ [Accessed 12 March 2017].

Leonard, T., 2018. He banned the word mankind and cried when he met his wife… Is Canada's PM Justin Trudeau the world's most PC politician? [online]. *Daily Mail*, 9 March. Available from: www.dailymail.co.uk/femail/article-5480029/Is-Canadian-PM-Justin-Trudeau-PC-politician.html [Accessed 15 March 2018].

Levin, D., 2017. Barred from Canadian embassy parties: cardboard Trudeau [online]. *New York Times*, 21 March. Available from: www.nytimes.com/2017/03/21/world/canada/canada-justin-trudeau-cardboard-cutout.html [Accessed 10 February 2018].

Martin, D., 2018. If this is Trudeau putting Canada "back" on the world stage, we should get off [online]. *CTV News*, 22 February. Available from: www.ctvnews.ca/politics/don-martin-blog/don-martin-if-this-is-trudeau-putting-canada-back-on-the-world-stage-we-should-get-off-1.3815230 [Accessed 15 May 2018].

Meskhi, M., 2018. Not everyone at NYU is excited to see Justin Trudeau at graduation [online]. *NYU Local*, 19 April. Available from: https://nyulocal.com/not-everyone-at-nyu-is-excited-to-see-justin-trudeau-at-graduation-7da0c0354900 [Accessed 19 April 2018].

Meyer, C., 2018. Canadian government spent over $7 million to advertise on social media in 2016–17 [online]. *National Observer*, 5 February. Available from: www.nationalobserver.com/2018/02/05/news/canadian-government-spent-over-7-million-advertise-social-media-2016-17 [Accessed 23 March 2018].

Michaud, N., 2007. Values and Canadian foreign policy: inspiration or hindrance? In: Bratt, D. and Kukucha, C.J. eds. *Readings in Canadian foreign policy: classic debates and new ideas.* Don Mills: Oxford University Press, 341–356.

Morris, L., 2018. The high price of feminism in the "new" Saudi Arabia [online]. *Washington Post*, 21 May. [Accessed 21 May 2018].

Mulroney, D., 2018. Trudeau is delivering the foreign policy Canadians deserve [online]. *Globe and Mail*, 25 February. Available from: www.theglobeandmail.com/opinion/trudeau-is-delivering-the-foreign-policy-canadians-deserve/article38103174/?cmpid [Accessed 15 May 2018].

Nadeau, J., 2004. Branding Canada: can we brand a country? *Canadian Diversity*, 3(2) (Spring), 94–96.

Naumetz, T., 2018. Government yet to establish benchmarks for Mali mission success [online]. *iPolitics*, 18 May. Available from: https://ipolitics.ca/2018/05/18/government-yet-to-establish-benchmarks-for-mali-mission-success/ [Accessed 21 May 2018].

Nimijean, R., 2005a. Articulating the "Canadian Way": Canada™ and the political manipulation of the Canadian identity. *British Journal of Canadian Studies*, 18(2), 26–52.

Nimijean, R., 2005b. The paradoxical nature of the Canadian identity. *Teaching Canada*, 23, 25–31.

Nimijean, R., 2006. The politics of branding Canada: the international-domestic nexus and the rethinking of Canada's place in the world. *Revista mexicana de estudios canadienses*, 11, 67–85.

Nimijean, R., 2014. Domestic brand politics and the modern publicity state. In: Kozolanka, K. ed. *Publicity and the Canadian state.* Toronto: University of Toronto Press, 172–194.

Nimijean, R., 2015. Electoral reform will test Trudeau's leadership, and his values. In: *The Monitor*. Ottawa: Canadian Centre for Policy Alternatives, 12–14.

Nimijean, R., 2017. Migrant spirit contested: competing visions of Canada's national identity in the 2015 federal election. *TransCanadiana*, 9, 335–352.

Nossal, K.R., 2003. "The world we want"? The purposeful confusion of values, goals, and interests in Canadian foreign policy [online]. Available from: http://cdfai.org/currentpublications.htm [Accessed November 13 2003].

Paris, R., 2014. Are Canadians still liberal internationalists? Foreign policy and public opinion in the Harper era. *International Journal: Canada's Journal of Global Policy Analysis*, 69(3), 274–307.

Percival, V., 2018. On global health, Canada is not "back" [online]. *Globe and Mail*, 21 February. Available from: www.theglobeandmail.com/opinion/on-global-health-canada-is-not-back/article38032659/?cmpid [Accessed 15 May 2018].

Potter, E.H., 2009. *Branding Canada: projecting Canada's soft power through public diplomacy*. Montreal: McGill-Queen's University Press.

Rabson, M., 2018. Major audit finds Canada and provinces have no real idea what might be needed to adapt to climate change [online]. *National Observer*, 27 March. Available from: www.nationalobserver.com/2018/03/27/news/major-audit-finds-canada-and-provinces-have-no-real-idea-what-might-be-needed-adapt [Accessed March 31 2018].

Rankin, L.P., 2012. Gender and nation branding in "The true north strong and free". *Place Branding and Public Diplomacy*, 8(4), 257–267.

Rose, J., 2010. The branding of states: the uneasy marriage of marketing to politics. *Journal of Political Marketing*, 9(4), 254–275.

Smith, M.-D., 2018. Trudeau tweet caused influx of refugee inquiries, confusion within government, emails reveal [online]. *Ottawa Citizen*, 3 April. Available from: http://ottawacitizen.com/news/politics/trudeau-tweet-caused-influx-of-refugee-inquiries-confusion-within-government-emails-reveal/wcm/71f4c183-4a71-4bfc-b845-36232f227a99 [Accessed 15 May 2018].

Stairs, D., 2003. Myths, morals, and reality in Canadian foreign policy. *International Journal: Canada's Journal of Global Policy Analysis*, 58(2), 239–256.

Toope, S., 2016. Canada isn't back … yet [online]. *Globe and Mail,* 12 February. Available from: www.theglobeandmail.com/news/world/world-insider/on-the-world-stage-canada-isnt-back-yet/article28742020/ [Accessed 31 May 2018].

van Ham, P., 2001a. Interview with the Author [online]. *Foreign Affairs*. Available from: www.foreignaffairs.com/articles/global-commons/2001-09-01/interview-author [Accessed October 2001].

van Ham, P., 2001b. The rise of the brand state: the postmodern politics of image and reputation. *Foreign Affairs*, 80(5), 2–6.

Way, L., 2011. An energy superpower or a super sales pitch? Building the case through an examination of Canadian newspapers coverage of oil sands. *Canadian Political Science Review*, 5(1), 74–98.

Wells, P., 2016. Justin Trudeau defends Saudi deal — "We're not a banana republic' [online]. *Toronto Star*, 10 June. Available from: www.thestar.com/news/canada/2016/06/10/trudeau-defends-saudi-deal-were-not-a-banana-republic-wells.html [Accessed 23 July 2016].

Wherry, A., 2015. For the record: Justin Trudeau on liberty and the niqab [online]. *Maclean's*, 10 March. Available from: www.macleans.ca/politics/for-the-record-justin-trudeau-on-liberty-and-the-niqab/ [Accessed 4 October 2016].

## 2 The brand image of Canadian Prime Minister Justin Trudeau in international context

Alex Marland

**ABSTRACT**
This policy commentary outlines the components of a political brand and explores the brand attributes of Canadian Prime Minister Justin Trudeau on the international stage. It is difficult for any Canadian leader to attract sustained, positive international media attention as Trudeau has done. It is argued that his image is anchored in the brand of his father Pierre Trudeau and in stereotypes of Canada. Moreover, his style of political image management plays well among liberal elites in metropolitan cities, and in the light entertainment programming and social media selfies that augment his celebrity status.

**RÉSUMÉ**
Ce commentaire politique présente les composantes d'une marque politique et explore les caractéristiques de celle du Premier ministre canadien Justin Trudeau sur la scène internationale. Pour tout autre leader canadien, il serait difficile de susciter un intérêt positif et soutenu des médias internationaux avec autant de succès que Trudeau. Certains avancent que son image est ancrée dans la marque de son père, Pierre Trudeau, et dans des stéréotypes du Canada. De plus, son style de gestion d'image politique s'intègre bien parmi les élites libérales des métropoles, ainsi qu'au programme léger de divertissement et aux selfies des médias sociaux qui renforcent son statut de célébrité.

Getting noticed in a positive manner on the global stage is difficult for the leader of a non-superpower. Canadian Prime Minister Justin Trudeau is among a small number whose celebrity leaps from domestic politics into international pop culture. But what image does the Trudeau brand project, exactly?

It is impossible to construct a definitive description. Brands are the sum of all communication exposure and touchpoints. Consumers form an emotional attachment to certain brands, becoming loyal to a brand and its symbols, preferring it over the alternatives even during a crisis (e.g. Hoeffler and Keller 2003). Branding a politician is complex, given that humans are not inanimate and malleable, as with soap or soda. With politicians, there are so many more stimuli. Some of these variables are reasonably fixed (e.g. party affiliation, jurisdiction, demographic characteristics), some can be adjusted (e.g. clothing, mannerisms, tone of voice) and some require group effort (e.g. public policy, spokespersons). Expert use of a marketing mix is no guarantee that desired messages will cut through the barrage of communication that citizens around the world are exposed to each day. Most of them pay scant attention to politics; even if they do, global news coverage typically ignores Canadian politicians. Moreover, voters process information in diverse ways. In Canada, a Liberal Party supporter is predisposed to see their leader much differently than other partisans do. In other countries, people will harbor opposing impressions about Trudeau based on ideology, or interest in Canada.

The brand of any Canadian leader is indelibly associated with stereotypes of Canada itself. Canada evokes a nicer, kinder version of the United States. Words used to describe Canada in the FutureBrand Country Brand Index include friendly, fun, freedom, clean and snow (FutureBrand 2015, p. 25). A Canadian prime minister is thus internationally typecast as the leader of a nation of polite, law-abiding citizens who play hockey, enjoy a high standard of living and live in a safe environment of natural beauty. The Trudeau brand is gentile but it defies the more rugged stereotypes. To conservatives, he is the leader of a socialist hotbed of high taxes, a substandard medical system, lax drug laws and political correctness. Among progressives, he is a tonic for the populism of Brexit, the Donald Trump presidency, anti-immigration sentiments and right-wing rhetoric. There are more impressions: environmentalists see Canada as a climate change dinosaur because of oil/tar sands emissions, internationalists lament that Canadian politicians prioritize domestic policy over global activism, and so on. All such thoughts about Canada and global politics bear on the Trudeau brand.

Above all, Justin Trudeau's image is an extension of that of his famous father, former Prime Minister Pierre Trudeau. From a marketing point of view, the son leverages the brand equity of the parent brand (Marland 2016, pp. 126–134). He benefits by hugging the positive attributes while developing his own persona and disassociating himself from negatives. Liberal partisans' attachment to the Trudeau family brand – which has gravitated from representing national unity to embodying the values of the Canadian Charter of Rights and Freedoms – constrains abilities to pivot in the public consciousness. Understanding the current Canadian prime minister's persona therefore requires familiarity with his namesake. A similar playbook is being executed in different technological terrain.

Media and public fascination with Pierre Trudeau in the late 1960s reached such a frenzy that the phenomenon was dubbed Trudeaumania. His sex appeal embodied a mod subculture of trendy music, stylish suits, pop art and a cosmopolitan world outlook in a country that was breaking free from its colonial roots (Litt 2016). Young Liberal women chased him in front of cameras. He dated entertainers such as Barbara Streisand. On international trips, he was accorded celebrity treatment. There are parallels with the early years of Justin Trudeau's time in the same role. Richard Nimijean (2017) is among those who observe how the younger Trudeau graced the cover of *Vogue* magazine, uses fancy socks as a diplomatic tool, and is described on American talk shows as the world's sexiest politician. Other examples of Justin Trudeau's international fame abound, including his bromance with Barack Obama (a Democrat), his mingling with Hollywood A-listers, and being mobbed at international events by delegates and journalists seeking a photograph with him. Trudeau was so eager to project an image of democratic accessibility that he quickly became known as the selfie prime minister. This last point is a demarcation from his father's era. Smartphones and social media result in images in faraway places traveling the world instantly. Digital photos and video are created daily and circulate via Facebook, Instagram and Twitter (see Lalancette and Raynauld 2017). Political paparazzi and social media users are drawn to beautiful people, and celebrity and pop culture, particularly when combined with an image of accessibility. In the global political entertainment marketplace, attention is paid to lifestyle and human-interest stories; public policy is an afterthought. Millions more people in faraway places will be exposed to a shirtless Trudeau photobombing a wedding as compared with the small number who will examine his government's policies. American television host Ellen DeGeneres' tweet that Trudeau was an "inspiration" for his government's public apology to LGBTQ Canadians who faced persecution over their sexual orientation is the exception rather than the rule.

So, the Liberal Party of Canada has produced another debonair cosmopolitan who projects the idealism of the liberal elites who are largely concentrated in metropolitan cities. They care about Canada's international image and role in foreign affairs. These global thinkers find prestige in Canada having a seat on the United Nations (UN) Security Council. When a Republican is in the White House they chafe against closer ties with Washington, and when a Democrat is in office they fawn over Canadian connections. These are among the varied reasons why Stephen Harper and the Conservative Party prioritized domestic policy and exhibited apparent disdain for global political institutions. When George W. Bush (a Republican) was president, Conservatives urged Canadians to support the troops in Afghanistan, a patriotic stance that exhibited awareness that Bush was unpopular in Canada. Conservative foreign policy stances sought to appeal to segments of the electoral market at home. Strong stands in support of Israel and Ukraine, for example, resonated with targeted voter cohorts in Canada. The liberal elites were apoplectic when Prime Minister Harper skipped opportunities to address the UN General Assembly, once attending the opening of a Tim Hortons restaurant in Oakville instead, a forum that Conservative voters were more likely to relate to. Harper was playing to his political constituency which did not include those who prize global statesmanship. Likewise, Justin Trudeau connects with his own base when seeking out international forums and fame, a recognition that Liberals are more likely to see themselves as global citizens.

Contrasts between Prime Ministers Harper and Trudeau extend beyond policy and practice. To the global media, Harper was just another middle-aged white guy in a suit with no pizazz or celebrity appeal. Conversely, his successor is handsome and on the right side of political correctness. This makes Trudeau attractive to light entertainment programming, ranging from *Vanity Fair* to TMZ. "Why can't he be our president?" asks the cover of *The Rolling Stone* in August 2017. The prime minister rationalizes attention paid to him and wife Sophie Grégoire Trudeau as a good way to generate international exposure of Canada, particularly among those who ordinarily do not pay attention to Canadian politics. Bureaucrats in Global Affairs Canada have discussed framing the country's foray into UN peacekeeping operations as "building on Brand Trudeau" (Blanchfield 2016). In many respects, he is marketing magic.

Trudeau's policies draw attention in more highbrow outlets, such as *The New York Times* and *The Guardian*. The most lauded is his feminism, symbolized best by his appointment of a gender-balanced cabinet. Visuals of the prime minister handing out coats to Syrian refugees arriving in Canada struck an emotional chord too. On some files, Trudeau has tried to avoid making the news, such as free trade negotiations with the United States, because of the risk of falling on the wrong side of President Trump. A notable misstep was a statement about Fidel Castro's death proclaiming the Cuban dictator as a "remarkable leader." It was a case of hugging the parent brand too closely: Castro was a family friend who attended his father's funeral. Both Trudeaus have faced controversy for expressing fondness for communist China.

Political celebrity is prone to ebb and flow, to be fêted or derided. Justin Trudeau's international brand luster is arguably waning. In 2016, he attended the World Economic Forum annual meeting, known as the Davos Summit. The event brings together high-profile business, political, entertainment and other leaders. Canadian media reported that their new prime minister was treated as a rock star. He met with business personalities and mingled with celebrities such as Bono, Leonardo DiCaprio and Kevin Spacey. A year later the political winds were changing. Going to Davos amid a spurt of anti-elitism would not do, particularly when Trudeau was under fire at home for vacationing in the Bahamas on a private island owned by the Aga Khan, another family friend. Instead, Trudeau embarked on his first prime ministerial cross-country charm offensive, effortlessly projecting a democratic ethos in town halls with Canadians. Later in 2017, Australian and New Zealand media lit into Trudeau for skipping a meeting of Trans-Pacific Partnership leaders. No longer a fresh face, in 2018 Trudeau and his family faced worldwide ridicule for wearing traditional Indian outfits in blatant photo ops, and his administration was criticized for inviting a Sikh extremist to an official function in New Delhi. One Canadian political talk show host argued that the

> far-too-long tour of India by a prime minister looking for campaign-friendly photo-ops has become a cross between the Keystone Cops and Mr. Dressup. Poor advance team scouting, lousy political intelligence-gathering, awkward fashion advice and a major security breach have turned a minor snub at the arrival gate into a sustained epic failure. (Martin 2018)

His second cross-Canada town hall also had less of the fawning adulation that characterized the first tour. If history is any indication, Trudeau is walking the same path as his father and President Obama before him: the media shine wears off as the thorny business of governing takes over. In opposition, a leader represents hope and optimism. Once in power, a leader's image absorbs attributes of the establishment.

The accumulation of controversial decisions, broken promises, pseudo-scandal, unethical behavior and negative news will accumulate and damage the Trudeau brand. Idealism attached to a rising star is gradually replaced by the realism that a prime minister is a human being with flaws who is advancing a political agenda. To some extent, domestic frustrations have little bearing outside of Canada. External awareness of Trudeau is limited and familiarity is likely built through social media superficialities. This includes impressions in elite circles that the handsome, wholesome Canadian is a foil to a mean-spirited, unhinged President Trump. Trudeau also fits among a wave of young, charismatic leaders including Jacinda Ardern (New Zealand), Luigi Di Maio (Italy), Sebastian Kurz (Austria), Emmanuel Macron (France), Matteo Renzi (Italy), Taavi Roivas (Estonia) and Leo Varadkar (Ireland). The contrast with stodgy standoffish opponents and his Conservative predecessor makes for a good brand story. However, we must not overstate international interest in the Canadian prime minister. Global public opinion surveys about world leaders pay attention to countries with more clout, such as China, Germany, Russia, the United Kingdom and the United States (e.g. Gallup International 2017). The old order still dominates world politics. No matter what socks Trudeau wears, Canada is simply not the global player that some Canadians imagine.

So what do Canadians think of their political heartthrob? The contrast with President Trump and political turmoil in the United States makes Canada's leader look like a global statesman. There is smugness that despondent Americans can find refuge up north. Some crave the diplomatic clout that comes with being a middle power. To them, fawning international media attention is a political bargaining tool, and it is good for investment and tourism. Indeed, an Angus Reid Institute survey found that more than half of Canadians believe that Trudeau's fame is a net positive for Canada (Angus Reid Institute 2017). However, the same poll found that just as many Canadians think that the Trudeau government places excessive attention on public relations and photo-ops, and that it is not getting things done. Further, the India trip was such a public relations disaster that it may mark the end of the prolonged Trudeau love-in. For the first time, a majority of Canadians disapproved of his performance as prime minister, a level of popularity worse than Harper's at the same point in their tenures (Angus Reid Institute 2018).

International stardom and adulation cannot be Justin Trudeau's endgame. The citizens of New York City and Manila have no say in whether the Trudeau Liberals are returned to office. His image at home rather than abroad will be of growing importance as the 2019 federal election approaches. Remaining in power is a precondition to any leader's ability to leverage political capital on the international stage.

## Notes on contributor

*Alex Marland* studies political marketing in Canada. His book *Brand command: Canadian politics and democracy in the age of message control* (UBC Press, 2016) won the Donner Prize for best public policy book by a Canadian.

## Disclosure statement

No potential conflict of interest was reported by the author.

## References

Angus Reid Institute, 2017. 'Charismatic' and 'modern' or 'arrogant' and 'flaky'? Canadians weigh in on the Trudeau brand. [online] 19 October. Available from: http://angusreid.org/trudeau-brand/ [Accessed 22 February 2018].
Angus Reid Institute, 2018. Scheer's delight? If an election were held tomorrow, CPC could have a shot at majority government. [online] 19 March. Available from: http://angusreid.org/federal-issues-march2018/ [Accessed 23 March 2018].
Blanchfield, Mike, 2016. Canada mulled using 'Brand Trudeau' to help pitch world on peacekeeping return. *Toronto Star*, December 30. Available from https://www.thestar.com/news/canada/2016/12/30/canada-mulled-using-brand-trudeau-to-help-pitch-world-on-peacekeeping-return.html [Accessed 1 March 2018].
FutureBrand, 2015. Country brand index 2014–15. Available from: https://www.futurebrand.com/uploads/CBI2014-5.pdf [Accessed 22 February 2018].
Gallup International, 2017. Global leaders: Gallup International's 41st annual global end of year survey. Available from: http://www.gallup-international.com/wp-content/uploads/2017/12/2017_Global-Leaders.pdf [Accessed 1 March 2018].

Hoeffler, S. and Keller, K.L., 2003. The marketing advantages of strong brands. *Journal of Brand Management*, 10 (6), 421–445.

Lalancette, M. and Raynauld, V., 2017. The power of political image: Justin Trudeau, Instagram, and celebrity politics. *American Behavioral Scientist*. Available from: doi/pdf/10.1177/0002764217744838 [Accessed 22 February 2018].

Litt, P., 2016. *Trudeaumania*. Vancouver: UBC Press.

Marland, A., 2016. *Brand command: Canadian politics and democracy in the age of message control*. Vancouver: UBC Press.

Martin, D., 2018. If this is Trudeau putting Canada 'back' on the world stage, we should get off. *CTV News*, February 22. Available from https://www.ctvnews.ca/politics/don-martin-blog/don-martin-if-this-is-trudeau-putting-canada-back-on-the-world-stage-we-should-get-off-1.3815230 [Accessed 1 March 2018].

Nimijean, R., 2017. A portrait of Justin Trudeau. Canadian Centre for Policy Alternatives [online]. 24 August. Available from: https://www.policyalternatives.ca/publications/monitor/portrait-justin-trudeau [Accessed 22 February 2018].

# 3  All about that base?

Branding and the domestic politics of Canadian foreign aid

Stephen Brown

**ABSTRACT**
How do left- and right-leaning governments differ in their provision of foreign aid? As the case of Canada confirms, it is not clear that either type gives more aid or that they spend it significantly differently. This article examines the claim that Stephen Harper's government played to its Conservative base and compares its record to that of Liberal governments. It finds that all governments over the past few decades have tried to brand their aid initiatives in ways that will appeal to their respective bases. These changes are based on domestic electoral considerations, rather than the needs and priorities of aid recipients, and are a distraction from and impediment to aid effectiveness considerations. In spite of their rhetorical differences, successive governments actually exhibit great continuity in their aid programs, regardless of which party is in power.

**RÉSUMÉ**
Comment les gouvernements de gauche et de droite diffèrent-ils dans la fourniture de l'aide au développement ? Comme le confirme le cas du Canada, il n'est pas certain que l'un ou l'autre octroie davantage d'aide ou qu'ils la dépensent de façon sensiblement différente. Cet article examine l'affirmation selon laquelle les politiques du gouvernement Harper ont visé sa base électorale conservatrice et compare ses pratiques à celles des Libéraux. Il constate que tous les gouvernements au cours des dernières décennies ont essayé de présenter leurs initiatives d'aide de manière à faire appel à leur base respective. Ces changements sont fondés sur des considérations électorales nationales, plutôt que sur les besoins et les priorités des bénéficiaires de l'aide, et constituent une distraction et une entrave à l'efficacité de l'aide. En dépit de leurs différences rhétoriques, les gouvernements font preuve d'une grande continuité dans leur programme d'aide, quel que soit le parti au pouvoir.

© 2018 The Author(s). Published by Informa UK Limited, trading as Taylor & Francis Group
This is an Open Access article distributed under the terms of the Creative Commons Attribution-NonCommercial-NoDerivatives License (http://creativecommons.org/licenses/by-nc-nd/4.0/), which permits non-commercial re-use, distribution, and reproduction in any medium, provided the original work is properly cited, and is not altered, transformed, or built upon in any way.

## Introduction

During the decade that the Conservative government of Prime Minister Stephen Harper was in power in Canada (2006–2015), analysts frequently commented that the key to understanding the government's policies – especially the ones commentators disapproved of – was how it played to Conservative Party's electoral base, including in relation to Canadian foreign aid policies. Interestingly, mainstream commentators have criticized its successor, Justin Trudeau's Liberal government, much less frequently for similar actions, for instance when it announced that "Canada is back" (for an exception, see Akin 2015), and rarely if at all when it issued its Feminist International Assistance Policy.

This article explores the prevalence and impact of "playing to the base" – that is to say, a government seeking to please its core groups of supporters – and electoral politics more broadly in Canadian aid policies. To what extent does domestic politics influence Canadian aid priorities and practices? How does the recently completed decade of Conservative government compare to other Canadian governments? What impact does the targeting of categories of voters via aid "branding" have on the effectiveness of aid?

It argues that the Harper government's bias toward its base is indeed visible in its aid initiatives. However, Liberal governments have also demonstrated their own bases and biases, all of which distract from evidence-based decision-making. Though the Harper government's pandering to its base was often highlighted, academics and political commentators, in their general disapproval of the Harper government's policies, tend to minimize and even ignore the importance of domestic politics in setting aid policies under other governments as well. In fact, changes to date under the Trudeau government seem to be more at the rhetorical level than in practice – that is to say, mainly a branding exercise. Moreover, in several instances, Liberals and Conservatives pander in similar ways to Canadian voters beyond their respective traditional bases, which can also have negative effects on aid effectiveness.

To make this argument, the article begins by reviewing the literature on political party ideology and its effect on foreign aid, particularly regarding disbursement levels and underlying motives. Next, it introduces the Harper government and its oft-cited electoral base and contrasts it with the more loosely defined Liberal base. It then traces how recent Conservative and Liberal governments have played to their respective bases in their aid policies, through an examination of five key issue areas that can be linked to bases of electoral support: the role of women in development, the funding of Canadian development non-governmental organizations (NGOs), geographic priorities, humanitarian assistance, and aid budgets. For each area, it illustrates how, to varying degrees, governments led by both parties have framed their aid and played to their respective bases, as well as used aid policy for electoral purposes, to the detriment of aid effectiveness. This mainly qualitative study of Canadian aid provides new insights into the branding of international assistance and the domestic dynamics of aid policy that is in large part motivated by electoral considerations.

Branding initiatives can target both domestic and international audiences. For instance, the "Canada is back" pronouncements were ostensibly aimed at the international community, presumably linked to the Trudeau government's desire to be elected to the United Nations (UN) Security Council in 2021. However, the Liberals also wanted to signal to Canadian voters that they, unlike the Conservatives, were internationalists and intended to make important contributions on the world stage. Similarly, new aid policies seek to send messages to Canadians and to international actors, be they donor peers or recipient countries. Without meaning to deny the importance of the role of branding in Canada's international image and projection of soft power (Potter 2009) or the need to analyze the interconnection of the national and international dimensions of branding (Nimijean 2006, Rankin 2012), this article follows Marland (2016), Nimijean (2005) and others in focusing primarily on domestic dynamics.

## Political parties, ideology and the domestic determinants of foreign aid

Domestic politics clearly matter when donors decide how to allocate their foreign aid (Kleibl 2013). Most studies of foreign aid focus on donor country motives and geographical aid allocation patterns, treating the donor state as a unitary actor and failing to examine variations based on leadership and ideology within the donor government (Dreher *et al.* 2015). Similarly, although numerous studies focus on the determinants of the size of a donor government's aid budget, fewer consider differences between left- and right-leaning governments. Of those, a handful make the rather intuitive argument that left-wing governments tend to provide more foreign aid both in specific case studies (Milner and Tingley 2010, Travis 2010) and more generally among Organisation for Economic Co-operation and Development (OECD) donors (Imbeau 1988, Thérien and Noël 2000, Thérien 2002, Tingley 2010, Brech and Potrafke 2014). However, Fuchs *et al.* (2014, p. 177) reviewed eight such publications and found the evidence "inconclusive," as the various studies reached a range of different and even contradictory conclusions (see also discussion in Dreher *et al.* 2015, pp. 163–164). Surprisingly, Conservative-led governments in the United Kingdom after 2010 have been as supportive of high levels of aid spending as their Labour Party predecessors (Heppell and Lightfoot 2012, Mawdsley 2017). Fuchs *et al.*'s (2014) own study failed to find any statistically significant difference between left- and right-wing governments in the case of Germany.

A quick look at Table 1, which traces the evolution of the ratio of official development assistance (ODA) to gross national income (GNI) – the standard measure of donor generosity – confirms that there is no clear link between aid volume and ideology over the past three decades in Canada. For instance, the average ODA/GNI ratio between 1985 and 1993, during which time the Progressive Conservatives were in office, was 0.47 per cent, close to historical highs. However, 1994–2005, under the Liberals, and 2006–2015, when the Conservatives held power, the average level of ODA was identical: 0.30 per cent of GNI. After the Liberal government of Justin Trudeau was elected, the ratio fell to 0.26 per cent in 2016 and will remain around that level for the foreseeable future, according

**Table 1.** Relative generosity of Canadian governments, 1985–2016.

| Years | Party in power | Prime Minister | Average ODA/GNI (%) | Range of ODA/GNI (%) |
|---|---|---|---|---|
| 1985–1993 | Progressive Conservative Party | Brian Mulroney, Kim Campbell | 0.47 | 0.44–0.50 |
| 1994–2005 | Liberal Party | Jean Chrétien, Paul Martin | 0.30 | 0.22–0.43 |
| 2006–2015 | Conservative Party | Stephen Harper | 0.30 | 0.24–0.34 |
| 2016 | Liberal Party | Justin Trudeau | 0.26 | 0.26 |

Source: Data from OECD (2018b), with calculations by the author.

to the government's 2018 budget. Furthermore, these averages belie wide fluctuations while a single party is in power, especially the deepest cuts ever under Liberal Prime Minister Jean Chrétien in the 1990s.

If left- and right-wing governments do not systematically appear to spend different *amounts* of aid, it still could be that they spend the aid budget *differently*, whatever their level of generosity. For instance, conservative governments are generally considered more likely to use aid to promote their commercial interests, which has been confirmed in some case studies (e.g. Fleck and Kilby 2006), but not in others (such as Dreher *et al.* 2015, Sohn and Yoo 2015).

Other publications have argued that the Canadian government, under the Harper Conservatives, "instrumentalized" (Brown 2016b) and "recommercialized" (Brown 2016c) the aid program. However, there were always close ties between aid and Canadian business interests under previous Liberal governments as well. This article adopts a somewhat different albeit complementary approach. It assesses the common accusation that the Harper government was "playing to its base" in the realm of foreign aid and how applicable the phenomenon has been under Liberal governments as well. In doing so, it treats the Harper government as less of a *sui generis* case and explores the extent to which the Canadian government adopts such a strategy regardless of which party is in power. First, however, it examines the parties' respective bases.

## Conservative and Liberal bases

As mentioned above, from 2006 to 2015, while Prime Minister Stephen Harper and his Conservative Party were in power in Ottawa, analysts frequently commented that the key to understanding the government's policies was how it played to the Conservative Party's electoral base, be it in general (e.g. Malloy 2010, Wells 2013) or regarding its foreign policy (Jones 2014, Nossal 2014), and specifically with respect to foreign aid (Brown 2015b, Audet and Navarro-Flores 2016, Black 2016, Goyette 2016). This base has been described in geographic, religious and ideological terms: Western Canadian, especially Alberta-based (the home province of all four leaders to date of the Conservative Party and its predecessor, the Reform Party/Canadian Alliance), evangelical Christian, and neoconservative, with important support from certain "diasporic" ethnic communities. Observers have implicitly and explicitly contrasted this not only with the party's previous "Progressive Conservative" incarnation, including under the government of Prime Minister Brian Mulroney (1984–1993), but also with various Liberal governments, including under Jean Chrétien (1993–2003), Paul Martin (2003–2006) and Harper's successor, Trudeau (2015 to present).

The Conservatives' base, as described above, does not accurately describe all of its electoral support, as the party has also held strong appeal among non-evangelical, social and fiscal small-c conservatives. They have also attracted voters from across the country who might not want to support the Liberals, who had previously been in power for 13 years, and to whom the leftist New Democratic Party does not hold much appeal. For instance, in the 2011 general elections, the Conservatives dominated in Western Canada, but also obtained a large majority of seats in Ontario, significantly extending their electoral sway in the province's rural and suburban areas. The need to appeal to voters outside the party's traditional base can serve as a brake on appeals that seek to please that base.

For instance, the Conservative Party leadership did not want to try to restrict access to abortion, roll back LGBT rights or appear too anti-immigrant, fearing it would alienate potential voters.

By way of contrast, the Liberal Party's traditional base has been located primarily in Quebec, Ontario and the Atlantic provinces. Immigrants have also been an important source of Liberal support, especially those from developing countries (White 2017), although the Harper government made strategic inroads into more socially conservative immigrant communities. The Liberal base is more cosmopolitan and internationalist in perspective, often associated with the legacy of Lester B. Pearson, including United Nations peacekeeping. Especially under Justin Trudeau, the Liberals have particularly appealed to and, in fact, targeted women voters, notably under a Prime Minister who proudly proclaims himself a feminist and regularly emphasizes his support for a woman's right to choose.

## Playing to the base

Just as many of the Harper government's foreign policy positions – such as unconditional support for Israel – can be traced to a desire to appeal to specific members of the party's base (evangelical Christians) and/or expand it (e.g. to Jewish voters in key urban ridings), numerous initiatives in the realm of foreign aid reflected a desire to please or enlarge the party's appeal to voters. According to Nossal (2014, pp. 15–16), "during the period of minority government from 2006 to 2011 [...] electoral politics not only loomed large, but trumped virtually all other strategic considerations" and "even with a majority [government], foreign policy decisions continued to be framed with the ballot box primarily in mind." Though less clearly linked to electoral considerations, at least in the public eye, the Trudeau government has also adopted foreign policy positions and labels meant to please its base, including more action on climate change, a "progressive" trade agenda, a "feminist" foreign policy and an explicitly Feminist International Assistance Policy (FIAP), issued in June 2017 (Canada 2017).[1]

This section compares successive governments' actions in the five foreign aid policy areas identified in the introduction and assesses their impact on aid effectiveness.

### Women in development

The role of women in development has been a priority of Canadian aid since the mid-1980s. Successive policy documents have all identified women and/or gender equality as a priority area, often labeled a crosscutting issue. Thus, the focus is not a new one, but the way it is framed has shifted repeatedly.

In January 2010, Harper announced that maternal, newborn and child health (MNCH) would be an importance focus of the Group of Eight (G8) summit to be hosted by Harper in June of that year at a resort in Huntsville, in the Muskoka region of Ontario. At the summit, he launched the Muskoka Initiative for MNCH, with the goal of mobilizing an extra CAD$5 billion for development assistance in this area. The Conservatives followed this up in 2014 with a global summit on MNCH, held in Toronto, also personally hosted by Harper, with a commitment to spend another CAD$3.5 billion over five years.

The government apparently chose to champion MNCH specifically to soften the Conservatives' – and Harper's – "nasty brand," to use Marland's (2016, p. xiv) expression. After all, who could object to a literal motherhood issue? However, even before the Muskoka summit, controversy erupted. Foreign Minister Lawrence Cannon and Minister of International Cooperation Bev Oda initially stated that the initiative would not provide any funding for contraception. After a public outcry, the government announced that contraception would be included, but not abortion, even where legal.[2] Public objections continued, but the government maintained that abortion services, though available in Canada, were too divisive an issue domestically to fund abroad. Conservative Senator Nancy Ruth publicly advised NGO representatives to "Shut the fuck up on this issue" or risk a backlash (quoted in Clark 2010, Delacort 2010). Most NGOs did precisely that. They avoided criticizing the government for its restrictive approach to MNCH and contented themselves with accessing the funds to be used for the government-identified priorities. Despite the eventual inclusion of contraception in the Muskoka Initiative, only 1.4 per cent of Canada's funding was spent in this area, demonstrating how low a priority it was (Payton 2015).

The ban on MNCH funding for abortion, even where legal, can easily be interpreted as playing to the Conservatives' socially conservative base, especially evangelical Christians, while also appealing to Catholics. The marginalization and possible initial exclusion of contraception also fit well within that frame. Moreover, the Harper government adopted a Christian charity-influenced approach of "saving women and children," who were portrayed as passive victims, as opposed to seeking to empower women and promote gender equality (which would address some root causes of poor MNCH, rather than treat symptoms), and tended to reduce women's role to "walking wombs" (Tiessen 2015; see also broader discussion in Rankin 2012).

Though the Muskoka Initiative has no doubt funded numerous important programs, its restrictive approach, which drew criticism from United States Secretary of State Hillary Clinton, United Kingdom Foreign Secretary David Miliband and leading British medical journal *The Lancet*, prevented it from having as positive an impact as it could have (Brown and Olender 2013, p. 169). For instance, under the Conservatives, it was of little assistance to the 220 million women who lack access to contraception and did nothing to prevent the 13 per cent of maternal deaths that are due to unsafe abortions (Payton 2015). Moreover, the high proportion of Canadian aid earmarked to the Muskoka Initiative, CAD$8.5 billion between 2010 and 2020, represents roughly 20 per cent of Canada's total aid. In a context of stagnant and even shrinking aid budgets, the focus on MNCH has necessitated cuts to aid in other vital sectors.

The Liberal Party sought to distinguish itself from the Conservatives' approach. While the party's 2015 electoral platform avoided using the term "abortion," it promised to

> ensure that Canada's valuable aid initiative on Maternal, Newborn and Child Health (MNCH) is driven by evidence and outcomes, not ideology. Closing existing gaps in reproductive rights and health care can and will save lives. We will cover the full range of reproductive health services as part of MNCH initiatives. (Liberal Party of Canada 2015, p. 65)

After their electoral victory, Prime Minister Justin Trudeau gave a mandate to Minister of International Development Marie-Claude Bibeau that included "ensuring that Canada's valuable development focus on Maternal, Newborn and Child Health is driven by evidence and outcomes, not ideology, including by closing existing gaps in reproductive rights and health care for women" (Trudeau 2015), repeating the same somewhat coded language. Here, the Liberals were signaling to those who were familiar with the controversy that abortion would be added to the Muskoka Initiative, and possibly that more emphasis would be placed on contraception as well.

The 2017 FIAP took a bolder approach. It explicitly stated that Canada would "support increased access to a full range of health services, including [...] safe and legal abortion, and post-abortion care" (Canada 2017). It also made "Gender equality and the empowerment of women and girls" the policy's "core action area" and committed to allocating no less than 95 per cent of Canadian bilateral aid by 2022 to initiatives that either targeted this priority area or integrated it into their objectives. The new aid policy even had its own designated hashtag, which cleverly rhymes in both official languages: #HerVoiceHerChoice and #SaVoixSonChoix.

The Liberals were playing to their pro-choice, pro-feminist base, while initially avoiding words and specifics that would attract opprobrium from opponents. Interestingly, they went out of their way to praise their predecessors' "valuable" MNCH program, also seeking to envelop themselves in the cloak of this motherhood issue – although that emphasis seems to be decreasing as the Liberal government reframes its work in this area. Having completely dropped any mention of the Muskoka Initiative – what Marland (2016, p. 326) refers to as "brand evisceration" – the Trudeau government now uses the more encompassing label of "sexual and reproductive health and rights" or SRSH, a somewhat awkward, weaker brand.

The Trudeau government has emphasized the need to, in Bibeau's words, "empower women and girls and protect their rights, as they are equal agents of change in the development of their communities and countries" (Global Affairs Canada 2016, p. 3). These words and the promise to apply a "feminist lens [...] throughout all of Canada's international assistance activities" (Global Affairs Canada 2016, p. 10) contrast starkly with the "saving victims" approach of the Harper government. However, it remains to be seen what actual impact this will have on aid programming (Brown and Swiss 2017). Though branded differently, projects announced since the Trudeau government came to power – including those specifically targeting women and girls – do not have particularly different underlying approaches from those under the Conservatives.[3] The language, however, is likely to appeal to the female-dominated and internationalist base, and potentially attract support away from the New Democrats.

### *Support to Canadian development NGOs*

The funding of development NGOs became increasingly politicized under the Harper government, as it ceased funding a number of organizations that had been critical of government policy, especially regarding the activities of the Canadian extractive industry or Canada's position on Palestinian rights. Many well-regarded NGOs, including KAIROS, Alternatives, Development and Peace, MATCH International and the Mennonite Central Committee, as well as the sector's umbrella organization, the Canadian Council for International Co-operation, had their funding proposals rejected, often with spurious justifications. One cannot underestimate the chilling effect this had on the NGO sector and advocacy work in particular, further magnified by what appeared to be vindictive, onerous income tax audits of critical NGOs. By way of contrast, when the media reported on a homophobic Christian evangelical NGO receiving funding for its work in Uganda, the government merely suspended its funding pending an investigation – and resumed it almost immediately (Mackrael and Ling 2013).

A study published in the *Canadian Journal of Development Studies* in 2013, and earlier leaked to the press, fed the perception that the Harper government was disproportionally allocating aid funds to NGOs that represented its base. It found that, when compared to Liberal governments in 2001–2005, the Conservative government over the period 2006–2010 increased funding to faith-based NGOs by 42 per cent, especially proselytizing ones, whose funding increased by 75 per cent, many of which were based in Western Canada. By way of contrast, grants to religious NGOs under the Liberals had declined by five per cent. Conversely, the previous Liberal government had increased funding to secular NGOs by 27 per cent and the Conservatives subsequently by five per cent (Audet *et al.* 2013). These patterns strongly support the thesis that the Harper government was seeking to please its base.

Such conclusions must be tempered by a parallel study by Ray Vander Zaag (2013) that found no such trend and Vander Zaag's (2014) strong critique of Audet *et al.*'s study. However, even if the results are accurate, they might not be as conclusive as they appear at first blush regarding Conservatives playing to their base. It could be that the previous Liberal governments had been playing to or otherwise biased toward their secular, non-Western base – and the Conservatives merely restored a more balanced distribution of funding. Still, according to Vander Zaag's (2013, p. 327) calculations, faith-based NGOs received 34 per cent of aid funds channeled through Canadian NGOs between 2005 and 2010, though they constituted 25 per cent of NGOs.

Lacking both clear data on funding trends and, furthermore, any sense of what would be a good (let alone optimal) distribution of funds among types of NGOs and their regional headquarters, it is hard to demonstrate that the Harper Conservatives were particularly biased toward their base – or their Liberal predecessors either. Also, it is not clear what the effect on aid effectiveness is, even if the proportion of aid to religious organizations did increase, as there is no robust evidence on the relative effectiveness of the various types of NGOs.

Nonetheless, perceptions matter beyond empirical facts. The impression or even belief remained that the Harper government was favoring the West and faith-based organizations, which could curry favor with the Conservative base. The flip side of the coin was, in particular, the sense that it discriminated against Quebec-based NGOs. In large part in reaction to Quebecers' disagreement with the Canadian government's aid priorities (and to stoke Quebec nationalist sentiment), the Quebec government announced in 2014 that it would set up its own official aid organization, the *Agence québécoise de solidarité internationale*, an initiative strongly supported by Quebec-based development NGOs, and try to "repatriate" Quebec's share of the Canadian aid budget (Arsenault 2014).

In response to the Quebec government's activist agenda, to the crisis in the Harper government's relations with NGOs more generally and to garner electoral support in Quebec in particular as the 2015 general elections approached, the Conservatives adopted a new International Development and Humanitarian Assistance Civil Society Partnership Policy in February 2015. It promised to restore funding to NGOs, improve the funding allocation mechanisms and treat NGOs as development actors in their own right, rather than mere subcontractors. However, it was never put into practice, either by the Conservatives in their remaining months in power or by the subsequently elected Liberals. In the meantime, Quebec elected a new government, which implemented an austerity budget and shelved the plan of creating its own aid agency. Two and a half years after the Conservatives launched their policy, the Liberals released a new one that made repeated reference to "a feminist approach," but otherwise differed very little in terms of principles or objectives (Bacher 2017).

Not only could this be considered wasted time, Canadian NGOs are also still waiting (as of March 2018) for the government to announce what the FIAP promised would be "more predictable, equitable, flexible, and transparent funding mechanisms" (Canada 2017). In the meantime, a new problem has arisen: How will the government assess NGO project proposals that were submitted to Global Affairs Canada in response to calls for proposals prior to the launching of the FIAP, but do not meet the latter's subsequent requirements, notably evidence of having held consultations with local women's groups? As was the case under the Harper Conservatives, a large number of proposals for funding seem to be languishing on the minister's desk. Once a critical mass of NGO funding approvals emerges, it will be interesting to see how the Trudeau government's funding patterns compare to previous ones.

### *Geographic priorities*

Since 2002, Canada has identified priority countries for its development assistance. It modifies the list every few years, including under the newly elected government of Paul Martin in 2005 and by the Harper government in 2009 and 2014. The Conservatives' changes in 2009 controversially dropped eight low-income African countries, including several francophone ones, and added middle-income countries in the Americas. In 2014, it restored two of the francophone African countries – Benin and Burkina Faso – that it had dropped in 2009, and added a few new countries, including the Democratic Republic of the Congo, Mongolia, Myanmar and the Philippines.

In many instances, the Harper government's additions conspicuously aligned with the Canadian government's trade agenda, especially the middle-income countries in Latin America with which it was pursing free-trade agreements, and the mineral-rich countries of Congo, Mongolia and Myanmar that Canadian extractive companies were keen to do business in. Accompanied by ministerial pronouncements and party platforms that emphasized the need for Canadian companies to benefit from Canadian foreign aid, these changes can be seen as playing to Canada's pro-business, more self-interested base (Goyette 2016), and to a certain extent the Western Canada base (where much of the extractive industry is headquartered), but not the religious base per se. It is closely linked to the "recommercialization" of Canadian aid (Brown 2016c) and the broader instrumentalization of foreign aid under the Harper government (Brown 2016b). In the run-up to the 2015 general elections, the addition of the Philippines in 2014 can be interpreted as an attempt to win over Filipino-Canadian voters, and the simultaneous restoration of the two French-speaking African countries to appeal to Quebec voters (as was the case for the new civil society partnership policy mentioned above).

The Harper government was not the first to use its geographic aid priorities to try to influence domestic politics. In the 1970s, Pierre Trudeau's Liberal government increased aid to francophone African countries to counter the growth of Quebec's own independent diplomatic relations and development assistance, a threat that resurfaced in 2013–2014, as discussed above. In addition, just as the Conservatives de-emphasized Africa, in its rhetoric if not in actual aid flows, the Liberals have periodically touted their emphasis on Africa in a "serial morality tale" (Black 2015), using aid to Africa as a way of demonstrating its compassion. In this way, the Liberals have used Africa to play to their more humane internationalist base.

Justin Trudeau's government similarly engaged in virtue signaling when it announced in the FIAP that "Canada will ensure that no less than 50 percent of its bilateral international development assistance is directed to sub-Saharan African countries by 2021–22" (Canada 2017). This new commitment, however, was less bold than it seemed, as that target had already been met as recently as 2013 and would require very little new spending to reach again (Calleja 2017).

Moreover, both Conservative and Liberal governments have placed both Haiti and Ukraine among the 10 largest recipients of Canadian ODA, motivated in large part by the presence of voters with diasporic ties to those countries.[4] Haiti is a natural fit for Canadian aid, as it is a low-income country in Canada's neighborhood and one with which Canada shares an official language, otherwise uncommon in the Americas, and a long history of development cooperation. Still, one cannot ignore the fact that Haitian-Canadians are an important minority in vote-rich Montreal. The emphasis Liberal and Conservative governments have placed on Ukraine, however, is much harder to justify on developmental grounds. It is far less clear that Canada should prioritize this middle-income, post-Soviet country. As Ukraine shares a border with the European Union and could eventually join the EU, a partnership with European countries makes a lot more sense, one that goes far beyond traditional aid. However, about one million Canadian voters are of Ukrainian descent and both the Liberals and the Conservatives are keen to court their vote.

Aid to one particular region or country is not *ipso facto* more effective than aid to another. Much depends on what the project or program seeks to accomplish and how well designed it is. *A priori*, assuming an altruistic overarching goal, foreign aid should target the countries where the needs are greatest and focus on poverty reduction (as mandated by Canadian law). Still, important contributions can be made in reducing poverty and inequality in marginalized communities even in middle-income countries. Conversely, aid in a low-income country is not always well spent. It is especially risky in fragile and conflict-affected states, but those are the states that have the least access to other sources of development finance and are at greatest risk of being left behind. What is clear, however, is that constantly shifting countries of focus harms aid effectiveness, as unpredictability and volatility prevent the long-term programming and partnerships that are key to having a lasting impact. Both the Liberals and the Conservatives are guilty of that.[5]

### *Humanitarian assistance*

According to a recent study, while the Harper government was in power, the number of faith-based organizations participating in the government/NGO humanitarian response network grew rapidly, despite the fact that many of them actually had little experience in the sector. The study's authors attribute this increase to the Conservatives "probably seeking to please their electoral base" (Audet and Navarro-Flores 2016, pp. 181–182). Moreover, the relative size of Canadian humanitarian assistance doubled: During its decade years in power (2006–2015), the Harper government committed an average of 14 per cent of its aid budget to humanitarian assistance, more than twice the six per cent that the Liberals had in 1994–2005.[6]

Together, the increased role of religious NGOs and the prominence accorded to humanitarian aid can be linked to the Conservative base, though a bit more tenuously in the second case. In particular, the Harper government's emphasis on humanitarian assistance, including the sharp increase in spending, fits well with a (Christian) charity-based approach to aid – giving victims the food, water, blankets or shelter they need – as opposed to longer term, solidarity-based development cooperation that would appeal more to Liberal and New Democratic Party supporters (Black 2016, p. 23).

There is no doubt that humanitarian assistance is greatly needed around the world. UN appeals are frequently undersubscribed. Climate change appears to be increasing the number of weather-related natural disasters and thus the demand for humanitarian aid, as has the current crisis in Syria and neighboring countries. Although Canada's growing emphasis on humanitarian assistance parallels global trends, it actually exceeds them (Brown 2016b). Moreover, in the Canadian context, where the Harper government froze and then cut its aid budget after 2010, the growing proportion of humanitarian assistance has required an even further reduction in other forms of aid, including programming that could help *prevent* future emergencies. In terms of aid effectiveness, this could be counterproductive.

The Trudeau government has retained and even increased the Harper government's emphasis on humanitarian aid, committing a record 27 per cent of ODA to the humanitarian sector in 2016 (OECD 2018b). The FIAP refers to humanitarian action more often than any previous Canadian aid policy document. Its frequent mention of forcibly displaced people is a reminder of the Trudeau government's prominent commitment to helping refugees, including its signature promise to quickly settle 25,000 Syrians in Canada. In fact, refugee resettlement, which is counted in ODA figures, may explain the rapid increase in humanitarian assistance flows in 2016. In late 2017, Canada announced CAD$38 million in support to Myanmari Rohingya refugees in Bangladesh, highlighting how it would "address the gender-specific needs of women and girls" as part of a feminist approach (Global Affairs Canada 2017; see also Harris 2017). Clearly, the Trudeau government has started to brand its humanitarian assistance and use it to appeal to its pro-refugee, liberal internationalist base.

## *Aid budgets, "real" results and business as usual*

As was the case for other Western donor countries, Canada significantly increased its foreign aid allocations in the early 2000s, after a period of steep decline. The Liberals under Prime Minister Paul Martin promised to double aid spending, a commitment that was kept by the Conservative government that replaced it. No sooner had the latter done so, however, then it first froze aid budgets and then decreased spending. The Trudeau government increased aid only slightly in its three federal budgets – barely enough to keep up with inflation. As the result of economic growth, the ODA/GNI ratio will remain stagnant at around 0.26 per cent – the lowest average of any Canadian government since the 1960s. The unwillingness to commit significant new resources to foreign aid contrasted strongly with the 70 per cent increase in the defense budget, announced in 2017 (Reuters 2017).

To justify this relative stinginess – when compared both with donor peers in the OECD and against Canada's commitment in 1970, repeated countless times since then, for ODA to reach 0.7 per cent of GNI – the Harper and Trudeau governments have made almost identical claims in terms of results and global leadership.

Members of the Harper government constantly emphasized the fact that they prioritized obtaining results – or even "real results," the pleonasm frequently used by Canadian International Development Agency President Robert Greenhill (quoted in Berthiaume 2007), Minister of International Cooperation Oda (2009), her successor Fantino (2013), Governor General Johnston (2013, p. 20) and Harper himself (quoted in CBC News 2010). This focus on results and, more broadly, accountability resonated with the Conservative base because accountability was a leitmotif of the party's successful campaign to defeat the Liberals in the 2006 elections, making hay of bribery scandals that hounded the Liberals.

A prominent focus on results also spoke to the Conservative base that was more suspicious regarding the effectiveness of foreign aid, more likely to believe that it was often wasted abroad and would be better spent at home. The emphasis on visible results was meant to please or at least placate skeptical journalists, parliamentarians and voters. The increased emphasis on humanitarian assistance mirrors this preoccupation with quick, visible results.

When faced with criticism for Canada's lack of generosity, the emphasis on results and accountability served as a convenient fig leaf. For instance, in response to a question in the House of Commons about Canada's "withering" aid budgets, Minister Fantino replied, "It is not about shovelling money out the door; it is about ensuring Canadian taxpayer money is used properly and for legitimate reasons" (quoted in Hansard 2013). Similarly, Trudeau (2015) included a mention of the need to "deliver real results" in his mandate letters and, using the same false dichotomy – and a remarkably similar metaphor – as Fantino, defended aid budget stinginess by saying that "throwing buckets of money indiscriminately at a problem isn't necessarily the best solution" (quoted in MacCharles 2016). Likewise, the Liberal government's discussion paper, released as part of the pre-FIAP consultation process, dismissed significantly higher aid budgets as "unrealistic" and asserted that "it is just as important to consider how Canada's international contributions can best deliver results" (Global Affairs Canada 2016, p. 23). In a similar vein, Liberal Finance Minister Bill Morneau told Canadian NGOs that "we can do more with less" (quoted in Canadian Press 2017).

Although one can hardly deny the importance of results in foreign aid, an overemphasis on results, especially quantitatively measurable ones, has given the Canadian government a case of "Obsessive Measurement Disorder" (Smillie 2016). When combined with the risk aversion bred by extreme accountability pressures, this approach stifles innovation and paralyzes decision-making in an aid program known for its "excessive bureaucracy" (Brown et al. 2016, p. 1). Moreover, stand-alone aid programs selected for their rapid, visible impact attributable to one donor in particular contradict decades of learning on aid effectiveness. Collectively, development actors have understood that long-term programs based on broad partnerships, including with the host government, are more likely to produce long-lasting results, even if they are harder to attribute to a particular donor's inputs. High-profile flag-waving, domestic-audience-pleasing donor projects, such as Canada's three "signature projects" in Afghanistan, are not only ill advised, they can prove to be disappointing from a public relations perspective as well (Brown 2016a, pp. 125–127, 2016b, pp. 19–20).

The Trudeau government also justified its lack of additional aid money with its creation of a self-funding CAD$300 million Development Finance Institute, known as FinDev Canada, which seeks to promote private-sector investment in developing countries. The Liberals conveniently glossed over the fact that those funds had already been announced by the previous government, and declared that it would support the FIAP. This example epitomizes continuity under the Liberals with the Harper government's aid strategy, including its promotion of the role of the private sector in international development and counting on it to fill the funding gap. The FIAP, in fact, contains numerous references to the private sector, presenting it as an unproblematic agent for reducing poverty, fighting inequality and promoting gender equality, despite a very spotty record in at least the last two.

The February 2018 federal budget also contains a section on new approaches to development assistance, emphasizing the private sector and seeking "to attract insurance and pension funds to invest in [the] fight against global poverty" (Blanchfield 2018). Of the CAD $2 billion in planned extra aid spending over five years, a total of $1.5 billion will go to two "innovative" new programs.[7] The first, the International Assistance Innovation Program, will provide "flexible" forms of development financing that could well duplicate the functions of the newly created FinDev Canada. The second, the Sovereign Loans Program, will reintroduce ODA loans, a practice that was phased out decades ago because of unsustainable debt levels in the developing world. These programs provide further evidence of continuity of the Trudeau government's aid program with the Harper government's, putting into practice mechanisms that the latter had considered but never implemented. To make these programs sound more progressive and specifically Liberal, the Trudeau government is portraying them as feminist, referring to them as "an essential part of Canada's Feminist International Assistance Policy." However, the programs' descriptions make no actual mention of women, girls or gender equality (Canada 2018, p. 159).

Another subterfuge, practiced as much by the Harper Conservatives as the Trudeau Liberals, is to repeat to Canadians that the government is playing a crucial global leadership role and that this is more important than paying what could be considered its fair share of global foreign aid (Brown 2017a, 2017b) – as if one could do the former without the latter. The FIAP's "Achilles Heel," in particular, is its weak financial base (Brown and Swiss 2017, p. 118). The meager increase in the aid budget also means that any new initiative or priority must come at the expense of another one.

Thus the branding of Canadian aid, like other branding efforts, attempts to obscure the "rhetoric/reality gap" (Nimijean 2005), but its success in this area – as in other cases – appears limited. In fact, on the question of ODA budgets, the Liberal government seems to be at odds with its base, which is broadly supportive of aid and, in fact, exerting public pressure on the government to increase funding for aid. The reason for this discrepancy is not immediately obvious, but is probably related to senior Liberal politicians' own lack of commitment to ODA or the low priority that the government knows that voters attach to aid spending. For now, the feminist branding seems to have precluded stronger criticisms. Nonetheless, this disconnect could be exploited in the future by the New Democratic Party.

## Conclusion

Analysts are largely correct in asserting that many Harper government priorities sought to please its base, including in the realm of foreign aid. Its emphasis on "saving" women and children (under the Muskoka Initiative for Maternal, Newborn and Child Health) and innocent victims of humanitarian emergencies depoliticized aid by sidestepping causes and focusing on Christian charity to alleviate symptoms. The explicit exclusion of support to abortion services, even where legal, and the reluctance to support contraception also clearly play to the Conservative base. The emphasis on visible results, including lives saved, as well as increased self-interest (including in the choice of priority countries), played well to a base suspicious of the effectiveness of foreign aid. The Harper government also targeted critical NGOs, seeking to silence their advocacy work, while favoring or at least appearing to favor – the evidence is not especially clear – faith-based NGOs, especially Western Canada-based Christian ones, in development and humanitarian assistance.

While the Harper government and, in the case of MNCH, Harper himself, sought to project an image of caring for innocent victims, Liberal governments have also portrayed themselves as preoccupied with the most marginalized, including through a focus on Africa and, most recently, on women and girls. When in power, both parties have shuffled the list of priority countries, using them to signal their political identities and please their respective core supporters. Liberals have emphasized Africa, especially francophone countries, in line with their base's priorities, while the Harper government focused on countries with better trade and investment opportunities for Canadian companies and investors – although they also tried to steal from the Liberal playbook as the 2015 elections approached. Both parties favored Haiti and Ukraine for electoral reasons, though the latter case is hard to justify more objectively.

In many instances, such as MNCH, the promotion of the private sector and the emphasis on "real results" and on self-proclaimed leadership instead of restoring funding to previous levels or meeting the commitment of 0.7 per cent of GNI, the Trudeau Liberals have largely retained Conservative practices, contenting themselves with reframing some of the language (e.g. mentioning women's rights and feminism; dropping the Muskoka label), without necessarily modifying practice very much.

Although the Liberals' new Feminist International Assistance Policy is likely to modify the face of Canadian aid, with its ambitious quantitative targets for assistance to women and girls, both the policy itself and the funding announced to date are much more about helping them rather than achieving gender equality. Despite a clear change in language (such as referring to "empowering" instead of "saving"), the difference with the previous government's approach is not yet visible in practice. To date, there is no sign of anything as transformational as the feminist label would suggest.

"Feminist international assistance" is the latest in a long list of flavors-of-the-month in Canada's aid program over the past two decades. It should have more staying power than past priorities, for instance not being dropped after the next Cabinet shuffle, and will probably last for the duration of the current Liberal government. However, its branding as "feminist" and its close association with the Liberals make it highly likely to be axed if and when the Conservatives return to power and put in place their own brand evisceration strategies.

Although foreign aid can be of great assistance, the politicization of aid by both parties is harmful to its effectiveness, whether when policies and priorities are frequently changed for political imperatives or when more fundamentally selected with political, rather than developmental, objectives in mind. It should not be surprising that governments want to please voters and attract new ones, but it is particularly important to understand how pandering to the base can undermine efforts to reduce poverty and inequality abroad, which requires long-term engagement and dependable partnerships.

Just as the governments of Paul Martin and Stephen Harper did in their own way after being elected, the Trudeau government has announced that "Canada is back." In the realm of foreign aid, such a claim is hard to justify, given the high degree of continuity and especially the Liberals' decision to maintain relatively low levels of spending – which contrasts sharply with the previous two governments' budget increases early in their respective mandates, and with the Trudeau government's willingness to massively increase spending in other areas, notably defense. The Liberals' refusal to buttress their "Canada is back" rhetoric with concrete resources – in particular for foreign aid, but in other areas as well, such as peacekeeping – will undermine the claim, as well as the government's attempts to increase Canada's "soft power" on the international stage, including its chances of being elected to the UN Security Council.

The Trudeau government seems to be counting instead on the branding of its high-profile thematic priority to please its base in the realm of foreign aid. In doing so, it continues the tradition of shifting priorities and frames, which distracts public attention and can please core supporters. However, improving the effectiveness of Canadian aid will require more substantive changes that do not reflect primarily domestic political imperatives, but rather respond to the needs and priorities of developing countries themselves. In fact, the feminist label, though not the focus on women *per se*, may actually serve as an impediment to partnerships with governments for whom the term holds no appeal.

These findings have relevance beyond the study of Canadian aid. Given that the literature is not conclusive on whether left- or right-wing parties give more aid or even spend aid differently, the Canadian case suggests that more attention should be paid to how the primary difference may actually be how they brand their aid as part of an effort to please their base and attract new voters, as well as to improve their international image, a line of inquiry that falls outside this article's purview. Rather than highlight differences, such an approach would underscore the remarkable continuity of donor countries' aid practices, despite high-profile changes in their rhetoric.

## Notes

1. It is important to note that these are labels that the Trudeau government applies to its own policies. The extent to which they are accurate is rather debatable. See, for instance, Vucetic (2017).
2. It is not clear why the two government ministers stated that contraception would be excluded – whether that was actually the government's initial intention or whether the ministers simply confused contraception with abortion.

3. To be fair, given the long lead-time between project identification and announcement, most projects announced to date were originally designed under the previous government. It is all the more striking, however, that the Trudeau government has nonetheless framed these project announcements under the FIAP brand since June 2017, which demonstrates how rhetorical differences can be much more significant than substantive ones. A systematic comparison of concrete differences between projects developed before and after the FIAP's adoption would be an important topic for future research. Swiss (2018) outlines three strategies that the government could adopt to meet the target of 95 per cent of aid to focus on women, girls and gender equality, highlighting the constraints imposed by a lack of new resources under what he terms "miserly feminism."
4. In 2015–2016, for instance, Ukraine was the top recipient of Canadian aid, having received 3.3 per cent of total ODA, while Haiti ranked seventh, at 1.7 per cent (OECD 2018a).
5. The same can be said about the shifting of official priority themes, areas or sectors every few years, which is more about branding than about responding to changing needs. See discussion in Brown (2015a).
6. These figures were calculated using data from OECD (2018b).
7. The government took care to specify that the CAD$1.5 billion will not come from the additional $2 billion, but rather "from existing unallocated International Assistance Envelope resources" (Canada 2018, p. 159). However, given the fungibility of funds, it is not clear that this distinction is meaningful.

## Acknowledgements

The author is very grateful to the three institutions that hosted him during the various stages of researching and writing this article: the United Nations University World Institute for Development Economics Research (UNU-WIDER) in Helsinki, the University of Birmingham's Institute of Advanced Studies and International Development Department, and the Institut d'étude du développement économique et social at the Université Paris 1 Panthéon-Sorbonne. He received helpful suggestions from participants at the workshop on "The Domestic Dimensions of Development Cooperation," held at the Institute of Development Policy and Management, University of Antwerp, Belgium, 24–25 October 2016, especially from Jörg Faust, as well as from Richard Nimijean, David Carment, Megan Pickup, Stéphanie Bacher and two anonymous reviewers. He also thanks Dane Degenstein for research assistance, and apologizes to Meghan Trainor for the article's title.

## Disclosure statement

No potential conflict of interest was reported by the author.

## Funding

This work was supported by the Social Sciences and Humanities Research Council of Canada under grant number 435-2013-0283.

## Notes on contributor

*Stephen Brown* is professor of political science at the University of Ottawa. He is the author of numerous publications on foreign aid, especially Canada's. More information is available at www.stephenbrown.xyz.

## ORCID

*Stephen Brown* http://orcid.org/0000-0002-7084-9726

## References

Akin, David, 2015. Liberals boast Canada is back! To what? Breaking our word? *Toronto Sun*, 9 November. Available from: http://torontosun.com/2015/11/09/liberals-boast-canada-is-back-to-what-breaking-our-word/ [Accessed 28 March 2018].

Arsenault, Julien, 2014. Solidarité internationale: le Québec veut sa propre agence. *Presse canadienne*, 24 February. Available from: www.lapresse.ca/actualites/politique/politique-quebecoise/201402/24/01-4742041-solidarite-internationale-le-quebec-veut-sa-propre-agence.php [Accessed 6 October 2016].

Audet, François, and Navarro-Flores, Olga, 2016. The management of Canadian development assistance: ideology, electoral politics or public interest? *In*: Stephen Brown, Molly den Heyer, and David R. Black, eds. *Rethinking Canadian Aid*. 2nd ed. Ottawa: University of Ottawa Press, 171–186.

Audet, François, Paquette, Francis, and Bergeron, Stéfanie, 2013. Religious nongovernmental organisations and Canadian international aid, 2001–2010: a preliminary study. *Canadian Journal of Development Studies*, 34 (2), 291–320.

Bacher, Stéphanie, 2017. Nouvelle Politiques [sic] des partenariats: l'attente injustifiée. *Huffington Post Québec*, 26 November. Available from: http://quebec.huffingtonpost.ca/un-seul-monde/nouvelle-politiques-des-partenariats-lattente-injustifiee_a_23253337/ [Accessed 27 January 2018].

Berthiaume, Lee, 2007. CIDA Boss Hints at Shift to Stable Nations. *Embassy*, 27 June.

Black, David R., 2015. *Canada & Africa in the new millennium: the politics of consistent inconsistency*. Waterloo, ON: Wilfrid Laurier University Press.

Black, David R., 2016. Humane internationalism and the malaise of Canadian aid policy. *In*: Stephen Brown, Molly den Heyer, and David R. Black, eds. *Rethinking Canadian Aid*. 2nd ed. Ottawa: University of Ottawa Press, 17–35.

Blanchfield, Mike, 2018. Aid minister aims for more private sector investment in foreign aid. *Financial Post*, 28 February. Available from: http://business.financialpost.com/pmn/business-pmn/aid-minister-aims-for-more-private-sector-investment-in-foreign-aid [Accessed 24 March 2018].

Brech, Viktor and Potrafke, Niklas, 2014. Donor ideology and types of foreign aid. *Journal of Comparative Economics*, 42 (1), 61–75.

Brown, Stephen, 2015a. Aid effectiveness and the framing of new Canadian aid initiatives. *In*: Duane Bratt and Christopher J. Kukucha, eds. *Readings in Canadian foreign policy: classic debates and new ideas*. 3rd ed. Don Mills, ON: Oxford University Press, 467–481.

Brown, Stephen, 2015b. Canada's development interventions: unpacking motives and effectiveness in Canadian foreign aid. *In*: Fen Osler Hampson and Stephen M. Saideman, eds. *Canada Among nations 2015. elusive pursuits: lessons from Canada's interventions abroad*. Waterloo, ON: Centre for International Governance Innovation, 139–159.

Brown, Stephen, 2016a. From Ottawa to Kandahar and back: the securitization of Canadian foreign aid. *In*: Stephen Brown and Jörn Grävingholt, eds. *The securitization of foreign aid*. Basingstoke, UK: Palgrave Macmillan, 113–137.

Brown, Stephen, 2016b. The instrumentalization of Canadian foreign aid under the Harper government. *Studies in Political Economy*, 97 (1), 18–36.

Brown, Stephen, 2016c. Undermining foreign aid: the extractive sector and the recommercialization of Canadian development assistance. *In*: Stephen Brown, Molly den Heyer and David R. Black, eds. *Rethinking Canadian aid*. 2nd ed. Ottawa: University of Ottawa Press, 273–294.

Brown, Stephen, 2017a. Harper lite? The Trudeau government on foreign aid. Centre for International Policy Studies Blog, 2 April. Available from: www.cips-cepi.ca/2017/04/02/harper-lite-the-trudeau-government-on-foreign-aid/ [Accessed 27 January 2018].

Brown, Stephen, 2017b. "The System is Broken": Canada's Latest Rationale for Stinginess. Centre for International Policy Studies Blog, 2 October. Available from: www.cips-cepi.ca/2017/10/02/the-system-is-broken-canadas-latest-rationale-for-stinginess/ [Accessed 27 January 2018].

Brown, Stephen, den Heyer, Molly, and Black, David R., 2016. Why rethink Canadian aid. *In*: Stephen Brown, Molly den Heyer, and David R. Black, eds. *Rethinking Canadian aid*. 2nd ed. Ottawa: University of Ottawa Press, 1–13.

Brown, Stephen and Olender, Michael, 2013. Canada's fraying commitment to multilateral development cooperation. *In*: Hany Besada and Shannon Kindornay, eds. *Multilateral development cooperation in a changing global order*. New York: Palgrave Macmillan, 158–188.

Brown, Stephen and Swiss, Liam. 2017. Canada's Feminist International Assistance Policy: game changer or fig leaf? *In*: Katherine A.H. Graham and Allan M. Maslove, eds. *How Ottawa spends, 2017–2018*. Ottawa: Carleton University, 117–131.

Calleja, Rachael, 2017. FIAP and Sub-Saharan Africa: ambitious new target? *Canadian International Development Platform*, 24 October. Available from: http://cidpnsi.ca/fiap-sub-saharan-africa/ [Accessed 27 January 2018].

Canada, 2017. *Feminist International Assistance Policy*, 9 June. Ottawa: Global Affairs Canada. Available from: www.international.gc.ca/gac-amc/campaign-campagne/iap-pai/index.aspx?lang=eng [Accessed 27 January 2018].

Canada, 2018. *Budget 2018: Equality and Growth for a Strong Middle Class*, 27 February. Available from: https://www.budget.gc.ca/2018/docs/plan/toc-tdm-en.html [Accessed 27 February 2018].

Canadian Press, 2017. Do more with less foreign aid, Morneau urges development agencies. *Globe and Mail*, 27 March. Available from: www.theglobeandmail.com/news/politics/do-more-with-less-foreign-aid-morneau-urges-development-agencies/article34437061/ [Accessed 27 January 2018].

CBC News, 2010. Harper tells UN to focus on aid results, 2 September. Available from: www.cbc.ca/news/world/harper-tells-un-to-focus-on-aid-results-1.922048 [Accessed 7 October 2016].

Clark, Campbell, 2010. Feminist senator Nancy Ruth tells aid groups to drop abortion fight. *Globe and Mail*, 3 May. Available from: www.theglobeandmail.com/news/politics/feminist-senator-nancy-ruth-tells-aid-groups-to-drop-abortion-fight/article563557/ [Accessed 6 October 2016].

Delacort, Susan, 2010. Aid groups advised to "shut the f--- up" on abortion. *Toronto Star*, 3 May. Available from: www.thestar.com/news/canada/2010/05/03/aid_groups_advised_to_shut_the_f_up_on_abortion.html [Accessed 6 October 2016].

Dreher, Axel, Nunnenkamp, Peter and Schmaljohann, Maya, 2015. The allocation of German aid: self-interest and government ideology. *Economics & Politics*, 27 (1), 160–184.

Fantino, Julian, 2013. Canada's foreign aid is getting results. *Huffington Post*, 3 January. Available from: www.huffingtonpost.ca/the-honourable-julian-fantino/cida-co-operation-private-sector_b_2398198.html [Accessed 7 October 2016].

Fleck, Robert K., and Kilby, Christopher, 2006. How do political changes influence US bilateral aid allocations? Evidence from panel data. *Review of Development Economics*, 10 (2), 210–223.

Fuchs, Andreas, Dreher, Axel and Nunnenkamp, Peter, 2014. Determinants of donor generosity: a survey of the aid budget literature. *World Development*, 56, 172–199.

Goyette, Gabriel C., 2016. Charity begins at home: the extractive sector as an illustration of the Harper government's de facto aid policy. *In*: Stephen Brown, Molly den Heyer and David R. Black, eds. *Rethinking Canadian aid*. 2nd ed. Ottawa: University of Ottawa Press, 255–271.

Global Affairs Canada, 2016. *International assistance review discussion paper*. Ottawa: Government of Canada.

Global Affairs Canada, 2017. Minister Bibeau announces final tally for Myanmar Crisis Relief Fund. *News Release*, 13 December. Ottawa: Global Affairs Canada. Available from: www.canada.ca/en/global-affairs/news/2017/12/minister_bibeau_announcesfinaltallyformyanmarcrisisrelieffund.html [Accessed 27 January 2018].

Hansard, 2013. 41st parliament, 1st Session, Edited Hansard, Number 242, House of Commons Debates, 29 April. Available from: www.parl.gc.ca/HousePublications/Publication.aspx?DocId=6114837 [Accessed 7 October 2016].

Harris, Kathleen, 2017. Canada's response to Rohingya humanitarian crisis tops $50M. *CBC News*, 13 December. Available from: www.cbc.ca/news/politics/canada-aid-rohingya-myanmar-bangladesh-1.4446139 [Accessed 27 January 2018].

Heppell, Timothy, and Lightfoot, Simon, 2012. "We will not balance the books on the backs of the poorest people in the world": understanding Conservative Party strategy on international aid. *The Political Quarterly*, 83 (1), 130–138.

Imbeau, Louis M., 1988. Aid and ideology. *European Journal of Political Research*, 16 (1), 3–28.

Johnston, David, 2013. Seizing Canada's Moment Prosperity and Opportunity in an Uncertain World, Speech from the Throne to Open the Second Session of the Forty-First Parliament of Canada, 16 October. Available from: www.afn.ca/uploads/files/throne-speech.pdf [Accessed 7 October 2016].

Jones, Peter, 2014. Canada's bitter, small-minded foreign policy. *Globe and Mail*, 2 January. Available from: www.theglobeandmail.com/opinion/canadas-bitter-small-minded-foreign-policy/article16147665/ [Accessed 24 March 2018].

Kleibl, Johannes, 2013. Tertiarization, industrial adjustment, and the domestic politics of foreign aid. *International Studies Quarterly*, 57 (2), 356–369.

Liberal Party of Canada, 2015. *Real change: a new plan for a strong middle class*. Available from: www.liberal.ca/files/2015/10/New-plan-for-a-strong-middle-class.pdf [Accessed 6 October 2016].

MacCharles, Tonda, 2016. Trudeau calls UN goal to boost aid spending "too ambitious." *Toronto Star*, 10 May. Available from: www.thestar.com/news/canada/2016/05/10/justin-trudeau-un-goal-to-boost-spending-on-aid-too-ambitious-for-canada-right-now.html [Accessed 7 October 2016].

Mackrael, Kim, and Ling, Justin, 2013. CIDA defends support of organization that made anti-gay comments. *Globe and Mail*, 11 February. Available from: www.theglobeandmail.com/news/politics/cida-defends-support-of-organization-that-made-anti-gay-comments/article8477787/ [Accessed 6 October 2016].

Malloy, Jonathan, 2010. Playing to his base: two books track the rise of Christian and social conservatism in Harper's Ottawa. *Literary Review of Canada*, 18 (6), 24–25.

Marland, Alex, 2016. *Brand command: Canadian politics and democracy in the age of message control*. Vancouver: UBC Press.

Mawdsley, Emma, 2017. National interests and the paradox of foreign aid under austerity: conservative governments and the domestic politics of international development since 2010. *The Geographical Journal*, 183 (3), 223–232.

Milner, Helen V., and Tingley, Dustin H., 2010. The political economy of U.S. foreign aid: American legislators and the domestic politics of aid. *Economics & Politics*, 22 (2), 200–232.

Nimijean, Richard, 2005. Articulating the "Canadian Way": Canada™ and the political manipulation of the Canadian identity. *British Journal of Canadian Studies*, 18 (1), 26–52.

Nimijean, Richard, 2006. The politics of branding Canada: the international-domestic nexus and the rethinking of Canada's place in the world. *Revista Mexicana de Estudios Canadienses*, 11, 67–85.

Nossal, Kim Richard, 2014. *Primat der Wahlurne*: explaining Stephen Harper's foreign policy. Paper presented at the annual meeting of the International Studies Association, Toronto, 29 March.

Oda, Beverley J., 2009. A new effective approach to Canadian aid. Speaking Notes for the Honourable Beverley J. Oda Minister of International Cooperation at the Munk Centre for International Studies, Toronto, 20 May. Available from: www.acdi-cida.gc.ca/acdi-cida/acdi-cida.nsf/eng/NAT-5208469-GYW [Accessed 7 October 2016].

OECD, 2018a. Table 32 - Major Recipients of Individual DAC Members' Aid. *Statistics on resource flows to developing countries*. Paris: OECD. Available from: www.oecd.org/dac/financing-sustainable-development/development-finance-data/statisticsonresourceflowstodevelopingcountries.htm [Accessed 24 March 2018].

OECD, 2018b. *Query wizard for international development statistics*. Paris: OECD. Available from: http://stats.oecd.org [Accessed 27 January 2018].

Payton, Laura, 2015. Canada's foreign aid commitment to contraception low despite great need. *CBC News online*, 25 June. Available from: www.cbc.ca/news/politics/canada-s-foreign-aid-commitment-to-contraception-low-despite-great-need-1.3123144 [Accessed 6 October 2016].

Potter, Evan H., 2009. *Branding Canada: projecting Canada's soft power through public diplomacy*. Montreal and Kingston: McGill-Queen's University Press.

Rankin, L. Pauline, 2012. Gender and nation branding in "The True North Strong and Free." *Place Branding and Public Diplomacy*, 8 (4), 257–267.

Reuters, 2017. Canada to boost military budget by 70% after pressure from US to spend more. *The Guardian*, 7 June. Available from: www.theguardian.com/world/2017/jun/07/canada-increase-military-spending-nato [Accessed 12 June 2017].

Smillie, Ian, 2016. Results, risk, rhetoric and reality: the need for common sense in Canada's development assistance. *In*: Stephen Brown, Molly den Heyer and David R. Black, eds. *Rethinking Canadian aid*. 2nd ed. Ottawa: University of Ottawa Press, 89–104.

Sohn, Hyuk-Sang, and Yoo, Nari, 2015. Motivation for aid allocation and political ideology: a case study of South Korea. *Pacific Focus*, 30 (3), 344–371.

Swiss, Liam, 2018. Feminism on the cheap: can Canada achieve its ambitious gender equality aid targets with no new money? *GRoW Research Bulletin*, 5, 3–5.

Thérien, Jean-Philippe, 2002. Debating foreign aid: right versus left. *Third World Quarterly*, 23 (3), 449–466.

Thérien, Jean-Philippe, and Noël, André, 2000. Political parties and foreign aid. *American Political Science Review*, 94 (1), 151–162.

Tiessen, Rebecca, 2015. "Walking wombs": making sense of the Muskoka Initiative and the emphasis on motherhood in Canadian foreign policy. *Global Justice*, 8 (1), 1–22.

Tingley, Dustin, 2010. Donors and domestic politics: political influences on foreign aid effort. *The Quarterly Review of Economics and Finance*, 50 (1), 40–49.

Travis, Rick, 2010. Problems, politics, and policy streams: a reconsideration US foreign aid behavior toward Africa. *International Studies Quarterly*, 54 (3), 797–821.

Trudeau, Justin, 2015. *Minister of International Development and La Francophonie Mandate Letter*. Available from: http://pm.gc.ca/eng/minister-international-development-and-la-francophonie-mandate-letter [Accessed 6 October 2016].

Vander Zaag, Ray, 2013. Canadian faith-based development NGOs and CIDA funding. *Canadian Journal of Development Studies*, 34 (2), 321–347.

Vander Zaag, Ray, 2014. Trends in CIDA funding to Canadian religious development NGOs: analysing conflicting studies. *Canadian Journal of Development Studies*, 35 (3), 458–474.

Vucetic, Srdjan, 2017. A nation of feminist arms dealers? Canada and military exports. *International Journal*, 72 (4), 503–519.

Wells, Paul, 2013. *The longer I'm prime minister: Stephen Harper and Canada, 2006–*. Toronto: Random House Canada.

White, Stephen E., 2017. Canadian ethnocultural diversity and federal party support: the dynamics of Liberal partisanship in immigrant communities. *PS: Political Science and Politics*, 50 (3), 708–711.

# 4   Canada's Feminist International Assistance Policy
To whom is Canada back?

Rebecca Tiessen and David Black

## Introduction

Several notable announcements, beginning at the very outset of the Liberal government elected in 2015, have signaled a focussed Canadian commitment to gender equality. These have included the 2015 appointment of 50% or more cabinet posts to women, ongoing efforts to ensure that 50% of ambassadors are women, Prime Minister Justin Trudeau's self-declaration as a feminist at the United Nations in 2016, focused support for increased women's participation in peacekeeping through the Elsie Initiative,[1] expanded commitments to funding for sexual and reproductive health and rights, targeted funding for women's rights organizations, and an expanded effort to address the need for girls' education around the world. Among the most significant and prominent commitments introduced under the Liberal government, however, is the Feminist International Assistance Policy (FIAP) – a policy document that elevates Prime Minister Trudeau's personal narrative and values (noted above) to the level of a bold national policy vision for improved international assistance. Taken together, these commitments to gender equality have been central features of the Trudeau Liberal government's branding efforts, reinforcing and giving a particular focus to Canada's self-declaration of "being back" (Brown, this volume).

The specific rhetorical commitments to gender equality are a particularly prominent element in the framing of Canadian international values and virtue. The tone and sentiments have reinforced a more positive, activist image, diverging sharply from the previous Harper Conservative government's defensive orientation within a darker and narrower view of international relations, and "hinting at a return to the role of helpful fixer that many Canadians identified with" (Nimijean, this volume).

Analysing Canada's return to an activist orientation that places gender equality and feminist principles at the heart of all international assistance activities demands closer attention to how and for whom Canada is "back", both domestically and internationally. In short, we need to pay closer attention to the distinct audiences to whom these branding initiatives have been directed, how the 'sender' (i.e., the Canadian government) anticipates they will be received, and the implications of this messaging for the ongoing (re-)construction of our national identity.

Here we unpack the idea of Canada "being back" by analysing the identity construction emerging from this rhetoric and by disaggregating the branding surrounding what has become one of the most prominent exemplars of the return to a more liberal and justice-oriented international approach: gender equality programming and feminist principles in international development cooperation. This commentary documents the nature of the branding exercise undertaken through the introduction and rolling out of the FIAP, the implications of this discursive shift in terms of the idea of feminism adopted and projected, the audiences to whom this branding effort is targeted, and the possibilities of translating an aspirational feminist brand into concrete and sustained action.

## Building a new brand through the Feminist International Assistance Policy

The Canadian government has positioned itself as a global leader on gender equality through the FIAP, with its bold commitments to targeted funding for the empowerment of women and girls amounting to 15% of Canada's $2.6 billion bilateral development assistance program, and an overall commitment to ensuring that 95% of Canadian development programming supports "gender equality and the empowerment of women and girls by 2021/22" (Bibeau as cited in Gac, 2017, p. 3). Notably, the government has committed to allocating $150 million over five years to support local women's organizations in developing countries that are working to advance the rights of women and girls and promote gender equality (Canada, 2017a). The policy applies a "human-rights approach" to six focus areas, namely, (1) Gender equality and the empowerment of women and girls; (2) Human dignity; (3) Growth that works for everyone; (4) Environment and climate action; (5) Inclusive governance; and (6) Peace and security (GAC, 2017). Supporting gender equality and the empowerment of women and girls is identified as the surest way to build a more peaceful, inclusive and prosperous world. To do this, the FIAP supports targeted investments, partnerships, innovation and advocacy efforts, aimed at closing gender gaps and improving chances of success for all.

The FIAP, like other international policies, is largely about projecting Canadian values abroad. Indeed, international assistance policies are particularly amenable to 'values signalling', since their direct ramifications for Canadians are limited and therefore the room for policy manoeuvre is relatively great. This value-signalling role is manifested in a speech by Minister of Foreign Affairs, Chrystia Freeland, when she asserts that: "we (Canadians) are safer and more prosperous… when more of the world shares Canadian values. Those values include feminism and the promotion of the rights of women and girls" (Canada, 2017b). The specifics of the feminist values that Canada is projecting abroad are elaborated in the FIAP and summarized above.

To be sure, although the FIAP has been recognized as a potential 'game changer' (Brown and Swiss, 2017), a growing body of scholarship highlights the limitations and missed opportunities of this document (see Nacyte, 2018; Tiessen and Swan, 2018). Among the limitations highlighted by critics are the failure to define feminism and the specific feminist orientation of this policy, which targets women and girls in instrumentalist ways to achieve broader goals and objectives; the limited attention to diverse voices and groups, including LGBTI+ communities; the failure to articulate strategies and commitments for engaging men and boys; and the lack of comprehensive efforts to support transformative change addressing power relations, cultural barriers, and discriminatory practices. There is, moreover, a strong emphasis in the FIAP on its innovation and novelty, which has the distinct disadvantage of failing to acknowledge and build on Canada's longstanding commitments and priorities concerning gender equality programming.

Indeed, notwithstanding some notable gaps under the Harper Conservative government between 2006 and 2015 (Tiessen and Carrier, 2015), the Canadian brand has long positioned gender equality near the heart of Canada's national and international commitments. For example, as a self-proclaimed international leader in the promotion of gender equality (Tiessen, 2016), Canada placed itself on the cutting edge of commitments to gender equality with the introduction of its Gender Equality policy in 1999, which built in turn on the Women in Development (WID) policy initiated in 1976. In this sense, the FIAP should be understood not as a sharp break with the past, but rather as the latest chapter in a substantial (if flawed) history of gender prioritization.

Despite the limitations and critiques of the FIAP highlighted in recent literature however, the Liberal party's articulation of an overriding strategy to promote gender equality raises significant questions about the audience for whom "Canada" is back, and how this branding is strategically targeted and "received" by different audiences. In what follows, we highlight three such audiences: Canadian civil society, the international policy bureaucracy, and 'like-minded' governments abroad.

## For whom is Canada back, and to whom is Its feminist branding targeted?

The idea of "being back" resonated with many Canadians. Surely, for those who had grown (or had always been) disgruntled with the domestic and foreign policy and practice of the Conservative governments between 2006 and 2015, a return to Liberal party leadership signalled "being back" in relation to liberal values, strengthened humanitarian practices, more socially progressive ethical commitments, and principles of justice and equality. This rhetoric signalled a preoccupation with value politics and national identity construction, but also the way in which "brand politics" have become increasingly partisan, with different governing parties competing to render their partisan identities as synonymous with "Canadianness" (Nimijean, 2014).

Beyond appealing to the party's political base at home who might reflexively consider "Canada back" when the Liberal party is in power however, the FIAP reflects a broader sentiment aimed at a wider domestic audience who considered Canada's commitments to aid, humanitarian assistance, justice and equality to be lacking over the previous decade (Brown, this volume). More specifically and concretely, the extensive consultative process with civil society organizations during the protracted international assistance review (IAR) shifted the nature and focus of domestic dialogue considerably. The Harper Conservatives saw most Canadian civil society organizations (CSOs) as oppositional in nature and had limited engagement and consultation with them, effectively blacklisting some CSOs that did not conform to Conservative government priorities. The about-face of the Liberal government in the initial days after their election, and in the months that followed, can be understood as part of a rebranding exercise in which the Liberal government was showcasing their internationalist character to Canadians who were personally and/or professionally dedicated to having an impact on the world stage (Brown, this volume). In this sense, the Liberal rebrand was aimed directly at the extensive community of Canadian development NGOs and CSOs, many of whom were deeply committed to feminist principles and a core focus on gender (e.g., "A Feminist Approach", 2016). Appealing to this particular component of the domestic community also had the political virtue of muting criticisms from the NGO community of other aspects of international assistance – most notably the lack of substantial new funding commitments. With a large number of CSOs dedicated to feminist principles and gender equality, a feminist international assistance policy was warmly welcomed by many, and their praise for this boldly articulated policy turn did much to overshadow the government's "miserly" budgetary provisions (Swiss, 2018). Despite the FIAP's limitations, moreover, the language of feminism in Canada's official assistance policy does open new space for feminist CSOs to hold the government accountable for its rhetorical commitments.

A second, widely overlooked aspect of the FIAP's branding audience and impact was the federal government bureaucracy itself – notably though not only within the still-newly integrated structures of Global Affairs Canada. In short, the government's decision to 'double-down' on feminist principles through its International Assistance policy can be expected to affect both the perceptions and leverage of the development branch within Global Affairs. To be sure, as noted above, other dimensions of Canadian international policy – defence and security, trade, and diplomacy for instance – have featured an enhanced emphasis on gender equality.[2] None however has – or arguably *could* – focus as overwhelmingly on the government's feminist 'brand' as international assistance. Symbolically at least, the FIAP has become 'ground zero' for the government's feminist international policy aspirations.

The intra-governmental ramifications of this role as exemplar of Canada's feminist international brand are uncertain. Historically, development policy was the weakest link in Canada's international policy repertoire, with the then-Canadian International Development Agency (CIDA) chronically concerned to protect its limited policy prerogatives (see Black forthcoming). Now, within an integrated GAC, the development branch's status could be enhanced by the symbolic prominence provided by its feminist branding. More probably, however, and as indicated by the lack of new funding for international assistance,[3] it could reinforce the relative marginalization of development in relation to its more broadly focused counterparts in international trade, security, and diplomacy, and render it vulnerable if and when a change of government (and therefore policy priorities) occurs.

In addition to domestic branding, the FIAP represents an important branding opportunity in relation to international audiences. As Brown (this volume) argues, for example, the proclamation of Canada being back was linked to the Trudeau government's aspiration to seek election to the United Nations (UN) Security Council in 2021. Specific aspects of the FIAP, such as its support for girls' and women's education, have received particular emphasis as the government's Security Council campaign gets underway in earnest (Raj, 2018; Zilio, 2018).

Canada's feminist branding through the FIAP also helps position this government in line with other self-consciously progressive governments such as Sweden, which was the first country to introduce a feminist foreign policy, followed by other governments that have employed the language of feminism to exemplify progressive strategies in international aid. When Canada hosted the G7 meeting in 2018, gender equality and women's empowerment alongside Canada's commitments thereto were the focus of prominent public statements, and re-positioned Canada in relation to other donor nations, thereby shaping a national identity narrative shared with key domestic and international audiences alike. The importance of cultivating diverse allies in the G7 as well as other western groupings has heightened in light of currently strained relations with the United States. Overall, Canada's multilateral engagements are important and may partially disarm criticism from the OECD Development Assistance Committee (DAC) peer review report on Canada's desultory international assistance financing commitments (OECD 2018).

Understanding to whom branding is directed through feminist policy pronouncements and positioning is therefore important for making sense of the Trudeau government's priorities and strategies. Yet there are also substantial challenges associated with how this branding plays out and its implications for effective practice, consistent messaging, and appropriate commitments.

## Challenging the brand

While the FIAP is a self-proclaimed bold commitment to Canada and the world to actively engage with gender inequality and feminist principles in international assistance, the limitations of the policy and the messaging surrounding it demonstrate ambiguity and lack of clarity, in part because the branding has been cautious rather than bold – what might be described "tip-toe feminism". A branding exercise must appeal to as wide an audience as possible. In other words, ambiguity in the messaging can be an effective strategy for selling a particular approach that appeals to a broad base.

Nevertheless, a feminist branding exercise can also be divisive. Feminism, often jokingly referred to as the other "F word", is regularly and wrongly demonized in popular media for amounting to a zero-sum game in which gains for women or other marginal groups equal losses for others. The problematic assumptions and lack of informed understanding of feminism remain a distinct challenge for advocates of feminist principles but also for a government that uses feminism as part of its branding strategy. Failures of understanding concerning feminism and the misinterpretations of this social justice concept persist within Canada and around the world. Consequently, the use of feminism in branding may impact Canada's relations with countries that do not subscribe to feminist principles and/or feminist language. President Trump, for one, has publicly declared that he is not a feminist, with specific implications for branding in the context of maintaining his support base in the United States. Strikingly, moreover, the 'global South' countries with whom Canada must partner through its FIAP and related programs may also reject the language of feminism (Aksli, 2017). Importantly, there are diverse constituencies within these partner countries with whom the messaging of feminism will resonate differently. For example, feminist organizations, women's rights groups and gender equality movements around the world will surely welcome a feminist approach to international collaboration, even if they may also have vitally important insights on the most effective means to advance these objectives. Some may challenge the potential hypocrisy of feminist principles embedded within international aid, while others will embrace the language of feminism to galvanize their commitments to poverty reduction efforts that meet the needs of all people, and especially those who are disproportionately impacted by poverty and inequality. Regardless of these important differences, however, ownership of the language of feminism and the principles and priorities of a FIAP will remain an important consideration in Canada's work. Branding that prioritizes audiences within Canada and elsewhere in the global North risks misconstruing the needs of those for whom it is ostensibly intended, thereby alienating them.

More broadly, a branding exercise that employs the language of feminism must also ensure that commitments to feminist principles remain at the heart of the work that the government and its partners do in the name of international assistance. Employing the language of feminism for instrumental reasons of branding Canada without delivering on these principles can trivialize feminism. The branding of national identity must not become an alternative to clearly defined public policy; indeed, a persistent gap between brand and policy will undermine the power and attractiveness of the brand (Nimijean, 2014).

An overarching feminist international policy also requires thoughtful consideration of all aspects of international policy, and needs to be comprehensive and coherent to avoid the hypocritical tensions that arise from a rhetoric of feminist values combined with anti-feminist practices in other policy domains. A prominent example is the often-referenced contradiction between Canada's public stance on human rights and gender equality in Saudi Arabia and its ongoing arms sales to Saudi Arabia, used for what can only be understood as anti-feminist ends. As a branding exercise, feminist priorities also run the risk of being treated as a fad that lacks sustained commitment and impact, especially by other political parties that will almost certainly wish to advance an alternative brand.

## Living up to the brand

The true test of a feminist commitment to international assistance is in the delivery of programming. A successful branding exercise must lead to a sound "product" and concrete action that is consistent with the nation's brand. Without action that matches the rhetoric, the brand is diminished (Nimijean, this volume).

Moreover, Canada's branding through the FIAP raises concerns about a shallow emphasis on novelty versus the strength to be gained from an approach that consciously builds on Canada's longstanding commitments and experiences in gender policy and programming. Canada's current feminist commitments can credibly build on decades of dedicated gender equality efforts, and should aspire to promote transformative changes that move beyond superficial efforts to target women and girls. Branding has been – and will remain – an important strategic dimension of any government's international policy. Understanding more precisely the "targets" and objectives of such branding efforts should also enable a closer consideration of the *limitations* of the branding exercise, and challenge governments to move beyond posturing for targeted audiences to ensure more robust, comprehensive, and sustainable commitments over time.

## Notes

1 https://pm.gc.ca/eng/news/2017/11/15/elsie-initiative-women-peace-operations
2 On defence policy, for example, the government's 2017 policy document, *Strong, Secure, Engaged* promises to increase the percentage of women in the Canadian Forces from 15% to 25% by 2026.
3 Juxtaposed with the planned surge in defence spending, for example. See Brown and Swiss (2017), pp. 127–128; also OECD (2018).

## Sources

Aksli, M. 2017. "Canada's Feminist International Assistance Risks Not Being Relevant to Its Development Partners and Not Enjoying Strong Local Ownership." *Policy Options*, 17 October.
"A Feminist Approach to Canada's International Assistance." 2016. A submission to the International Assistance Review. Online: www.oxfam.ca/sites/default/files/file_attachments/a_feminist_approach_-_final.pdf
Bibeau, M.-C. 2017. "Canada launches new Feminist International Assistance Policy", *Global Affairs Canada News Release*, 9 June. Ottawa: Global Affairs Canada.
Black, D. (forthcoming 2019). "Canadian Aid to Africa in the 1990s: A Crisis of Confidence." In G. Donaghy and D. Webster (eds.), *A Samaritan State Revisited*. Calgary, University of Calgary Press.
Brown, S. and Swiss, L. 2017. "Canada's Feminist International Assistance Policy: Bold Statement or Feminist Fig Leaf." In K. Graham and A. Maslove (eds.), *How Ottawa Spends, 2017–2018*, chapter 10,

pp. 117–131. Online: www.researchgate.net/publication/320779507_Canada%27s_Feminist_International_Assistance_Policy_Bold_Statement_or_Feminist_Fig_Leaf

Canada. 2017a. "Canada's Feminist International Assistance Policy". 9 June. Online: http://international.gc.ca/world-monde/issues_development-enjeux_developpement/priorities-priorites/policy-politique.aspx?lang=eng

Canada. 2017b. "Address by Minister Freeland on Canada's Foreign Policy Priorities." Speech, June 6, 2017, Ottawa Canada. Online: www.canada.ca/en/global-affairs/news/2017/06/address_by_ministerfreelandoncanadasforeignpolicypriorities.html

GAC (Global Affairs Canada). 2017. "Canada launches new Feminist International Assistance Policy", *Global Affairs Canada News Release*, 9 June. Ottawa: Global Affairs Canada.

Nacyte, L. 2018. Canada's Feminist International Assistance Policy: Security for Whom? *LSE Engenderings*. Online: http://blogs.lse.ac.uk/gender/2018/01/22/canadas-feminist-international-assistance-policy-security-for-whom/

Nimijean, R. 2014. "Domestic Brand Politics and the Modern Publicity State." In K. Kozolanka (ed.), *Publicity and the Canadian State*. Toronto: University of Toronto Press, pp. 172–194.

OECD Development Assistance Committee. 2018. *OECD Development Assistance Committee Peer Reviews: Canada 2018*, Paris: OECD Publishing.

Raj, A. 2018. "Canada Deserves UN Security Council Seat, Envoy Marc-Andre Blanchard Argues to the World." *HuffPost*, 1 October. www.huffingtonpost.ca/2018/10/01/canada-un-security-council_a_23547715/

Swiss, L. 2018. "Feminism on the Cheap: Can Canada Achieve its Ambitious Gender Equality Aid Targets with No New Money?", *GrOW Research Bulletin*, Issue 5, Montreal: McGill University Publications.

Tiessen, R. 2016. "Gender Equality and the 'Two CIDAs': Success and Setbacks, 1976–2015." In S. Brown, M. den Heyer and D. R. Black (eds.), *Rethinking Canadian Aid*. Ottawa: University of Ottawa Press, pp. 195–210.

Tiessen, R. and Carrier, K. 2015. "The Erasure of 'Gender' in Canadian Foreign Policy under the Harper Conservatives: The Significance of the Discursive Shift from 'Gender Equality' to 'Equality between Women and Men'." *Canadian Foreign Policy Journal*, Vol. 21, Issue 2, pp. 95–111.

Tiessen, R. and Swan, E. 2018. "Canada's Feminist Foreign Policy Promises: An Ambitious Agenda for Gender Equality, Human Rights, Peace and Security." In N. Hillmer and P. Lagassé (eds.), *Justin Trudeau and Canadian Foreign Policy*, New York: Palgrave Macmillan, pp. 187–205.

Zilio, M. 2018. "Trudeau to Lead Canada's Campaign for a UN Security Council Seat in New York This Week." *Globe and Mail*, 24 September.

# 5  Friend or faux?

Trudeau, Indigenous issues and Canada's brand

Heather Exner-Pirot

**ABSTRACT**

Canada and Canadians often consider themselves to be a force for good in the world. Does that self-perception hold true with Indigenous issues? This article evaluates Canada's brand with respect to international Indigenous issues historically, as well as contemporarily under the leadership of the Trudeau government, with a focus on the United Nations Declaration on the Rights of Indigenous Peoples and the Arctic Council. Canada's record is shown to be mixed, with a history of diminishment of Indigenous rights on the world stage, paired with real leadership and commitment to partnership in regional Arctic governance. However, there is little evidence that Canada's treatment of its Indigenous peoples, which has risen as a key domestic policy issue in the wake of the Truth and Reconciliation Commission, has affected its international brand. More concretely, domestic angst and discomfiture with regards to Canada's relationship with its Indigenous peoples could lead to a downplaying of Canada's reputational strengths of diversity and tolerance.

**RÉSUMÉ**

Le Canada et les canadiens se considèrent souvent comme une force au bénéfice du bien dans le monde. Cette auto-perception se vérifie-t-elle en ce qui concerne les questions liées aux autochtones ? Cet article évalue le label canadien vis-à-vis des questions autochtones sur la scène internationale, d'un point de vue historique, mais aussi contemporain - sous le leadership du gouvernement Trudeau - en se concentrant sur la Déclaration des Nations-Unies sur les droits des peuples autochtones et sur le Conseil de l'Arctique. Le bilan du Canada se révèle comme étant mitigé, avec une histoire de diminution des droits des autochtones sur la scène internationale, associée à de véritables leadership et engagement, en termes de partenariat, au sein de la gouvernance régionale de l'Arctique. Cependant les données sont rares sur la manière dont le Canada traite ses populations autochtones, et dans le prolongement de la Commission de vérité et réconciliation, ce point a émergé comme une question majeure de politique domestique et terni l'image internationale du pays. Plus concrètement, l'angoisse et la déconfiture concernant le rapport du Canada avec ses populations autochtones pourrait conduire à une minimisation des forces de diversité et de tolérance qui forgent la réputation du pays.

Well, if we're just looking at it from a circumpolar perspective, I think Canada is looked upon positively, because of the issues that they deal with at the Arctic Council level. But I think there's so much more potential – and hopefully this new Canadian government looks at it as an opportunity to enhance some of their activities.

—Duane Smith, Chair and Chief Executive Officer (CEO) of the Inuvialuit Regional Corporation and former President of Inuit Circumpolar Council Canada, January 2016a

## Introduction

Between Trump's antics and Brexit angst, North Korea's nuclear threats and Russia's increasing brazenness, the international order is experiencing a level of turbulence unknown since at least the attacks of 9/11. For Indigenous peoples in Canada and globally, however, instability and conflict are predominant features of their existence within the Westphalian international system.

Canada and Canadians often consider themselves to be a force for good in the world. Based on Canada's reputation among other nations and nationals, it seems most others agree. But does that reputation hold true with Indigenous issues?

This article evaluates Canada's brand with respect to international Indigenous issues, historically as well as contemporarily under the leadership of the Trudeau government. Canada's efforts to promote Indigenous inclusion in Arctic regional politics, including in the Arctic Council, and to adopt the United Nations Declaration on the Rights of Indigenous People (UNDRIP) are adopted as case studies to illustrate Canada's record.

Canada's record on international Indigenous issues is mixed; but its impact on Canada's reputation is marginal. Indigenous issues have gained political significance domestically, particularly since the release of the Truth and Reconciliation Commission's Calls to Action in 2015, but they are still peripheral internationally. Furthermore, there has been more consistency on Indigenous issues in Canadian international policy across successive governments than domestic rhetorical differences might suggest.

## Canada's Indigenous brand problem in context

It is fair to assert that Canada has been seen in increasingly glowing terms internationally since the election of the Liberals and Justin Trudeau as Prime Minister (Nimijean 2017), although the luster is showing signs of waning (e.g. Wu 2018).

However, Canada's reputation as benign, welcoming and tolerant has often been compromised by its dislocation and marginalization of Indigenous peoples, even if some prominent Canadian politicians, including former Prime Minister Stephen Harper and former Cabinet member Pierre Pettigrew, have asserted that Canada "has no colonial past" (Pettigrew 1999, Ljunggren 2009). An otherwise fawning cover story on Canada's "example to the world" in *The Economist* in October 2016, for example, made a point of referencing Canada's "shameful treatment of Indigenous peoples" (The Economist 2016).

As Whitney Lackenbauer and Andrew Cooper (2007, p. 99) articulate it, Indigenous issues are the "Achilles heel" of Canada's international image, with "the gap between Canada's self-image as a good international citizen and the flaws in its own record highlighted by Indigenous issues." Savvy Indigenous leaders have long leveraged Canada's desire to be considered a good and positive force in international relations for domestic ends. As First Nations leader Ovide Mercredi described it: "Given that Canada prides itself on its international human rights commitments, raising issues at the international level has been an important way for us to gain attention for our grievance" (cited in Lackenbauer and Cooper 2007, p. 99).

The Indigenous challenge to Canada's global brand is as old as Canada itself. As Niezen (2000, p. 123) documents, Indigenous leaders from Canada and New Zealand aired their grievances about the governments in their respective nation-states to the British monarch as early as the mid nineteenth century, though they elicited little more than polite hearings.

Competing depictions of Indigenous life in a young Canada were on display at the Chicago World Fair of 1893. While the official Canadian "live exhibit" portrayed Indigenous children from a rotation of eight residential schools in a mock schoolroom to highlight Canadian civility, the "authentic" Kwakwaka'wakw exhibit organized by anthropologists featured a graphic *hamatsa* performance that included the cutting and biting of human flesh, much to the outrage and embarrassment of Canadian officials (Raibmon 2000).

Also notable was the appeal by Levi General Deskaheh of the Six Nations (located now in Ontario) in 1923 to the nascent League of Nations for self-determination. Canada's "Achilles heel" was evident early on, with Herbert Ames, the Canadian representative at the League of Nations, alerting Prime Minister William Lyon Mackenzie King in December 1923 that:

> During the Assembly [of the League of Nations] a picturesque delegation of Iroquois Indians, with their chief, Deskehah [sic], were here in Geneva addressing meetings and interviewing delegates. They aroused a certain amount of sympathy among people who heard their side only. Since the Assembly, I understand that they have been following up this initiative by visiting several European countries ... I think that really it will be necessary to pay some attention to this lest our apparent indifference be misinterpreted and thus our excellent reputation over here suffer somewhat. (Ames 1923 cited in Niezen 2000, p. 125)

That Canada's structural inability to effectively address the "Indian problem" – or, as Newhouse and Belanger (2016) have redefined it, the "Canada problem" – has made it vulnerable to embarrassment and pressure from Indigenous leaders on the global stage is perhaps best exemplified by Canada's efforts to intercede in South African politics during its apartheid era. When John Diefenbaker opposed South African membership in the Commonwealth in 1961 due to their policy of apartheid, they retorted that Indians lacked political representation in Canadian parliament. Diefenbaker had set about granting franchise to Indians, in 1960, partly on the grounds that it would "remove in the eyes of the world any suggestion that in Canada colour or race places any citizen in an inferior category to other citizens of the country" (cited in Lackenbauer and Cooper 2007, p. 102).

During the Mulroney era, Canada's efforts to impose sanctions on South Africa led to further criticism. Chief Louis Stevenson invited South African Ambassador to Canada Glenn Babb to Peguis First Nation in Manitoba in 1987, and formally requested CAD$99 million from South Africa in foreign aid, in an explicit attempt to embarrass the Canada government: "I felt it's a strong attempt to put pressure on Canada's federal government and will make them think about cleaning up its own backyard. People should not throw stones if they live in a glass house." Though the visit was controversial – with one oppressed group seeming to disregard the plight of another oppressed group for their own purposes – Stephenson argued:

> I have successfully accomplished my objective of drawing national, if not international attention, to the plight of Canada's Native people by having Babb visit my reserve. I know my decision was not popular, but at least it lit a fire under the provincial and federal governments and the public at large in coming to terms to do something about the Indian issues. (cited in Compton 1987)

Another high-profile event occurred in 2001, when Assembly of First Nations (AFN) National Chief Matthew Coon Come spoke at the World Conference Against Racism in Durban, South Africa. Coon Come compared Canada's policies toward its Aboriginal people to South Africa's apartheid, saying that Canada was slow to address the social problems experienced by First Nations people "because we are Indians" and that government policies meant Indigenous people in Canada were being "pushed to the edge of extinction" (cited in Barnsley 2001). The Minister of Indian Affairs at the time, Robert Nault, decried the speech, saying there was "no proof of this in the modern time" and that his comments were "not acceptable for any national leader to make in an international forum" (as quoted in Mackey 2002). The AFN released a press release at the event, noting the prominence of the Indigenous Peoples' Caucus at the World Conference, and that Chief Coon Come was "being interviewed extensively by media such as BBC World Service, Italian, Canadian and South African national TV news" (AFN 2001).

It is important to acknowledge that while Canadian Indigenous leaders have been known to use their global platform to criticize Canadian policies, Canada is still viewed as one of the leading nations in terms of recognizing and supporting Indigenous rights. Anecdotally, Canada is often seen as falling shy of the status of New Zealand, with its politically powerful Maori, but ahead of Indigenous peoples in Australia, who historically had no treaties with the Crown and thus weaker legal outlets for reparations, and the United States, where Indigenous issues are much less urgent politically for federal and state governments. State responsiveness to Indigenous issues in these four Anglosphere countries corresponds roughly to the proportion of their population that is Indigenous. Sami in northern Europe enjoy what are probably the highest standards of living of any Indigenous group. However, perhaps due to their small population, their long shared history with the dominant ethnic group, and the unitary systems of government found in the Nordic states, they have not achieved the same level of constitutional recognition and status.

## *Canada's Indigenous brand under Trudeau*

The Harper government came to be almost universally disliked by Indigenous Canadians (e.g. Galloway 2017) due to, among other things, the scrapping of the Kelowna Accord, the unwillingness to call an inquiry into Missing and Murdered Indigenous Women and Girls, the First Nations Financial Transparency Act and Bill C-45, an omnibus bill that made amendments to the Indian Act, Fisheries Act, Canadian Environmental Protection Act and Navigable Water Protection Act and that triggered the Idle No More movement.

The election of Justin Trudeau and his Liberal government in October 2015 offered the opportunity for Canada to remediate its relationship with its Indigenous peoples. Indeed,

Trudeau's positive global image did trickle over initially into international Indigenous affairs. The annual International Work Groups for Indigenous Affairs (IWGIA) publication, *The Indigenous World* (Vinding and Mikkelsen 2016), for example, highlighted Trudeau's election in its 2016 edition in a section on "positive developments at the national level," stating that:

> In Canada, the newly elected Prime Minister Justin Trudeau expressed his strong commitment to improve the relationship to indigenous peoples. Trudeau furthermore has prioritized the implementation of the Truth and Reconciliation Commission's Calls to Action, including the implementation of the UN Declaration on the Rights of Indigenous Peoples (UNDRIP) (p. 12).

It further highlighted the announcement by the Liberals that they would establish an inquiry into Murdered and Missing Indigenous Women and Girls (MMIWG), the inclusion of Canada's relationship with Indigenous peoples in Ministers' mandate letters, and the appointment of two Indigenous members to the Cabinet. "Canada has a long history of failed commitments to Indigenous peoples ... however early signs are hopeful" the report noted (p. 56).

Despite high hopes, and the high expectations the Liberals set for themselves on the Indigenous relations file, two and a half years on there is a sense among many Indigenous Canadians that few concrete achievements have been made. As a headline from the *National Post* articulated it, "Trudeau's rhetoric on First Nations [is] out of step with reality" (Akin 2016). A sense of unfulfilled promise in Indigenous issues extended to the foreign policy sphere, most prominently with UNDRIP.

The following sections evaluate Canada's international record on Indigenous issues with respect to UNDRIP and the Arctic Council. These provide high-profile examples of Indigenous engagement in Canada's international relations in recent years. They conclude with an evaluation of the performance of the Trudeau government on those particular files.

## Arctic Indigenous peoples and political empowerment

The 1941 signing of the Atlantic Charter by Franklin Roosevelt and Winston Churchill, the 1942 Declaration by the United Nations, and the subsequent establishment of the United Nations and its Charter legitimatized and popularized the concept of self-determination. This led to an intense period of decolonization and national independence in which the number of United Nations members grew from 60 in 1950 to 184 in 1993; it now sits at 193 member states. At the same time, the civil rights movement in the United States provided a model for domestic civil action. This led to a rise in organization, advocacy and action against the internal colonization of Indigenous peoples around the world, and demands for their own self-determination. At the same time, the welfare state, and its expansion of government services, reached into corners of Canada it had not known before, including northern Indigenous communities, increasing political contact and triggering institutional convergence.

The modern land claims era began in Canada with the signing of the James Bay and Northern Quebec Agreement (JBNQA) in 1975. This had a substantial impact on Inuit organizational ambitions and capacity. John English (2013) describes the importance of the Makivik Corporation, established to protect the rights, interests and financial compensation provided by the JBNQA, in developing Inuit leadership. Among its alumni, Charlie Watt, a founder of Makivik Corporation, went on to become a member of the Canadian Senate and a co-founder of the Inuit Circumpolar Conference (now Council; ICC). Mary Simon, who was Vice-President of Makivik Corporation in 1978, and later served as its president until 1995, became Executive Council member, President and Special Envoy of the ICC; Canada's first Circumpolar Ambassador and Chair of the Arctic Council; President of Inuit Tapiriit Kanatami from 2006–2012; and most recently Indigenous and Northern Affairs Canada (INAC) Minister's Special Representative to the Arctic. Sheila Watt-Cloutier, who was Corporate Secretary for Makivik Corporation from 1995–1998, later became President of ICC-Canada from 1995 to 2001, and then International Chair of the ICC between 2002 and 2006.

Inuit in Alaska and Greenland were going through their own rapid political development in the 1970s. Building on national discussions and progression of Indigenous self-determination, an Arctic Peoples' Conference was held in Copenhagen in 1973 that brought together Inuit and Sami. Subsequently, Eben Hopson, the mayor of the North Slope Borough, gathered Inuit from Alaska, Canada and Greenland in mid-1977 in Barrow, Alaska. This was the first Inuit Circumpolar Conference (ICC) (English 2013). This coincided with a period of devolution of authority to Indigenous peoples of the Arctic, including the finalization of the Alaska Native Land Claims Settlement in 1971; the granting of Home Rule in Greenland in 1979; and the establishment of Nunavut in the Canadian Arctic in 1999. These events served to increase the political capacity of Arctic Indigenous peoples, and also prompted interaction with one another along circumpolar East/West lines rather than the usual North/South interactions with political and administrative centers.

It was within this context that Canada assumed leadership in the development of an Arctic inter-governmental forum, including a push for formal and high-level Indigenous involvement.

## *Canada, Inuit and the Arctic Council*

Following Soviet leader Mikhail Gorbachev's 1987 Murmansk Speech, calling for the Arctic to become a "zone of peace," a group of academics and non-governmental organizations (NGOs) in Canada held a number of sessions looking at the idea of an Arctic Basin Council. Ultimately dubbed the "Arctic Council Panel," it included Rosemarie Kuptana, an Inuk woman from Sachs Harbor, as co-Chair alongside University of Toronto Professor Franklyn Griffiths.

The Arctic Council was a wholly Canadian initiative in the early days, and included a proposal to include formal Aboriginal participation, as well as one to address matters of military security, both of which caused concern to other states (English 2013, p. 172). Canada was under significant domestic pressure to advocate for the inclusion of Aboriginal participants in a potential council, coming in the wake of the Berger Inquiry, which investigated the social, environmental and economic impact of a proposed gas pipeline through the Mackenzie River Valley; the negotiations to establish Nunavut; and the constitutional revision to the Charlottetown Accord that required Aboriginal support.

Canada organized an experts' meeting on 5–6 May 1992 to discuss the Arctic Council proposal with delegates from all of the eight states with territory in the Arctic Circle

(Canada, Denmark, Finland, Iceland, Norway, Russia, Sweden and the United States). Several Indigenous representatives attended as part of national delegations; however, Mary Simon, the president of the ICC, was the only non-state delegate at the table. By the end of the meeting, it had been decided that the ICC and the Nordic Sami Council would participate in the work of the Council as "permanent observers" (English 2013, p. 176). Later, in a January 1993 report of the Arctic Council Panel, a draft Terms of Reference stated that: "In addition to the Arctic government, Aboriginal northern international organizations, such as the Inuit Circumpolar Conference and the Sami Council, will participate in the work of the Council as *Permanent Participants*" (English 2013, p. 184, emphasis in original).

The Canadian government assumed a full "marketing" role regarding the idea of an Arctic Council after that. It funded Mary Simon to convene a meeting in March 1993, in Yellowknife, to develop a unified and joint position among Inuit and other Canadian Aboriginal leaders as well as their Sami colleagues. The Russian Association of Indigenous Peoples of the North (RAIPON) attended an Arctic Council meeting for the first time in May 1993. As English articulates,

> There was no mention of Indigenous interests in Brian Mulroney's [1989] Leningrad speech, and Indigenous leaders were initially indifferent to the proposal. By the Spring of 1993, however, both Indian Affairs and Northern Development and External Affairs were funding, consulting with, and deferring to Indigenous interests in the drafting of the terms of reference for the new council. It was a distinction that had become a substantial difference. (p. 188)

In 1994, Mary Simon was appointed Canada's Ambassador for Arctic and Circumpolar Affairs, with instruction to work to establish an Arctic Council. It was eventually established in 1996 with a mandate to address the environmental protection issues identified in the 1991 Arctic Environmental Protection Strategy, as well as a more community oriented focus on sustainable development advocated by Canada. Although a Sustainable Development Working Group was eventually established, it took two years to develop its Terms of Reference (Finkler and Kadas 2016). Staples (1998, p.15) asserts that:

> The Canadian Arctic experience with sustainability emerged as issues of community development and community empowerment – an experience that has been dramatically mirrored in [Canada's] land claim agreements of the [previous] two decades ... In contrast the Scandinavian and European experiences were defined generally as the vertical integration and coordination of actions and responsibilities across national, regional and local governments.

### *Current Indigenous issues and the Arctic Council*

As demonstrated above, Canada and its northern Indigenous peoples, and their relationship, played a very significant role in the development of the Arctic Council and its unique focus on Indigenous issues and participation. Keskitalo (2007, p. 198) notes that critics of the Arctic Council Initiative "saw it more as a Canada-based proposal than as an internationally viable proposal" and that the Canadian focus on the Arctic could be "seen as a result of its domestic Indigenous situation."

Scrivener (1996, p. 13), more plainly, argued that:

> Generally, Arctic issues were less prominent in the domestic politics of the Arctic states, compared with the Canadian case. In some ways, the whole Arctic Council idea could be seen as an external projection of the internal political processes related to Indigenous peoples of the Canadian North.

Canada continued in its role as a reliable promoter and supporter of Indigenous and human issues in the work of the Arctic Council after its establishment. This position assumed a higher profile during Canada's 2013–2015 Arctic Council Chairmanship. Former Prime Minister Stephen Harper made the bold decision to appoint Leona Aglukkaq, the Member of Parliament (MP) for Nunavut and federal Minister for Health, and later Environment, as Chair of the Arctic Council, a position normally reserved for Foreign Ministers.

Aglukkaq made "Development for the People of the North" the theme of the Canadian Arctic Council Chairmanship. Given Canada's historical interests and contemporary challenges in the region, this was not an unexpected theme. Canada also pushed efforts to establish a fund to build the capacity of Permanent Participants to contribute to the work of the Arctic Council, promoted the incorporation of traditional knowledge in the work of the Council, and prioritized efforts to address mental health and suicide in Arctic communities.

Concerns about the Harper government's track record on issues such as climate change and resource development led to suspicion, however, about the Council's perceived shift in priority from environmental protection and scientific work to economic development. Matthew Willis (2013) called the Canadian vision an "Arctic Indigenous Canadian vision" which treated "the Arctic as a place for those living in it":

> "Outside" actors are allowed in, but only to support and serve Northern interests ... The idea that anything much remains to be discussed, or that non-Northerners have a natural role to play in any discussion that might break out, is nowhere to be found ... To call the Canadian vision unfashionable (except in the North) would therefore be an understatement.

This was precisely Canada's goal, in 2013 as it was in 1996, and which continues today: to push the Arctic Council's focus from science and environment toward local and Indigenous interests. And if it has at times been contested, a number of retrospections provided on the occasion of the council's 20th anniversary in 2016 specifically identified the inclusion of Indigenous voices as one of the primary achievements and characteristics of the forum (e.g. Brigham et al. 2016, Koivurova and Smieszek 2016).

Canada has developed a reputation, in the Arctic Council at least, as a key proponent of Indigenous engagement and inclusion.

### *Trudeau and the Arctic*

Trudeau's record in Arctic affairs more generally is mixed. A surprising focus of United States–Canada bilateral cooperation during the short window in which the Obama and Trudeau mandates overlapped was on Arctic issues. On 10 March 2016, concomitant with the state dinner held by Obama for Trudeau, the leaders issued a "US–Canada Joint Statement on Climate, Energy and Arctic Leadership," which was received positively by northern and Indigenous leaders (e.g. Inuit Circumpolar Council 2016a).

However a follow-up – the "United States–Canada Joint Arctic Leaders' Statement," launched on 20 December 2016 – was not received nearly as well. It seemed rushed, an effort by the Obama administration to push forward a number of initiatives during the transition to a Trump presidency. The usual, high consultation standards that Global Affairs Canada had observed on Arctic Council activities were replaced by high-level, top-down decision-making by the Prime Minister's Office (PMO) in an effort to accommodate their American partners. Several northern and Indigenous leaders, across Alaska, Yukon, the Northwest Territories and Nunavut, publicly expressed disappointment that they had learned about the statement and its initiatives only hours before it was announced – particularly the bombshell announcement of a moratorium on Arctic offshore oil and gas leases on both the American and Canadian sides (see Exner-Pirot 2016).

This was made all the more unseemly given the appointment of Mary Simon in Indigenous and Northern Affairs Canada as the Minister's Special Representative to the Arctic in August 2016, with the explicit mandate, flowing from the commitments made in the March 2016 joint statement, to engage with "territorial governments, Indigenous governments and organizations, and northerners to seek innovative ideas for advancing a Shared Arctic Leadership Model" (INAC 2017). In Simon's interim report of October 2016, submitted less than two months before the controversial December arctic statement, Simon emphasized the Prime Minister's desire to "reach out, listen and learn," and set out principles of partnership:

> A new Arctic Leadership Model needs to establish principles around involving Arctic governments and indigenous leaders from the outset in developing the model. Partnership is not just about the duty to consult. True partnership with Arctic peoples means active involvement from start to finish. There is also an expectation that traditional indigenous and local knowledge is recognized, respected, promoted, valued and used in processes and decision-making. Setting new expectations on the principles of partnership is core to getting an Inuit-to-Crown or Nation-to-Nation relationship right. (Simon 2016)

Duane Smith, CEO of the Inuvialuit Regional Corporation, articulated in a letter to Prime Minister Trudeau in January 2017 what many Northerners felt:

> This lack of meaningful communication is startling given your Government's stated commitment to improved Inuit–Crown relationships ... [our] rights require a balancing of interests, in which Inuvialuit must be involved for it to have meaning. Inuvialuit cannot support such unilateral decision-making. Indeed, it seems to be a step backward. (Smith 2017)

Canada is currently in the process of "co-developing" a new Arctic Policy Framework (APF) with Northerners, territorial and provincial governments, and First Nations, Inuit, and Métis people. Extensive consultations have occurred with northern stakeholders on what the direction of Canada's Arctic foreign policy should look like and achieve. It is expected to be launched in the latter half of 2018. Because the APF will integrate both domestic and international components of Canada's Arctic policy, it is likely to reflect, certainly from other states' point of view, a heavy focus on northern and Indigenous self-determination and well-being. While Trudeau's moratorium miss-step affected his reputation with Canadian northern stakeholders, the Liberals' APF is likely to entrench rather than challenge Canada's reputation for being Indigenous-centric in international Arctic circles.

## Canada and the United Nations Declaration on the Rights of Indigenous Peoples

Canada's record on international Indigenous issues outside the Arctic tells a different story. In terms of the highest profile international documents related to Indigenous rights, Canada has not yet ratified the 1989 International Labour Organization (ILO) Convention 169, consisting of 44 articles organized in 10 categories that outline the minimum standards of the rights of Indigenous peoples; and was one of only four countries that voted against UNDRIP in 2007. UNDRIP has become a salient political issue of late, as the Truth and Reconciliation Commission calls on the government to adopt and implement it in full, which the Liberals committed to doing in their 2015 electoral campaign. This section will examine UNDRIP's impact on Canada's brand from an Indigenous perspective.

## *The development of UNDRIP*

In 1982, the United Nations Economic and Social Council (UNESCO) established a Working Group on Indigenous Populations. Over the course of a decade, the text for a draft articulating international Indigenous human rights was agreed to and then submitted to the Sub-Commission on the Prevention of Discrimination and Protection of Minorities, and later the UN Commission on Human Rights. The latter established a Working Group on the draft Declaration on the Rights of Indigenous Peoples in 1994.

Around the same time, the First International Decade of the World's Indigenous People (pointedly, not "Peoples") was proclaimed by the United Nations General Assembly for the years 1995–2004. The "adoption of the draft United Nations Declaration on the Rights of Indigenous Peoples and the further development of international standards as well as national legislation for the protection and the promotion of Indigenous people" was proclaimed as a specific objective (Engle 2011, p. 144). As there was still no consensus on a text by the end of that Decade, a Second International Decade of the World's Indigenous People was proclaimed for 2005–2015.

Among the more contentious articles, Article 3 of the 1993 draft stated: "Indigenous peoples have the right to self-determination. By virtue of that right, they freely determine their political status and freely pursue their economic, social and cultural development." There were concerns that the conception of "self-determination" could include the right to statehood. Despite those concerns, the article remained intact in the 2007 Declaration, though it prompted the African Union to oppose the Declaration through a non-action resolution in 2006, and prompted Canada, the United States, Australia and New Zealand to vote against its final adoption in 2007 (Engle 2011, p. 145).

For Canada, there was a clear potential for incompatibility between UNDRIP and its domestic laws and rights. As Minister of Indian Affairs and Northern Development Jim Prentice stated in the House of Commons in 2006, five months after the Conservatives were elected to power:

> The proposed wording is incompatible with our Constitution, the Canadian Charter of Rights and Freedoms, various Supreme Court of Canada decisions, the National Defence Act and federal policies on Aboriginal land claims and self-government. We must work with other countries and the Standing Committee on Aboriginal Affairs and Northern Development to improve the drafting of such a declaration. (cited in Coates and Favel 2016, p. 17)

Similarly, John McNee, Canada's ambassador to the UN, iterated in 2007 that:

> Canada's position has remained consistent and principled. We have stated publicly that we have significant concerns with respect to the wording of the current text, including the provisions on lands, territories and resources; free, prior and informed consent when used as a veto; self-government without recognition of the importance of negotiations; intellectual

> property; military issues; and the need to achieve an appropriate balance between the rights and obligations of indigenous peoples, member States and third parties …
>
> Canada will continue to take effective action, at home and abroad, to promote and protect the rights of Indigenous peoples based on our existing human rights obligations and commitments. Such effective action, we must be clear, would not be undertaken on the basis of the provisions of this Declaration.
>
> By voting against the adoption of this text, Canada puts on record its disappointment with both the substance and process. For clarity, we also underline our understanding that this Declaration is not a legally binding instrument. It has no legal effect in Canada, and its provisions do not represent customary international law. (Coates and Favel 2016, p. 18)

This position eventually became untenable politically. The Harper government had endeavored to make several gestures of goodwill toward First Nations, Inuit and Métis groups, notably the Residential School Apology in 2008 and the concomitant establishment of the Truth and Reconciliation Commission of Canada. But the refusal to adopt the UNDRIP became a lightning rod in Aboriginal–Crown relations, even more so after Australia and New Zealand changed their positions and endorsed the Declaration in April 2009 and April 2010, respectively.

Canada thus committed to "endorse" the UNDRIP in its March 2010 Speech to the Throne, stating that:

> We are a country with an Aboriginal heritage. A growing number of states have given qualified recognition to the United Nations Declaration on the Rights of Indigenous Peoples. Our Government will take steps to endorse this aspirational document in a manner fully consistent with Canada's Constitution and laws. (Speech from the Throne 2010)

This was done formally on 12 November 2010. The INAC website explained the decision as such:

> After careful and thoughtful consideration, Canada has concluded that it is better to endorse the UNDRIP while explaining its concerns, rather than simply rejecting the overall document.
>
> Although the UNDRIP does not reflect customary international law or change Canadian laws, Canada believes that the UNDRIP has the potential to contribute positively to the promotion and respect of the rights of indigenous peoples around the world. (cited in CBC News 2010)

While Canada, the United States, Australia and New Zealand ultimately endorsed UNDRIP (as a declaration rather than a treaty, it does not merit ratification), none of them committed to fully enacting its provisions in their national constitutions or domestic laws. A key distinction made was that UNDRIP was "aspirational" and "non-binding." As Coates and Favel (2016, p. 19) explain, "the key implication was that the UN Declaration on the Rights of Indigenous Peoples was a target and a long-term roadmap that laid out national and Indigenous ambitions." This distinction satisfied few Indigenous groups.

### *UNDRIP and the Trudeau Liberals*

The relationship between Canada's Indigenous organizations and the Government of Canada continued to sour during Stephen Harper's tenure as Prime Minister. This was perhaps best encapsulated by the rise of the Idle No More movement and the hunger strike and occupation of Victoria Island, near Parliament Hill, by Attawapiskat First Nation Chief Theresa Spence.

The Liberals promised a different approach to Aboriginal–Crown relations and UNDRIP during the 2015 election campaign. Trudeau specifically promised in a speech to the Assembly of First Nations in July 2015 that:

> To support the work of reconciliation and continue the necessary process of truth telling and healing, we will work with you to enact the recommendations of the Truth and Reconciliation Commission, starting with the implementation of the United Nations Declaration on the Rights of Indigenous Peoples. (Trudeau 2015)

After the October 2015 election, in which the Liberals emerged victorious, Trudeau emphasized in his mandate letters to new Liberal Ministers the importance of their relationship with Indigenous peoples, based on recognition of rights, respect, cooperation and partnership. And in a statement marking the release of the final report of the Truth and Reconciliation Commission in December 2015, he reiterated his commitment to implementing – as opposed to merely endorsing – UNDRIP:

> [W]e will, in partnership with Indigenous communities, the provinces, territories, and other vital partners, fully implement the Calls to Action of the Truth and Reconciliation Commission, starting with the implementation of the United Nations Declaration on the Rights of Indigenous Peoples. (Prime Minister of Canada's Office 2015)

The Liberals made good on this promise with a dramatic speech by INAC Minister Carolyn Bennett to the United Nations Permanent Forum on Indigenous Issues. She announced "on behalf of Canada," on 10 May 2016, that:

> We are now a full supporter of the Declaration [UNDRIP], without qualification. We intend nothing less than to adopt and implement the Declaration in accordance with the Canadian Constitution ... Canada believes that our constitutional obligations serve to fulfill all the principles of the Declaration, including "free, prior and informed consent" ... Canada has already begun making real the Declaration on the Rights of Indigenous Peoples ... Let's be honest, implementing UNDRIP should not be scary. (Bennett, 2016)

The reaction to Bennett's speech from Canada's Aboriginal leaders was predictably positive. AFN National Chief Perry Bellegarde declared that "Canada is sending an important message to Indigenous peoples, to all Canadians and to the international community that Indigenous rights are human rights" (Assembly of First Nations 2016). Métis National Council President Chartier "expressed his appreciation for the Trudeau government's commitment to fully engage with the Métis Nation in the upcoming reconciliation process" (Métis Nations 2016). And Herb Nakimayak, the Vice-President of the ICC, applauded the speech, stating:

> Canada's commitment to withdraw its reservations to paragraphs 3 and 20 signals a 180° shift in its approach to Indigenous peoples. The commitments to obtain Indigenous peoples' free, prior and informed consent, before adopting and implementing legislative or administrative measures that would affect us, shows progressive action. (Inuit Circumpolar Council 2016b)

The glow was short lived. Only two months later, Justice Minister Jody Wilson-Raybould, a Kwakwaka'wakw woman and previous BC Regional Chief of the AFN, upturned the Liberals' commitment to fully implementing the UNDRIP at a speech to the AFN during their annual general meeting, on 12 July 2016:

So as much as I would tomorrow like to cast into the fire of history the Indian Act so that the Nations can be reborn in its ashes – this is not a practical option – which is why simplistic approaches, such as adopting the UNDRIP as being Canadian law are unworkable and, respectfully, a political distraction to undertaking the hard work required to actually implement it …

The way the UNDRIP will get implemented in Canada will be through a mixture of legislation, policy and action initiated and taken by Indigenous Nations themselves. Ultimately, the UNDRIP will be articulated through the constitutional framework of section 35. (Wilson-Raybould 2016)

It is unclear why the Liberals put themselves in such an unfavorable position. The arguments the Conservatives, other Anglosphere countries, and legal experts had used to depict UNDRIP as an "aspirational" document, and endorsing with reservations, were all publicly and clearly known. If the Liberals had devised no new strategy to address those legal reservations, they should not have made such a conspicuous commitment to doing so.

As UNDRIP persisted as a sore spot in the Liberals' efforts to improve Crown–Indigenous relations, the government's position shifted once more. A private member's bill, Bill-262, was introduced in April 2016 by New Democratic Party (NDP) MP Romeo Saganash (who was part of the team that initially crafted the declaration) that would force the government to implement the provisions of the declaration. After some initial reluctance, the Liberals decided to support the bill in November 2017. At the time of writing, it has passed its second reading in the House of Commons (Parliament of Canada 2018). Scholars Ken Coates and Dwayne Newman call the bill "overly simplistic" and assert that it "has the potential to unleash a legal struggle of titanic proportions, as each and every policy of the federal, provincial, and territorial governments is subjected to an international test that was not designed to match Canadian circumstances" (2018). But it is important politically with regards to Liberals' commitment to reconciliation.

## Indigenous issues and Canada's brand

Canada's reputation in the international system has long been esteemed, as evidenced in the Reputation Institute's annual survey of country reputations. This positive reputation precedes Trudeau, but his global popularity is likely to have entrenched it, with the Prime Minister the subject of Internet memes, magazine covers and fawning articles from the likes of *The New York Times* (see for example Kanter 2017), *Vogue* (Power 2015) and *Rolling Stone* magazine (Rodrick 2017). The juxtaposition with United States President Donald Trump has made a comparison seem especially favorable.

Tolerance and diversity are key components of Canada's brand (Nimijean 2005, p. 29). Yet Canada's oftentimes poor relationship with Indigenous peoples belies this self-image. Have Indigenous issues substantively affected Canada's brand with international stakeholders, and has Trudeau's record done anything to harm or improve it?

Three conclusions can be drawn. First, Indigenous issues are relatively marginal in international affairs and do not have a substantive impact on Canada's, or any Group of 20 (G20) country's, brand. With regards to UNDRIP, because the 2007 "against" vote was shared with New Zealand, Australia and the United States, any reputational hit that might have arisen was minimized. Canada's complicated approach to UNDRIP, from opposition to endorsement, to adoption and now implementation, is much more salient domestically than internationally, and very unlikely at this point to impact reputation.

The Arctic is somewhat of an exception. Canada's brand there is heavily aligned with the promotion of Indigenous inclusion and well-being. Canada's frequent policy development and alignment with Permanent Participants has arguably led to increased soft power in the Arctic Council due to the credibility that has imparted to its positions. It has also led to criticisms of parochialism.

Second, there has been no substantive difference in Canada's reputation or brand in Indigenous affairs internationally between the Harper and Trudeau governments. Domestic events such as the 2008 Residential School Apology, Idle No More, or the Gerald Stanley trial may momentarily hit international newsreels. But undoubtedly inuksuks, such as those highlighted during the 2010 Vancouver Olympics, are more salient than legislation such as Bill C-45 or C-262 in global associations with Canadian indigeneity. Canada's overall disposition to Indigenous rights and self-determination, including and especially in the Arctic region, has been marked by consistency across political lines.

Third, to the extent Indigenous issues will have an impact on Canada's brand during the current Liberal tenure, it will likely be from Trudeau's sensitivity to admonitions from First Nations, Métis and Inuit that Canada has failed in essential aspects of its celebrated diversity and tolerance. Whereas Harper was able to assume an unmitigated boosterism of Canada's greatness, Trudeau and his Liberal government must adopt a level of contrition for Canada's colonial history, as demonstrated in the Canada 150 celebrations. In one concrete example, Indigenous participants at a 2017 consultation on the international component of the Arctic Policy Framework asserted that Canada must "get its own house in order" before it claims a leadership role in the Arctic context, referring to the gaps in infrastructure, employment and education rates in the North (Exner-Pirot 2017, p. 14).

## Conclusion

Canada is perceived, and perceives itself, as a peaceful, tolerant and diverse nation. While its relationship with its Indigenous peoples, built on a foundation of colonization and marginalization, complicates this assessment domestically, it is difficult to assert that it has substantively impacted Canada's brand to a global audience.

By examining Canada's record with the development of UNDRIP and the Arctic Council, this article has attempted to illustrate Canada's international behavior in key Indigenous policy areas. It has been a leader in Indigenous engagement in the Arctic, and somewhat of a laggard in international documents. But Canada's general disposition to Indigenous rights and self-determination has been progressive from a global perspective, and consistent across successive governments. It does not challenge Canada's brand, and in the case of Arctic affairs, arguably strengthens it, if marginally.

That said, Canada's sensitivity to criticism of its core identity, and the foundation to its brand, has provided Indigenous Canadians with significant opportunities to influence Canadian foreign policy. The Canadian government's recent commitment to fully implement UNDRIP, and co-develop the international component of its Arctic Policy Framework, are prominent examples. The trend can be observed to have intensified under the Trudeau Liberals, but it did not begin with them.

Global branding is shown not only to involve a projection of values and identity outward, but to be a reciprocal process where the state is motivated to act domestically to justify and reinforce its brand.

## Disclosure statement

No potential conflict of interest was reported by the author.

## Notes on contributor

*Heather Exner-Pirot* is the Managing Editor of the Arctic Yearbook and a Strategist for Outreach and Indigenous engagement at the University of Saskatchewan.

## References

Akin, David, 2016. From housing to health, Trudeau's rhetoric on first nations out of step with reality, critics say. *National Post*, 23 November. Available from: http://nationalpost.com/news/politics/from-housing-to-health-trudeaus-rhetoric-on-first-nations-files-out-of-step-with-reality-say-some-critics [Accessed 19 March 2018].

Ames, Herbert, 1923. Letter to Right Hon. W. L. Mackenzie King. Ottawa, Canada, 28 December. League of Nations doc. no. 11/33556.

Assembly of First Nations, 2001. Coon come criticizes "official un discrimination" at world conference. Press release, 4 September. Available from: http://www.dialoguebetweennations.com/dbnetwork/english/MatthewCoonCome_PressReleaseSept4.htm [Accessed 15 February 15 2017].

Assembly of First Nations, 2016. Assembly of first nations welcomes Canada's unqualified support for UN Declaration on the rights of indigenous peoples, 10 May. Available from: http://www.afn.ca/en/news-media/latest-news/16-05-10-assembly-of-first-nations-welcomes-canadas-unqualified-suppor [Accessed 15 February 2017].

Barnsley, Paul, 2001. Racism? What racism? *Windspeaker*, 19 (6). Available from: http://www.ammsa.com/publications/windspeaker/racism-what-racism-0 [Accessed 15 February 2017].

Bennett, Carolyn, May 10, 2016. *Speaking notes: announcement of Canada's support for the united nations declaration on the rights of indigenous peoples*. New York City. Available from: http://www.metisnation.ca/wp-content/uploads/2016/05/Speech-Minister-Bennett-UNPFII-NEW-YORK-MAY-10-FINAL.pdf [Accessed 8 February 2016].

Brigham, Lawson, et al., 2016. The arctic council: twenty years of policy shaping. *In*: Lassi Heininen, Heather Exner-Pirot, and Joel Plouffe, eds. *Arctic yearbook 2016*. Akureyri: Northern Research Forum, 14–20.

CBC News, November 12, 2010. Canada endorses indigenous rights declaration. Available from: http://www.cbc.ca/news/canada/canada-endorses-indigenous-rights-declaration-1.964779 [Accessed 10 February 2017].

Coates, Ken and Favel, Blaine, May 2016. *Understanding UNDRIP*. Ottawa: Macdonald-Laurier Institute.

Compton, Catherine, 1987. South African ambassador visits reserve. *Windspeaker*, 5 (2). Available from: http://www.ammsa.com/publications/windspeaker/south-african-ambassador-visits-reserve [Accessed 14 February 2017].

Engle, Karen, 2011. On fragile architecture: the UN declaration on the rights of indigenous peoples in the context of human rights. *European Journal of International Law*, 22 (1), 141–163.

English, John, 2013. *Ice and water: politics, peoples and the arctic council*. Toronto: Allen Lane.

Exner-Pirot, Heather, 2016. Six takeaways from this week's U.S.-Canada joint arctic statement. *OpenCanada.org*. Available from: https://www.opencanada.org/features/six-takeaways-weeks-us-canada-joint-arctic-statement/ [Accessed 3 March 2017].

Exner-Pirot, Heather, December 13, 2017. *Summary report: roundtable on the international component of the arctic policy framework*. Report prepared for Global Affairs Canada. Author's copy.

Finkler, Harald and Kadas, Robert, 2016. Q & A: The 20th anniversary of the Arctic council. *In*: Lassi Heininen, Heather Exner-Pirot, and Joel Plouffe, eds. *Arctic yearbook 2016*. Akureyri: Northern Research Forum, 34–38.

Galloway, Gloria, 2017. Chiefs urge aboriginal people to vote against Harper government. *Globe & Mail*, 25 March. Available from: https://www.theglobeandmail.com/news/national/trudeau-to-roll-out-plan-to-bolster-funding-for-aboriginal-education/article25334759/ [Accessed 18 March 2018].

INAC, February 17, 2017. Shared arctic leadership model engagement 2016–2017. Available from: https://www.aadnc-aandc.gc.ca/eng/1469120834151/1469120901542 [Accessed 3 March 2017].

Inuit Circumpolar Council, 2016a. Inuit circumpolar council salutes the Canada-USA statement on arctic cooperation. Available from: http://www.inuitcircumpolar.com/uploads/3/0/5/4/30542564/icc_salutes_the_canada-usa_statement_on_arctic_cooperation_.pdf [Accessed 3 March 2017].

Inuit Circumpolar Council, 2016b. ICC Canada applauds Canada implementation action of UNDRIP: "it's a new beginning." Available from: http://www.inuitcircumpolar.com/uploads/3/0/5/4/30542564/press_release_-_10_may_2016_-_icc_canada_applauds_canada_implementation_action_of_undrip.pdf [Accessed 12 February 2017].

Kanter, James, 2017. Trudeau, praising the E.U., doesn't mention "brexit" or trump. *New York Times*, 16 February. Available from: https://www.nytimes.com/2017/02/16/world/americas/trudeau-speech-eu-strasbourg-canada-trade.html [Accessed 5 March 2017].

Keskitalo, Carina, 2007. International region-building: development of the arctic as an international region. *Cooperation and Conflict*, 42 (2), 187–205.

Koivurova, Timo and Smieszek, Malgorzata, December 7, 2016. The arctic council at 20: the value of flexibility. *World Policy*. Available from: https://worldpolicy.org/2016/12/07/the-arctic-council-at-20-the-value-of-flexibility/ [Accessed 9 February 2017].

Lackenbauer, P. Whitney and Cooper, Andrew F., 2007. The Achilles heel of Canadian international citizenship: indigenous diplomacies and state responses. *Canadian Foreign Policy Journal*, 13 (3), 99–119.

Ljunggren, David, September 25, 2009. Every G20 nation wants to be Canada, insists PM. *Reuters*. Available from: https://www.reuters.com/article/columns-us-g20-canada-advantages/every-g20-nation-wants-to-be-canada-insists-pm-idUSTRE58P05Z20090926 [Accessed 4 April 2018].

Mackey, Eva, 2002. *The house of difference: cultural politics and national identity in Canada*. Toronto: University of Toronto Press.

Métis Nation, May 10, 2016. Canada to fully adopt and implement UN declaration on rights of indigenous peoples. Available from: http://www.metisnation.ca/index.php/news/canada-to-fully-adopt-and-implement-u-n-declaration-on-rights-of-indigenous-peoples [Accessed 9 February 2017].

Newhouse, David and Belanger, Yale, 2016. The Canada problem in aboriginal politics. *In*: David Long and Olive Patricia Dickason, eds. *Visions of the heart*, 4th ed. Toronto: Oxford University Press, 352–380.

Newman, Dwayne and Coates, Ken, 2017. Bill on implementing UNDRIP "simplistic" and laden with "circular tensions." *The Hill Times*, 14 December. Available from: https://www.hilltimes.com/2017/12/14/bill-implementing-undrip-simplistic-laden-circular-tensions/128903 [Accessed 20 March 2018].

Niezen, Ronald, 2000. Recognizing indigenism: Canadian unity and the international movement of indigenous peoples. *Comparative Studies in Society and History*, 42 (1), 119–148.

Nimijean, Richard, 2017. A portrait of Justin Trudeau. *The Monitor*. (Ottawa: Canadian Centre for Policy Alternatives, September/October 2017): 26–31. Available from: https://www.policyalternatives.ca/publications/monitor/portrait-justin-trudeau [Accessed 19 March 2018].

Nimijean, Richard, 2005. Articulating the "Canadian Way": Canada$^{TM}$ and the political manipulation of the Canadian identity. *British Journal of Canadian Studies*, 18 (1), 26–52.

Parliament of Canada, 2018. Private members' bill C-262. *LEGISinfo*. Available from: https://www.parl.ca/LegisInfo/BillDetails.aspx?billId=8160636&Language=E. [Accessed 20 March 2018].

Pettigrew, Pierre, 1999. Canada's international personality. *In*: Phyllis Aronoff and Howard Scott, eds. *The New politics of confidence*. Toronto: Stoddart, 107–113.

Power, Justin, 2015. Justin Trudeau is the new young face of Canadian politics. *Vogue*, 9 December. Available from: https://www.vogue.com/article/justin-trudeau-prime-minister-canada [Accessed 20 March 2018].

Prime Minister's Office, December 15, 2015. Statement by prime minister on release of the final report of the truth and reconciliation commission. Available from: http://www.pm.gc.ca/eng/news/2015/12/15/statement-prime-minister-release-final-report-truth-and-reconciliation-commission [Accessed 9 February 2017].

Raibmon, Paige, June 2000. Theatres of contact: the kwakwaka'wakw meet colonialism in British Columbia at the Chicago's world fair. *Canadian Historical Review*, 81 (2), 157–190.

Rodrick, Stephen, 2017. Justin Trudeau: the North Star. *Rolling Stone*, 26 July. Available from: https://www.rollingstone.com/politics/features/justin-trudeau-canadian-prime-minister-free-worlds-best-hope-w494098 [Accessed 20 March 2018].

Scrivener, D., 1996. Environmental cooperation in the arctic: from strategy to council' paper submitted for publication to the Norwegian Atlantic Committee, Oslo.

Simon, Mary, October 31, 2016. *Interim report on the shared arctic leadership model*. Indigenous and Northern Affairs Canada. Available from: https://www.aadnc-aandc.gc.ca/eng/1481656672979/1485800424490 [Accessed 3 March 2017].

Smith, Duane, 2016. The need for an umbrella approach to Inuit relations and northern governance. In John Higginbotham and Jennifer Spence, eds. *North of 60: toward a renewed Canadian Arctic agenda*. Ottawa: CIGI (Centre for International Governance Innovation), 65–67.

Smith, Duane, 2017. *Letter in response to US-Canada joint arctic leaders' statement*. Available from https://assets.documentcloud.org/documents/3318896/IRC-Letter-to-PM-1.pdf [Accessed 3 March 2017].

Speech from the Throne. March 3, 2010. Available from: http://www.lop.parl.gc.ca/ParlInfo/Documents/ThroneSpeech/40-3-e.html [Accessed 14 February 2017].

Staples, L., 1998. Looking back, looking forward: sustainable development for the Arctic. *WWF Arctic Bulletin*, 2, 14–15.

The Economist, October 29, 2016. *Liberty moves north*. London: The Economist. Available from: http://www.economist.com/news/leaders/21709305-it-uniquely-fortunate-many-waysbut-canada-still-holds-lessons-other-western [Accessed 14 February 2017].

Trudeau, Justin, July 10, 2015. *Real change: restoring fairness to Canada's relationship with aboriginal peoples*. Available from: https://www.liberal.ca/justin-trudeau-at-assembly-of-first-nations-36th-annual-general-assembly/ [Accessed 9 February 2017].

Vinding, Diana and Mikkelsen, Caecilie, eds., 2016. *The indigenous world 2016*. Copenhagen: International Work Group for Indigenous Affairs.

Willis, M., 2013. Reflections on Canada's vision for the arctic council. *The Arctic Institute*. Available from: http://www.thearcticinstitute.org/2013/05/reflections-on-canadas-vision-for.html [Accessed 20 July 2015].

Wilson-Raybould, Jody, July 12, 2016. *Notes for an address: assembly of first nations annual general assembly*. Available from: https://drive.google.com/file/d/0B_bPXJbq-wgWenpoa2NlRmgwT2NlWkx3enNSWXJELTFSSzc4/view [Accessed 9 February 2017].

Wu, Huizhong, February 23, 2018. From "snub" to scandal, Trudeau's India trip sparks outrage. *CNN*. Available from: https://www.cnn.com/2018/02/22/asia/extremist-scandal-trudeau-india-visit-intl/index.html [Accessed 20 March 2018].

# 6 Predicting the North

Sovereignty and the Canadian brand in the Arctic

Mark Paradis, Richard D. Parker and Patrick James

**ABSTRACT**

Uncertainty sums up the Arctic of today, with significant implications for sovereignty and branding Canada. Climate change produces a level of interest in the North from a widening range of actors and confronts Canada with new challenges. The present study uses an expected utility forecasting model to assess the likely outcomes, under current conditions, across a range of substantively important issues in the Arctic. After an overview of the Arctic as an essential aspect of the Canadian brand, the work unfolds in four further stages. First, a forecasting model is introduced and linked to the present context. The second stage presents the expert-generated data used to forecast the future. Third, forecasts are produced and assessed in terms of implications for existing policy in areas ranging from search and rescue to transit of the Northwest Passage (NWP). The fourth and final stage offers conclusions about the Canadian brand in relation to the Arctic and suggests directions for future research.

**RÉSUMÉ**

L'incertitude résume bien la situation de l'Arctique d'aujourd'hui, avec des implications significatives pour la souveraineté et l'image du Canada. Le changement climatique suscite un niveau d'intérêt dans le Nord, parmi un nombre croissant d'acteurs, et met le Canada face à de nouveaux défis. Cette étude utilise un modèle de prévision d'utilité espérée pour évaluer les conséquences potentielles, dans les circonstances actuelles, de toute une série de problèmes sensiblement importants dans l'Arctique. Après une vue d'ensemble de l'Arctique en tant que trait essentiel de l'image du Canada, l'étude est présentée en quatre volets. D'abord, un modèle de prévision est présenté et mis en rapport avec le contexte actuel. Le deuxième volet introduit les données générées par des experts et servant à prévoir l'avenir. Le troisième expose des prévisions produites et évaluées, relativement aux implications pour les domaines politiques existants, allant des opérations de recherche et de sauvetage au transit dans le passage du Nord-Ouest (PNO). Le quatrième et dernier volet présente des conclusions sur l'image du Canada, relativement à l'Arctique, et propose des orientations pour les futures recherches.

Canadian identification with the North as a concept and the Arctic as a geographic region is an underlying reality for any study of the national brand. From centuries ago onward, "detached observers and patriotic spokesmen alike have fixed upon the northern character of Canada as one of the chief attributes of her nationality" (Berger 1966, p. 4, see also Francis 1997, p. 153; Bone 2009; Pigott 2011; White 2011; James and James 2014). "To a Canadian," Francis (1997, p. 152) observes, "North is more than a point on the compass. It is a region, a territory, a vast intimidating part of the country somewhere beyond easy comfort." Segal adds that the Arctic is a rarity, "a territory seen by so few" that is

> emotionally, spiritually, and personally so compellingly important to so many. Yet that is a modest and understated description of the relationship between Canadians and their Arctic region and territories. It is a passionate, possessive, patriotic, and nationalistic relationship second only to our embrace of hockey. (Griffiths et al. 2011, p. xi)

In sum, the Arctic is an essential component of the Canadian brand.

Yet in a twist of irony, the observed level of interest in the Arctic lags behind emotional attachment to it. For many years, "outsiders only paid attention to the Canadian North when an explorer got lost there" (Francis 1997, p. 163).[1] The northern theme "tended to identify the whole country with that region of it which contained the fewest of her people" (Berger 1966, p. 22). As Shields (1992, p. 164) asserts, "'The True North Strong and Free', a phrase from the English version of the Canadian national anthem, summarises many aspects of southern Canadian myths of the North." The anthem identifies the North with freedom and other positive traits. Yet the anthem is paradoxical because it reinforces "a sense of Canadian identity while disguising the simultaneous exploitation and underdevelopment of the North" (Shields 1992, p. 199). Ruhl (2008a, 2008b) draws attention to the neglect of indigenous voices from the North in tandem with the process of myth-making, which includes works of art along with the implementation of arrangements that work to the advantage of Canadians to the south. Thus, myth and reality sustain an uneasy coexistence.

Canadian nationalism, understood in terms of myth, legend and symbols, possessed a decidedly Northern character from the outset (Berger 1966, p. 24). Identification of Canada with the Arctic, however, goes beyond the thoughts of its citizens. For many around the world, the geography of Canada and the Arctic are synonymous. Visitors to the Canada pavilion at Epcot Center in Florida have the opportunity see a film about the nation that begins with a blinding snowstorm and a voiceover narration claiming Canada to be a land dotted with igloos and polar bears, where it snows "24 hours a day, every day of the year" (Disney Park Scripts 2017). Indeed, the view of Canada as an Arctic nation fits a global stereotype that is utterly pervasive. Even former Prime Minister Stephen Harper embraced it. He proclaimed in 2007 that "Canada has a choice when it comes to defending our sovereignty in the Arctic: We either use or lose it. And make no mistake this government intends to use it" (quoted in Le Mière 2013, p. 35). Popular perception and nationalist rhetoric aside, control over the Arctic is a serious contemporary issue on the Canadian foreign policy agenda, with significant implications for branding Canada.[2] "Canada," as observed by Potter (2009, p. 270) in an authoritative work on national branding, "has an opportunity to capitalize on its 'northernness' to promote its unique identity abroad. This northernness is probably the most understated and underutilized part of Canada's diversity brand."[3] Interest in the far north is building because of new possibilities for transportation and resource extraction; rising global energy prices and instability in the Middle East reinforce that trend (Hale 2012, p. 45, Cohen 2015). The situation, in a word, is complex and rapidly changing.

Now more than ever, states are paying greater attention to the Arctic. The maritime dimension is becoming increasingly important as nations that do not have a geographic or historic presence in the Arctic begin to work with countries that do. "China," for example, "marks the Arctic as a domain of strategic significance" and is developing stronger ties to smaller Arctic states such as Denmark and Iceland, "investing in joint energy, mineral exploitation and navigation projects" (Campagna et al. 2013, p. 26). Not surprisingly, many states are enhancing their military capabilities in the Arctic (Huebert 2011a, p. 197). All of this suggests that a new and more challenging era could be at hand for Canada as a major Arctic player. Thus, the Canadian brand as a whole will be impacted significantly by how these issues play out in the Arctic.

How do things stand right now? As noted by Nimijean (2006, p. 69), "leaders emphasize 'shared Canadian values' in response to political challenges," which include "concerns of Canadian sovereignty" in the international arena. The Arctic stands as a showcase for numerous "Canadian values," such as environmental protection and historic preservation. Thus, taking a stand politically on the nation's sovereignty in the region is a natural fit no matter what party controls the government in Ottawa.

What, then, might be said regarding the Harper era in relation to the comparatively short period of Prime Minister Justin Trudeau that so far has unfolded after it? During his tenure as Prime Minister Harper made very public annual, and costly, trips – amounting to more than CAD$3.4 million between 2006 and 2013 – to the Arctic to emphasize the region's importance to Canada (Boutilier 2015). Canadians and their leaders routinely reference the North as a source of uniqueness within North America (Francis 1997, p. 153). This is true across the ideological spectrum and can be expected to persist. "The myth of the North," observes Francis (1997, p. 171) with regard to Canadians, "is appealing because it promises to unite us, to dissolve all our differences in a great white hope for the future." To go even further, Canadian identity, when it is assertive, seeks not only distance from but even superiority in relation to the United States (Nimijean 2006, p. 77). Thus, attention toward the North can be expected to increase as a function of whatever might threaten such beliefs, with American interest in the Arctic as a likely stimulant (Francis 1997, p. 170). The Harper government, as one illustration, "elevated attention to bolstering Canadian claims to Arctic sovereignty in light of perceived threats from foreign powers" (Rankin 2012, p. 261). Even with Harper's replacement as prime minister by the much more liberal Trudeau, underlying commitment to an Arctic brand seems unlikely to change except in specific content and associated rhetoric.

Canada, already branded to some degree as a circumpolar nation, is "rediscovering itself" (Huebert 2011a, p. 216). This observation applies to both rising consciousness and resulting actions. Canadian activity in the Arctic is noteworthy over the last decade. Commercial and military activities in the region include a new military and civilian deepwater resupply center under construction on Baffin Island; an Arctic Training Centre in Resolute Bay for the army; and efforts toward enhanced surveillance capability by the Canadian Forces (CF) (Huebert 2011a, p. 215). Additionally, Canadian military cooperation in the region continues to be active as recently as March 2016, when assets of the United States Navy and CF cooperated in Ice Exercise 2016 (Commander, Submarine Force

Public Affairs 2016). These activities follow on from a highly viable but also controversial shift in the role of the CF during the era of the War in Afghanistan (Saideman 2016).

While budget constraints impose serious limits on activity (Grant 2010, p. 443, see also Koring 2018), Canadian initiatives continue to accumulate. Summarized in Lackenbauer (2011a, p. 433), *Canada's northern strategy: our north, our heritage, our future* is a government document from 2009 that confirms the rising significance of the Arctic on the Canadian policy agenda. Identifying potential for cooperation and conflict in the Arctic therefore becomes a significant priority in light of rapidly increasing interest from those identified, along with Canada, as Arctic states.[4] Most prominent among the potential flashpoints is the Northwest Passage (NWP; Grant 2010, p. 449, Huebert 2011a, p. 202, Lackenbauer 2011b, p. 237, Hale 2012, p. 146, James 2012, p. 118, Lajeuness 2016). With respect to this and other potential sovereignty-related matters for Canada, Lackenbauer (2011a, p. 425, see also Martin 2008, p. 324) goes as far as to identify a "use it or lose it" mindset. Ottawa must establish its presence in a more sustained way or risk erosion of its claim on the Arctic as a result of intrusions from other states. This is true especially of maritime regions (Huebert 2011a, p. 195, see also Parker and Madjd-Sadjadi 2010, p. 338). For example, non-Canadian vessels made at least two thirds of the 52 transits of the NWP in 2012–2013 (Chase 2014). At the same time, limitations in the military domain must be acknowledged as well; for example, Canada lacks even one warship or submarine that can operate within or under Arctic ice (Koring 2018, p. 3). And while Canada does maintain a noteworthy presence in the region through the activities of the Rangers, an organization described as "the eyes and ears of Canada's North," the Rangers are at best a part-time volunteer force that does not even qualify for the basic benefits, including health care and administrative support, afforded to the full-time active-duty Canadian Forces (Everson 2017).

While the North continues to define Canada, its importance now increasingly goes beyond identity. The geopolitical and economic significance of the Arctic is on the rise. Moreover, the North naturally emerges as part of a reconciliation project with indigenous peoples that remains far from fully realized. Canadian inactions have created a vacuum in the Arctic that other states, willing to expend greater resources, seem more than willing to fill. Uncertainty is greater than ever.

With rapid change underway and uncertainty on the rise, *forecasting* becomes a priority. Even among experts, uncertainty exists as to whether the Arctic will evolve into a zone of cooperation or discord (Huebert 2011a, p. 193, see also Emmerson 2010, p. 314 and Parker and Madjd-Sadjadi 2010). Although Arctic Council membership is "limited to the eight nations with land territory above the Arctic Circle: Canada, Denmark (via Greenland), Finland, Iceland, Norway, Russia, Sweden and the United States," 12 other nations have observer status (Balton and Thomas 2013, p. 21). These states, which include China, Italy, Singapore, Germany, France and Japan, certainly have commercial interests in the region as shipping lanes become increasingly navigable throughout the year. However, it also is not surprising that non-Arctic nations are becoming more involved in Arctic affairs, especially as Arctic Council members increase their stakes in the region. Denmark, for example, has embarked on its largest defense procurement project, tasking three frigates to focus on Copenhagen's interests in the High North (Le Mière 2013, p. 34). But Canada's actions are perceived as being "the exemplar" of confusion between the rhetoric of competitive arms procurement and willingness to employ instruments of national power in the region (Le Mière 2013, pp. 35–36). Forecasting is essential given the uncertainty about general tendencies toward discord or cooperation in resolution of matters related to sovereignty. Given renewed emphasis in Ottawa on public diplomacy (Trudeau 2015), all of that comes together under concern for the Canadian brand.

Debate over the future of Arctic sovereignty for Canada can be sharply worded. On one side, Huebert (2011b) sees a high risk of intrusion into the far north as climate change moves forward. On the other side, Griffiths (2011, p. 401) labels such concern a "pathetic fallacy." Both sides in the debate could benefit from the implementation of a rigorous model to produce support for their views about what will occur. This gap reinforces the policy relevance of the modeling exercise to be carried out here.

Lackenbauer (2011b, p. 227) calls for scenario-based thinking to derive an Arctic strategy.[5] In response to such priorities, the present study uses an expected utility forecasting model to assess likely outcomes across a range of substantively important issues in the Arctic. These issues are: search and rescue; environmental protection; control of seabed resources; fishing rights; and transit of military, private and scientific vessels. The findings will have academic value and also should inform policymakers and nongovernmental organizations (NGOs) concerned with more practical matters in the Arctic, such as the impact on the Canadian national brand. The work unfolds in four further stages. First, a forecasting model is introduced and linked to the present context. The second stage presents the expert-generated data used to forecast the future. Third, forecasts are produced and assessed in terms of implications for existing policy. The fourth and final stage offers conclusions about the Canadian brand and suggests directions for future research.

## The forecasting model

Bueno de Mesquita's expected utility model (1984, 1994, 2002, 2009, 2011, 2014) is reported to have had a success rate of approximately 90 per cent and is widely used and cited (2011). Importantly, the model outperforms expert predictions. A declassified Central Intelligence Agency study reports that the forecasting model "has hit the bull's-eye about twice as often as the government's experts who provided [Bueno de Mesquita] with data" (2009, p. 51).[6]

While a complete summary of the model (see Bueno de Mesquita 2011) is beyond the scope of this study, key features are introduced here in accessible terms. The model's purpose is to "predict the process and outcome leading to the resolution of complex negotiations or potentially coercive situations, including the possibility that they end with agreement, breakdown, or even the use of force" (p. 66). It is an iterative, as opposed to a repeated, model, which updates payoffs for participants based on the results of prior rounds (p. 67). Given its iterative nature, the model is able to predict both how and when the interaction is expected to end. The process ends when:

> either of two conditions is met: (1) the sum of player payoffs at the end of an iteration is greater than the projected sum of those payoffs in the next iteration, or (2) the sum of player utility, taking into account not only their payoffs from the game in which they are the primary players ... is greater in the current round than the projected sum of utilities in the next iteration. (p. 72)

Rational choice models, such as the expected utility forecasting model, assume complete and transitive preferences, unidimensional issues, and that "actors' preferences for possible outcomes diminish steadily with distance from their ideal outcomes" (James and Lusztig 2000).

In addition to a full list of players, the model requires data for five variables: player position, player influence, issue salience for the player, player resolve, and veto player status (Bueno de Mesquita 2011, p. 75). To obtain this information, we consulted two experts on the Arctic.[7]

Our first expert was tasked with identifying the primary Canadian foreign policy concerns regarding the Arctic. The expert identified sovereignty over territory – both land and water – and resources claimed by the Canadian government as the overarching foreign policy concern. Specifically, the government is concerned about maintaining control over: seabed resources, fishing rights (migratory and non-migratory), transit of science vessels, transit of military vessels, indigenous rights (recognition and decision-making powers), constabulary powers, and search and rescue.

Our second expert was tasked with coding the variables.[8] The expert had freedom to adjust the list of issues as deemed necessary during the coding process. To the list generated by the first expert, our second expert added concerns over controlling the transit of privately owned and operated ships, and pollution and environmental protection.

We relied heavily on *The predictioneer's game* website (Bueno de Mesquita 2013) to instruct our experts. We altered the instructions available there only to make language consistent with our own or if additional details were needed for a specific issue area. Consistent with other applications of forecasting models, we did not ask for their predictions (for example, see James and Lusztig 2000). Our full instructions are included in Appendix 1.

We told our experts that each issue had to be unidimensional. Our second expert was asked to identify the positions of each actor, as well as salient positions such as the status quo. Positions range from 0 to 100, the most extreme positions, with the other numbers being assigned in accordance with their substantive distance from both extremes. Players are defined as any group or individual with a stake in the outcome. In our case, actors could be national governments, subnational governments, international governmental organizations (IGOs), NGOs, or private actors.

Potential influence represents the ability of an actor to affect the outcome. Values range from 0 to 100. The scores are ratio-level data. Therefore, an actor with a score of 50 would possess half the influence of an actor at 100. Salience refers to importance of the issue vis-à-vis other issues. It represents the amount of time and energy that an actor is willing to devote to that issue. Each actor is assigned a salience score between 0 and 100.

Flexibility/resolve refers to the degree to which an actor is willing to be flexible in its position in order to ensure that an agreement is reached. Inputs for this variable can range from 0 to 100. A higher score refers to greater flexibility (lower resolve) and a lower score refers to higher resolve (lower flexibility).[9] Finally, the veto variable refers to the ability of an actor to veto any agreement. A veto player is assigned a 1 and a non-veto player is assigned a 0.

Any study that involves coding of data must deal with uncertainty about accuracy. While we recruited a highly qualified expert coder, gave her detailed instructions, and allowed the time needed to code each variable, uncertainty about estimates remains. Therefore, we assess how robust our findings are to variations in the inputs.

## Data

This section conveys data provided by our coder and a brief discussion of some of the factors that influenced coding. Given the type of data involved, such as national capabilities, the presence of a new government for one or more of the players will impact only at the margins and basic properties of the data will remain intact. For example, procurement issues suggest that Canadian military capabilities in the region will remain limited for the foreseeable future (Byers 2014, Simpson 2014). As another illustration, a bit later on, veto player status assigned by the model to Canada for an issue such as environmental protection will not change, if at all, for a very long time. Another instance concerns Canadian views toward sovereignty per se. Whether they tilt relatively left or right – Liberal or Conservative governments, respectively – concerns about Arctic sovereignty are maintained from one government to the next, even if for reasons that are not identical. While specific aspects are subject to change, the Arctic remains essential to the Canadian brand.

The data reveals that some of the models will not need to be run because only one actor has influence – when Canadian control over the issue area is uncontested or uncontestable. Some contestation remains possible – i.e. bureaucratic politics within Canada – but modeling a purely domestic process is beyond of the scope of this project.[10] Coding for each issue appears in Table 1.

### *Search and rescue*

The initial issue in the table is divided between land and water search and rescue. Both take place within the context of the 2011 Arctic Search and Rescue Agreement, which gives considerable influence to the Arctic Council. Canada's position tends not to differ greatly from that of the Arctic Council – consistent with the multilateral element in the Canadian brand. For simplicity's sake, land and water models appear in the same table because the only difference is whether the Canadian Coast Guard (CCG) or Royal Canadian Mounted Police (RCMP) has jurisdiction. Note the status of the Arctic Council as a veto player, consistent with a liberal point of view that emphasizes a central rather than epiphenomenal role for institutions in the bargaining process.[11]

### *Environmental protection*

For coding purposes, the issue of environmental protection is broken down into land, internal waters, territorial waters, exclusive economic zones (EEZ), and NWP. However, with the exception of the NWP (and some overlapping EEZ claims for Canada and the United States in the Beaufort Sea), Canadian control over the other areas is uncontested. Therefore, our expert only included coding for the NWP. The agreement between Canada and the Law of the Sea Conference (LOSC) signatories, both coded as 100 in the table, stems from the influence that Canada's Arctic environmental protection regulations (AWPPA) had on the LOSC's Article 234. The article "allows coastal states to enforce non-discriminatory environmental rules on shipping in ice-covered areas" (Emmerson 2010, p. 100). The United States is not a member of the LOSC, but Washington agreed voluntarily in 1992 that its commercial ships would be subject to AWPPA. While all three participants

**Table 1.** Expert coding.

| Player | Influence | Position | Salience | Flexibility | Veto |
|---|---|---|---|---|---|
| *Search and rescue* | | | | | |
| Arctic Council (Arctic S&R Agreement 2011) | 100 | 100 | 85 | 100 | 1 |
| Water: Canadian Coast Guard | 45 | 90 | 90 | 90 | 0 |
| Land: RCMP and any other local law enforcement agencies | | | | | |
| *Environmental Protection (NWP)* | | | | | |
| Canada | 50 | 100 | 99 | 10 | 1 |
| United States | 100 | 95 | 80 | 50 | 1 |
| UN/LOSC signatories | 50 | 100 | 60 | 50 | 1 |
| *Fishing rights and seabed resources* | | | | | |
| Canada | 90 | 100 | 99 | 10 | 1 |
| UN Commission on the Continental Shelf | 100 | 50 | 99 | 50 | 1 |
| United States (in any area in dispute w/ Canada) | 80 | 0 | 80 | 10 | 1 |
| *Transit of military and private vessels (NWP)* | | | | | |
| Canada | 50 | 100 | 99 | 10 | 1 |
| United States | 100 | 0 | 80 | 10 | 1 |
| LOSC signatories (particularly Arctic states) | 50 | 40 | 60 | 50 | 0 |
| UN | 50 | 50 | 60 | 50 | 0 |
| *Transit of non-military and private vessels (EEZ)* | | | | | |
| Canada (Article 234 and NORDREG) | 100 | 100 | 99 | 5 | 1 |
| Legal shippers | 50 | 75 | 80 | 50 | 0 |
| Illegal shippers | 0 – no influence over the formal outcome | 0 | ? | Not at any table for discussion of issues or positions | 1 (by ignoring the agreement or rules) |
| Insurance companies | 50 | 85 | 90 | 50 | 0 |
| *Transit of scientific vessels (NWP)* | | | | | |
| Canada | 100 | 100 | 90 | 35 | 1 |
| United States | 80 | 80 | 80 | 20 | 1 |
| UN/IMO (representing all other scientific vessels) | 100 | 50 | 60 | 20 | 1 |

Notes: S&R = Search and Rescue; RCMP = Royal Canadian Mounted Police; NWP = Northwest Passage; UN = United Nations; LOSC = Law of the Sea Conference; EEZ = Exclusive Economic Zone; NORDREG = Northern Canada Vessel Traffic Services Zone; IMO = International Maritime Organization.

are coded as veto players and low flexibility is attributed to the Canadian government, the nearly identical positions suggest a low likelihood of breakdown.

## Fishing rights

Fishing rights are divided initially between straddling and migratory stocks, and non-migratory stocks. For straddling and migratory stocks, there is no contestation of Canadian control, even if the NWP is found to be an international strait. For non-migratory stocks, the issue is further subdivided into internal waters, territorial waters, EEZs, and disputed continental shelf beyond the 200-nm limit. Like migratory stocks, control over internal waters, territorial waters and EEZs is uncontested.

For the disputed continental shelf, the actors are the Canadian government, the United Nations (UN) Commission on the Continental Shelf, and the American government. Canada and the United States are at opposite points on the issue; in fact, there are active boundary disputes between the two countries, specifically in that the maritime boundary between Alaska and Yukon has never been satisfactorily defined (Parker and Madjd-Sadjadi 2010, p. 339). The UN Commission is a (presumably) neutral body so its position falls in the middle, with a high degree of flexibility. All three participants are veto players, which will tend to promote confrontation.

### *Seabed resources*

Coding for seabed resources is identical to that for fishing rights. Therefore, they are reported together in Table 1. There is potential contestation over resources in the continental shelf beyond the 200-nm limit, with Canada facing possible disputes with the United States and Denmark (that is, claims remain uncertain). Canada's position is at the opposite end of the spectrum from that of the United States, with the UN in the middle. All three actors in this issue area are veto players. Similar to fishing rights, the UN has the greatest flexibility since its decision is based on multiple factors, including the quality of the claims submitted. Since Canadian and American influence on fishing rights and resources is partially based on evidence they provide to support their claims to the continental shelf, we will use a greater probability of shocks when running these models.

### *Transit of military vessels*

Military vessels in Arctic waters is a multifaceted issue. For internal waters, there is no debate. Military vessels are fully subject to Canadian jurisdiction. This also is the case for territorial waters, but our coder identified an interesting possibility. Since Canada is the only actor with influence over the region, there is no model to be run. Given Canadian participation with the United States Navy in ICEX 2016, and the possibility of future cooperation, Canadian flexibility for these waters is coded as 10, unlike the 0 for internal waters. The issue of military vessels in the NWP is more complex, with positions depending on whether it is viewed as Canadian waters or an international strait.

For military vessels in the NWP, the United States has taken the strongest view in favor of the NWP as an international strait. The UN's position is complicated. The International Court of Justice's (ICJ) Corfu Channel ruling puts the UN closer to the American position, but provisions in Article 234 for ice-choked areas place the UN closer to the Canadian position.[12] So far, the UN has remained silent on the NWP. Other states generally agree with the American position, but also do not wish to alienate Canada. The United States and Canada are veto players.

### *Transit of non-military and private vessels*

In terms of the transit of non-military and privately owned/operated ships, only control of the EEZ and NWP is contestable. Coding for the NWP is identical to that for military vessels in the NWP. Although legal shippers and insurance companies can impact the setting within which bargaining occurs through their choices and actions, they are not included because they have no influence over who controls the NWP. Instead, the model focuses on Canada, the United States, LOSC signatories, and the UN, with the Canadian and American governments as veto players.

In the EEZ, the Canadian government, legal shippers, illegal shippers, and insurance companies have some influence over the outcome. Ottawa is a veto player. Illegal shippers are not included in the model that we run, but are included in the coding to demonstrate the complexity of the issue. They do not possess any formal influence, but they do have a veto of sorts based on their disregard for any decision. Insurance companies and legal shippers differ from the Canadian position slightly in that they prefer lower regulations.

*Transit of scientific vessels*

Transit of scientific vessels is an issue divided into internal waters, territorial waters, EEZ and NWP. Canadian control of internal waters is uncontested. In territorial seas, the LOS stipulates that all vessels may have continuous and expeditious innocent passage. For the EEZ, Section XIII gives Canada the ability to set standards.

More complicated, as conveyed by the coding for this issue, is the situation in the NWP. The United States and Canada disagree over the status of the NWP. However, their agreement that United States Coast Guard Cutters (USCGC) will ask for permission and share scientific information in return for automatic approval has largely resolved the issue. The situation is less clear for non-USCGC vessels. Therefore, the United States is coded at 80. The International Maritime Organization (IMO)'s position, which represents all other scientific vessels, is complicated. It is a neutral actor that will not want to antagonize Canada or the United States. Despite the agreement, IMO's position is coded at 50. Other states may not want to follow the Canada–United States agreement, non-USCGC American vessels are not necessarily subject to the agreement, and the United States still fundamentally opposes the idea of the NWP being considered internal Canadian waters.

## Results from the forecasting model and analysis

The forecasting model provides a wealth of data.[13] For simplicity's sake, we focus on some of the most important output categories. We ran 10 rounds of each model. We begin with round-by-round player positions. In the initial round, the position is the one assigned by our coder. Subsequent positions reflect the results of previous rounds.

We also provide an issue forecast, which represents a weighted mean of all players' positions in that round. There are multiple versions of the issue forecast. We report the one favored by Bueno de Mesquita in the model's instructions: the smoothed version of the weighted mean. This measure is two-dimensional; it is a "weighted combination of their policy stance and their eagerness to reach an agreement or resist agreement" (Bueno de Mesquita 2013).

Finally, we report whether or not an end rule was satisfied. If an end rule has been met, the smoothed mean is reported in bold. While it is customary to assume that the game will end when the first end rule is met, there is no necessary reason to do so. Results for each model are reported in Table 2.

For each model, we also discuss the sensitivity of the model to shocks to any of the input variables. The use of shocks is important for two reasons. First, coding is inherently a subjective and difficult task. Second, unforeseen future events can alter one or more of the input variables. For each model, we ran an additional 20 simulations. In these shocked simulations, each input variable had a 10 per cent chance of being adjusted by 10 per cent

**Table 2.** Results.

| | Rd 1 | Rd 2 | Rd 3 | Rd 4 | Rd 5 | Rd 6 | Rd 7 | Rd 8 | Rd 9 | Rd 10 |
|---|---|---|---|---|---|---|---|---|---|---|
| *Search and rescue* | | | | | | | | | | |
| Round by round position | | | | | | | | | | |
| Arctic Council | 100 | 97.83 | 96.08 | 93.95 | 92.57 | 91.67 | 91.09 | 90.71 | 90.46 | 90.3 |
| Canada | 90 | 90 | 90 | 90 | 90 | 90 | 90 | 90 | 90 | 90 |
| Round by round forecast | | | | | | | | | | |
| Mean | 96.04 | 95.4 | **94.03** | 92.85 | 91.85 | **91.2** | 90.78 | 90.51 | 90.33 | 90.26 |
| *Environmental protection* | | | | | | | | | | |
| Round by round position | | | | | | | | | | |
| Canada | 100 | 100 | 99.86 | 99.86 | 99.86 | 99.86 | 99.86 | 99.86 | 99.86 | 99.86 |
| United States | 95 | 95.73 | 96.27 | 96.27 | 96.76 | 97.06 | 97.92 | 98.35 | 98.68 | 98.93 |
| UN | 100 | 99.7 | 99.33 | 98.84 | 98.51 | 98.39 | 98.46 | 98.68 | 98.9 | 99.08 |
| Round by round forecast | | | | | | | | | | |
| Mean | 97.65 | 97.75 | **97.88** | 97.96 | **98.03** | **98.28** | **98.56** | **98.86** | 99.07 | 99.17 |
| *Fishing rights and seabed resources* | | | | | | | | | | |
| Round by round position | | | | | | | | | | |
| Canada | 100 | 100 | 100 | 100 | 100 | 100 | 100 | 100 | 96.28 | 95.61 |
| UN | 50 | 50.65 | 60.78 | 70.01 | 77.86 | 84.16 | 88.98 | 92.49 | 94.92 | 95.34 |
| United States | 0 | 0.48 | 0.48 | 0.48 | 0.48 | 0.48 | 0.48 | 0.48 | 0.48 | 0.48 |
| Round by round forecast | | | | | | | | | | |
| Mean | 55.17 | 56.55 | **59.21** | 62.78 | 65.84 | 68.32 | 70.24 | 71.21 | **71.52** | **71.39** |
| *Transit of military and private vessels (NWP)* | | | | | | | | | | |
| Round by round position | | | | | | | | | | |
| Canada | 100 | 98.57 | 98.57 | 98.57 | 96.29 | 93.23 | 93.23 | 93.23 | 93.23 | 93.23 |
| United States | 0 | 0 | 0 | 0 | 0 | 0 | 0 | 0 | 0 | 0 |
| Arctic States | 40 | 45.64 | 56.65 | 64.41 | 69.1 | 59.65 | 51.35 | 52.91 | 53.66 | 54.2 |
| UN | 50 | 52.77 | 57.95 | 58.56 | 53.56 | 54.92 | 55.93 | 55.14 | 54.62 | 54.47 |
| Round by round forecast | | | | | | | | | | |
| Mean | **40.85** | 41.86 | 43.48 | **44.56** | 44.09 | 42.8 | 41.76 | **41.43** | **41.5** | **41.52** |
| *Transit of non-military and private vessels (EEZ)* | | | | | | | | | | |
| Round by round position | | | | | | | | | | |
| Canada | 100 | 100 | 100 | 100 | 100 | 100 | 100 | 100 | 100 | 100 |
| Legal shippers | 75 | 75 | 75 | 75 | 77.71 | 78.88 | 80.21 | 81.56 | 82.03 | 82.03 |
| Insurance companies | 85 | 84.48 | 83.58 | 81.84 | 80.68 | 82.22 | 83.59 | 82.75 | 82.16 | 82.1 |
| Round by round forecast | | | | | | | | | | |
| Mean | **90.83** | 90.74 | 90.48 | **90.37** | 90.54 | 91.06 | 91.51 | **91.73** | **91.74** | **91.72** |
| *Transit of scientific vessels (NWP)* | | | | | | | | | | |
| Round by Round Position | | | | | | | | | | |
| Canada | 100 | 100 | 100 | 100 | 100 | 83.25 | 76.26 | 81.13 | 84.57 | 86.98 |
| United States | 80 | 84.54 | 86.32 | 88.38 | 90.51 | 92.53 | 92.53 | 92.53 | 92.53 | 92.53 |
| UNIMO | 50 | 50 | 50 | 50 | 50 | 50 | 50 | 50 | 50 | 50 |
| Round by round forecast | | | | | | | | | | |
| Mean | 80.68 | **81.08** | 81.92 | 82.51 | 80.78 | 77.87 | **75.42** | 75.61 | 77.11 | 77.77 |

Notes: When an end rule has been met, the smoothed mean is reported in bold. NWP = Northwest Passage; UN = United Nations; EEZ = Exclusive Economic Zone; IMO = International Maritime Organization.

in any round.[14] A graphical representation of the sensitivity of the predictions to shocks is provided in Appendix 3.[15]

## *Search and rescue*

For search and rescue, given the initial similarity in the positions, it is somewhat surprising that the end rule is met in so few rounds. However, it is met by round 3 and the predicted end result of 94.03 is close to the mid-point between the official Arctic Council position of full access and the greater flexibility favored by the Canadian Coast Guard and law enforcement agencies. As rounds progress, the predicted value moves closer to that favored by Canada, but an end rule is not met between rounds 7 and 10. Canada can get a better result by avoiding the first round where the end rule is met, but should be cautious that misperception or greed does not lead to a failure to reach a cooperative solution to a relatively simple issue. Additional simulations provide considerable support for the base model, with very little difference between the predicted value and the mean value of the additional simulations. However, there is a higher level of variance as the rounds progress. While not surprising, the increasing variance urges caution in drawing inferences regarding the trajectory of the outcome beginning in later rounds.

### Environmental protection

For environmental protection, the model predicts a rather rapid resolution to this issue at 97.88. However, unlike the search and rescue model, the end result is met in several other rounds. While the end result is not met in every round, the predicted value hovers around the same amount. While it does increase in the base model each round, the simulations using shocked rounds do not give us confidence that this increase will definitely occur. The additional simulations do, however, show that the predicted values are confined to a small range. The initial positions, along with stability of the predicted means, suggest that a quick and cooperative resolution is in each actor's interest.

### Fishing rights and seabed resources

For the fishing rights and seabed resources models, the results follow an interesting trajectory from the Canadian perspective and suggest the potential for complications. There is an opportunity to reach an agreement in the third round at 59.21. This agreement is slightly more favorable to Canada, but is still a great distance from Ottawa's desired position. There is also room for agreement much later on in the process at a position much more favorable to Canada. However, all parties would need to endure several unsuccessful rounds to get there.

Given that many parties still are developing the cases to support their claims, we used a greater probability of shocks of a higher magnitude when running the additional simulations. The additional simulations for the two models produce slightly different results, but are close enough to draw similar conclusions. They suggest that while the upward trajectory of the round by round forecasts is likely to occur, base predictions in later rounds are near the upper extremes of all of the simulations. Therefore, there is a very real possibility that the upward trajectory will be less steep than the base model predicts. We did use a far more cautious test of sensitivity in this case, however, so we should not overstate the importance of the differences between the simulations.

### Transit of military and private ships in NWP

For the transit of military and private ships in the NWP models, there can be cooperative resolutions at a few different points. The weighted mean position begins in a favorable position for the Arctic states and the UN (40.85). Forecasts then rise slightly before returning to a point near the initial position. Each agreement position is rather close to that of many other states; they view the NWP as an international strait, but do not want to antagonize Canada. The best forecast for Canada is reached in the fourth round (44.56). Results of the shocked simulations suggest that while the pattern of a slight move toward the Canadian position followed by the return to the initial position is likely, we cannot come confidently to any conclusions about the exact round-to-round movement of the forecasts, except that they remain close to, but under, the midpoint. Our coder identified the possibility of Canada–United States military cooperation in the NWP. This activity potentially would satisfy American concerns and fits within a broader pattern for these two states. While it is difficult to assess exactly where cooperation would fall on the position line, these results suggest its possibility.

### Transit of private ships in EEZ

For the transit of private ships in the EEZ, satisfaction of the end rule is *extremely* volatile: only five of 10 rounds comply. While it appears possible to reach an agreement extremely quickly at 90.83, a position along the continuum that would see Canada granting some concessions to shippers and insurance companies over transit through Canada's EEZ, the majority of early rounds do not satisfy an end rule. A noteworthy pattern emerges when looking at the evolution of player positions. Canada continues to be rigid in its position, but those of the legal shippers and insurance companies move in opposite directions until they meet. Once their positions are sufficiently close, the end rule is satisfied with a far greater frequency. The results suggest that the legal shippers and insurance companies will come to an agreement of their own and this compromise position will be used in negotiations with Canada. Interestingly, throughout this entire process, the round-by-round forecast hovers around 91. In the simulations using shocked inputs, there is a small degree of increased volatility in the forecasts as the rounds progress, but none of the simulations predicts substantively different results. This is not surprising given that the initial discrepancy in position is relatively small.

### Transit of scientific vessels

For the transit of scientific vessels model, a high level of early instability is apparent – five of the first six rounds do not comply with either end rule. The forecasts show a slight downward trajectory away from the Canadian and American positions. Thus, from the Canadian and USCG's perspective, the earlier the agreement (that is, at 81.08 in round 2), the better, as the weighted mean issue position becomes increasingly less favorable as time goes on. This is particularly the case for Canada because the forecasts never diverge greatly from the USCG's position. It should be noted that while shocks do not greatly affect the predictions, volatility in later rounds is sufficient to make difficult any firm conclusions about the trajectory of the forecasts.

Table 3 conveys a summary of the results across the issues. Analysis of this table will provide a sense of the overall profile of the likelihood of cooperation and discord in the Arctic, with implications for the Canadian national brand as a whole. Overall, the results show that the process of managing these issues is likely to be cooperative. However, the results also show that the outcomes will be mixed for Canada's brand: Canada will need to accept a reduction in sovereignty in some issue areas. We now explore the results in terms of process, outcome and Canada's brand in more detail.

### Process

From the perspective of avoiding deadlock, the results in Table 3 are encouraging. In all of the issues areas examined, there is at least one possible agreement that can be reached between the parties involved. However, in terms of whether reaching a rapid conclusion –

**Table 3.** Summary of results – cooperation vs. deadlock.

| Issue | Rapid conclusion?[a] | Stability (number of agreement rounds) | Distance from Canadian position at agreement round | Does the Canadian position move less than that of main competitor? |
|---|---|---|---|---|
| Search and rescue | No (3) | Low (2) | Medium (5.97) | Yes |
| Environmental protection | No (3) | Low (5) | Low (2.12) | Yes |
| Fishing rights | No (3) | Low (3) | High (40.79) | Yes |
| Seabed resources | No (3) | Low (3) | High (40.79) | Yes |
| Transit of military vessels | Yes (1) | Low (5) | High (59.15) | No |
| Transit of private vessels (NWP) | Yes (1) | Low (5) | High (59.15) | No |
| Transit of private vessels (EEZ) | Yes (1) | Low (5) | Medium (9.17) | Yes[b] |
| Transit of scientific vessels | No (2) | Low (5) | High (18.92) | No[c] |

[a]An issue is considered to have a rapid conclusion if an end rule is reached in the first round. The first round where an end rule is reached is noted in parentheses.
[b]The Canadian position is compared to the average of the positions favored by the insurance companies and legal shippers.
[c]The Canadian position is compared to that of the United States.
Notes: NWP = Northwest Passage; EEZ = Exclusive Economic Zone.

assessed on the basis of whether an agreement can be reached in the first round – is possible for a given issue, Table 3 reveals this to be feasible in three of eight issues. All models satisfy at least one end rule by the third round. It should be noted that, when we refer to agreement, we do not necessarily mean that each actor is happy with the outcome, but that one of the end rules has been met.

Stability is assessed in Table 3 on the basis of the proportion of the 10 rounds in which at least one end rule is met: total (10), high (6–9) or low (0–5). The table reveals that *all* models have low stability. The five most stable issues have only five rounds in which an agreement is possible. In sum, we find a high degree of instability between rounds as to whether an end rule has been met. We find a tendency toward an end rule being satisfied in one or two early rounds, along with some successful rounds late in the model. It is likely often the case that the first possible satisfaction of the end rule is taken, but in some instances, continuing to future rounds is advantageous for one of the actors.

## *Outcomes*

What about distance of outcomes to the Canadian initial position? Results in Table 3 reflect the following coding: low (less than five units apart); medium (less than 10 units apart); high (10 or more units apart). While another coding scheme might produce somewhat different results by category, the overall pattern of mixed results is less encouraging for the Canadian brand: one low, two medium and five high. In one of those final five cases, Canada made a smaller adjustment in position than did its primary opponent. We also see the possibility of Canada–United States cooperation in the NWP, perhaps the most important of all issues from the standpoint of policy significance. The NWP is an issue on which the two countries hold completely opposing positions, but where they have managed to find creative ways to avoid discord in the past. Given the long history of military cooperation in North America and Canada's limited capacity in the Arctic, cooperation in the NWP may be an ideal solution for both parties. Cooperation may become more attractive as Russia reasserts itself. A reanalysis of this issue for the Donald J. Trump administration would be interesting.

Interesting to ponder in terms of a sense of urgency for Canada is the rather opposite-looking results pertaining to proximity to the Canadian position and change in outcomes across iterations. The forecasted results generally are at a distance from preferred

Canadian positions, yet some issues are moving across iterations in Canada's direction. This pattern would tend to support the value of negotiations across the board but without a rush to judgment.

## Canada's brand

How do the results from the model relate to the Arctic, in an encompassing sense, as an essential component of the Canadian brand? The presence of at least some uncontested issues points toward continuity. In a counter-intuitive way, veto players for some issues – a trait that might be associated with discord – instead may help to build a norm of consensus-seeking among those highly active in the Arctic. This could reinforce, rather than undermine, the long-term association of the Canadian brand with multilateralism. Things stand still otherwise.

Another positive aspect of the results concerns continuity vis-à-vis anticipated Canadian policy. The Canadian government's Arctic policies, which might have worried critics such as Rankin (2012) during the Harper era at least in terms of rhetoric, seem quite stable. Instead, the results of the model in an overall sense point toward pragmatic pathways for Canadian involvement in the Arctic. Moreover, it is likely that the warnings from Nimijean (2006) about the need to keep foreign and domestic policies in balance with each other can be heeded. This assertion would seem true at least in principle. Gyrations in domestic politics, such as the shift from Harper to Trudeau, appear unlikely to overturn a track record of pragmatic foreign policy in the Arctic.

Some negative implications also can be taken away from the model. Note in Table 1 the absence of Indigenous peoples from those listed as players. This is not a criticism of the expert, who generated the data from a well-informed position, but instead the tendency of Ottawa to act on the interests of the much larger segment of the Canadian population that dwells below the Arctic. The absence of Indigenous players from the expected utility model also reinforces points made by Ruhl (2008a, 2008b) about how icons are created regarding the Arctic, while at the same time it can be observed that a lack of agency among its people continues unabated for any number of issues. Finally, consider the paradox of a Canadian brand that includes attachment to the Arctic along with a lack of engagement (Berger 1966, Shields 1992, Francis 1997). The model suggests that it is likely to continue; most notably, issues from Table 2 reflect the interests of the Canadian government as opposed to society *per se*.

## The Canadian brand in the Arctic "the day after tomorrow"

White notes that "many, perhaps most, Canadians' perception of the Arctic owes more to mythology than to a solid understanding of real places with real and vexing social and political issues" (2011, p. 748). In order to help bring clarity to the future of the Arctic, this study has applied a forecasting model to a range of sovereignty-related issues. The results are mixed but generally favorable to continuation of Canadian sovereignty in the far north in terms of *process* and, to a lesser degree, *outcomes*. This suggests a somewhat complex pathway toward promoting the Canadian brand as an Arctic state: negotiations with other Arctic actors will yield results that are acceptable to the Canadian brand, but Canadians may need to reconceptualize some elements of Canada's Arctic identity. Nimijean (2006, p. 78) offers a point of caution here for leadership in particular: "The conscious effort to equate partisan political issues with national values is one of the dangers of national branding strategies." Thus Canada, if it hopes to succeed in national branding, must stay aware of the "international–domestic nexus" (Nimijean 2006, p. 80).

With respect to process, three issues are predicted to converge quickly toward cooperation: transit of military vessels in the NWP, and transit of private vessels in the EEZ and NWP. A cooperative solution can be found relatively quickly for the other issues. However, in several of the cases, it may take some time to reach an agreement if the first solution point is missed.

What about outcomes? Three issues – search and rescue, environmental protection, and transit of private vessels in the EEZ – feature forecasts that fall within 10 points of the Canadian position. The forecasts for five issues – search and rescue, environmental protection, fishing rights, transit of commercial vessels in the EEZ, and seabed resources – are closer to Canada's original position than to that of its primary opponent. Only the forecasts for the transit of military, commercial and scientific vessels in the NWPs are both more than 10 points from the Canadian position and closer to the position of Canada's opponent.

In the debate, involving Huebert (2011b) and Griffith (2011), over the sustainability of Canadian sovereignty in the Arctic, our process and outcome forecasts tend to support a middle ground. The processes lean toward a forecast of cooperation: all of the models reach at least one agreement round. However, in terms of outcomes, Canada gets close to its ideal point in a few issues, but the pulling and hauling of bargaining makes compromise at some distance from Canadian preferences the anticipated result most of the time. Thus, the recommendations from Lackenbauer (2011b, p. 219) ring true. He calls for a balanced policy, not "alarmism or pessimism," and advocates "bilateral and multilateral cooperation" (2011b, p. 241). This may the best way to pressure and build upon the Arctic component of the Canadian brand through sustained public diplomacy.

In light of the complex results from the preceding analysis, which vary significantly across issues, a prudent approach that acts upon the specific findings about timing and other tactical aspects would seem in order if Ottawa hopes to achieve the best overall outcome with regard to Arctic sovereignty and the national brand in an overall sense. This is in line with a hybrid environment for action, with elements of discord and cooperation at work simultaneously.

With regard to future research, it would be interesting to explore the causal mechanisms behind the results. The mixture of cooperation and discord also suggest a middle ground between realism and liberalism with regard to the Canadian brand. States that depend economically on resource rents and/or are autocratic become more likely to pursue exclusionary policies in the Arctic (Markowitz 2014). Both Canada and the United States fall at the low end of the scale on that dimension, which suggests that each will tend to eschew power projection and therefore remain relatively open to negotiated settlement of issues.[16] In sum, the overall implications of the forecasting results for the Arctic reveal that Canada possesses the opportunity to promote its national brand while also facing challenges across a complex set of issues.

## Notes

1. Francis (1997, p. 157) cites the discovery of gold in the Klondike of 1998 as a reason behind the high level of interest. The gold rush lasted briefly, but "many writers and, later, filmmakers were attracted to the story" (Francis 1997, p. 157).
2. Recent general works on Canadian foreign policy include Hale (2012), James (2012) and Nord and Smith (2013); for comprehensive histories of Arctic diplomacy and sovereignty, see Elliot-Meisel (1998), Smith (2014) and Lajeunesse (2016).
3. The literature on national branding is multifaceted; for examples, see Nimijean (2008) on Canadian studies in relation to cultural diplomacy and Rankin (2012) regarding gender and the Canadian national brand.
4. A summary of the new geopolitics of the region for all of the Arctic states appears in Huebert (2011a, pp. 205–216).
5. Byers (2009, pp. 131–141) reports on a scenario worked out with students that conveys a sense of urgency about possible loss of sovereignty regarding the NWP. This scenario, however, is unique and does not constitute reproducible evidence. Instead, scenario-based thinking focuses on potential adjustment of existing strategies and tactics in light of results from a forecasting model that is based on expert-generated data about actors, capabilities and preferences as they exist now.
6. James and Jones (2018) provide an exhaustive set of references and many illustrations regarding the highly successful expected utility model. It is beyond the scope of the present study to present the model in detail, but a user-friendly version also appears in James and Jones (2018).
7. Our first and second experts, respectively, are Carolyn C. James (Pepperdine University) and Elizabeth Elliot-Meisel (Creighton University).
8. While some readers may question consultation with just one expert to generate most of our data, evidence suggests that accuracy is *not* generally improved by using more than one coder (James and Lusztig, 2000; Bueno de Mesquita, 1994). Moreover, as described below, we use robustness checks to verify the stability of our results to variations in the data.
9. While actors may misrepresent their bargaining position, the expert coder *infers* sincere positions for participants on the basis of all available knowledge.
10. Constabulary powers are a largely uncontested area, with the possible exception of the NWP. However, even the United States, which is generally the main opponent to Canada's claim, would likely support Canadian constabulary efforts. Indigenous rights are an internal, "nation-to-nation" issue (Trudeau 2015).
11. Some controversy might ensue about granting this status to the Arctic Council because, to be exact, the treaty flowing from it *requests* better coordination involving national assets and policies.
12. It is understood that the ICJ is not *formally* part of the UN.
13. The output files are provided in Appendix 2.
14. The fishing and seabed resources models had a 30 per cent probability of a shock of a magnitude of 30 per cent. We used higher probabilities and magnitudes here due to the greater uncertainty over the inputs.
15. The graphs show the round-by-round smoothed mean for rounds that meet and do not meet the end rule along with the quartiles for smoothed means from the 20 additional simulations. We use quartiles instead of standard deviations because the clustering of the smoothed means from the shocked rounds is rarely normally distributed.
16. The need for posturing to please audiences at home, however, could stand in the way of cooperation with the United States (Bergh, 2012). Hale (2012) draws attention to the tendency in Canada to underestimate the importance of American domestic coalitions in constraining government action.

## Acknowledgements

This article was presented at the Annual Meeting of the International Society of Political Psychology, Herzliya, Israel, July 2013, and the Biennial Conference of the Association for Canadian Studies in the United

States, Tampa, Florida, November 2013. We are grateful to Bruce Bueno de Mesquita for use of his software in implementing our models, and to Michael D. Cohen, Elizabeth Elliot-Meisel Rob Huebert, Carolyn C. James, Tom Jamieson, Jonathan Markowitz and Simon Radford for helpful commentaries. We appreciate the help of Marc André Bodet and Melanee Thomas in identifying the main issues in Canadian foreign policy. Jinny Choi provided excellent research assistance and we thank her very much as well.

## Disclosure statement

No potential conflict of interest was reported by the authors.

## Notes on contributor

*Mark Paradis* holds a doctorate in political science and international relations from USC.

*Richard Parker* is the former president of the Southern Association for Canadian Studies and a graduate of McGill University.

*Patrick James* is Dornsife Dean's Professor of International Relations at USC.

## References

Balton, David and Thomas, Cari, 2013. Ocean governance in the high north. *U.S. Naval Institute Proceedings*, 139 (7), 18–23.
Berger, Carl, 1966. The true north strong and free. *In*: Russell Peter, ed. *Nationalism in Canada*. Toronto: McGraw-Hill, 3–26.
Bergh, Kristofer, 2012. The Arctic policies of Canada and the United States: domestic motives and international context. *SIPRI Insights on Peace and Security*, 1, 1–19.
Bone, Robert M., 2009. *The Canadian north: issues and challenges*. 3rd ed. Oxford: Oxford University Press.
Boutilier, Alex, 2015. Bill for Stephen Harper's annual Arctic trips tops $3.4 million. *Toronto Star*, January 27. Available from: https://www.thestar.com/news/canada/2015/01/27/bill-for-stephen-harpers-annual-arctic-trips-tops-34m.html [Accessed 27 January 2015].
Bueno de Mesquita, Bruce, 1984. Forecasting policy decisions: an expected utility approach to post-Khomeini Iran. *PS: Political Science & Politics*, 17 (2), 226–236.
Bueno de Mesquita, Bruce, 1994. Political forecasting: an expected utility model. *In*: Bruce Bueno de Mesquita and Frans Stokman, eds. *European community decision making*. New Haven: Yale University Press, 71–104.
Bueno de Mesquita, Bruce, 2002. *Predicting politics*. Columbus: Ohio State University Press.
Bueno de Mesquita, Bruce, 2009. *The predictioneer's game: using the logic of Brazen self-interest to see and shape the future*. New York: Random House.
Bueno de Mesquita, Bruce, 2011. A new model for predicting policy choices: preliminary tests. *Conflict Management and Peace Science*, 28 (1), 65–85.
Bueno de Mesquita, Bruce, 2013. Available from: www.predictionersgame.com.
Bueno de Mesquita, Bruce, 2014. *Principles of international politics*. 5th ed. Washington: CQ Press.
Byers, Michael, 2009. *Understanding sovereignty disputes in the north: who owns the Arctic?* Toronto: Douglas & McIntyre Publishers.
Byers, Michael, 2014. Why Canada's search for an icebreaker is an Arctic embarrassment. *The Globe and Mail*. January 21. Available from: http://www.theglobeandmail.com/news/national/the-north/why-canadas-search-for-an-icebreaker-is-an-arctic-embarrassment/article16425755/ [Accessed 21 January 2014].
Campagna, Paul F., McNulty, Dave, and Roscoe, Heath, 2013. When the ice melts. *U.S. Naval Institute Proceedings*, 139 (7), 24–30.
Chase, Steven, 2014. New deal nears on "polar code" to regulate Arctic shipping. *The Globe and Mail*. January 21. Available from: http://www.theglobeandmail.com/news/national/the-north/new-deal-nears-on-polar-code-to-regulate-arctic-shipping/article16443760/ [Accessed 21 January 2014].

Cohen, Ariel, 2015. Systemic violence threatens Middle East oil outlook. *Atlantic Council*. June 3. Available from: http://www.atlanticcouncil.org/blogs/new-atlanticist/systemic-violence-threatens-middle-east-oil-outlook [Accessed 3 June 2015].

Commander, Submarine Forces Public Affairs, 2016. *Navy submarines arrive in Arctic for ICEX 2016*. Available from: http://www.navy.mil/submit/display.asp?story_id=93648 [Accessed 18 March 2016].

Disney Park Scripts, 2017. *O, Canada! (Epcot)*. Available from: http://www.disneyparkscripts.com/o-canada-epcot/ [Accessed 4 March 2017].

Elliot-Meisel, Elizabeth, 1998. *Arctic diplomacy: Canada and the United States in the northwest passage*. New York: Peter Lang.

Emmerson, Charles, 2010. *The future history of the Arctic*. New York: Public Affairs.

Everson, Kristen, 2017. Canadian rangers lack support and health care access, military ombudsman says. *CBC News*. January 23. Available from: www.cbc.ca/news/politics/canadian-rangers-arctic-patrol-reserves-1.3938299 [Accessed 23 January 2017].

Francis, Daniel, 1997. *National dreams: myth, memory, and Canadian history*. Vancouver: Arsenal Pulp Press.

Government of Canada. 2009. *Canada's northern strategy: Our north, our heritage, our future*. Ottawa: Minister of Public Works and Government Services Canada.

Grant, Shelagh, 2010. *Polar imperative: a history of Arctic sovereignty in North America*. Vancouver: Douglas & McIntyre Publishers.

Griffiths, Franklyn, 2011. Pathetic fallacy: that Canada's Arctic sovereignty is on thinning ice. In: P. Whitney Lackenbauer, ed. *Calgary papers in military and strategic studies*, Occasional Paper No. 4. Calgary: University of Calgary, Centre for Military and Strategic Studies.

Griffiths, Franklyn, Huebert, Rob, and Whitney Lackenbauer, P., 2011. *Canada and the changing Arctic: sovereignty, security and stewardship*. Ontario: Wilfrid Laurier University Press.

Hale, Geoffrey, 2012. *So near yet so far the public and hidden worlds of Canada-US relations*. Vancouver: UBC Press.

Huebert, Rob, 2011a. Canada and the newly emerging international Arctic security regime. In: James Kraska, ed. *Arctic security in an age of climate change*. Cambridge: Cambridge University Press, 193–217.

Huebert, Rob, 2011b. Climate change and Canadian sovereignty in the Northwest passage. In: P. Whitney Lackenbauer, ed. *Calgary papers in military and strategic studies*, Occasional Paper No. 4. Calgary: University of Calgary, Centre for Military and Strategic Studies.

James, Patrick, 2012. *Canada and conflict*. Oxford: Oxford University Press.

James, Carolyn C. and James, Patrick, 2014. Canada, the United States and Arctic sovereignty: architecture without building? *American Review of Canadian Studies*, forthcoming.

James, Patrick and Jones, Randall J., 2018. IR's crystal ball: prediction and forecasting. In: Gofas Andreas, Hamati-Ataya Innana, and Onuf Nicholas, eds. *The SAGE handbook of the history, philosophy and sociology of international relations*. Thousand Oaks, CA: SAGE Publications.

James, Patrick and Lusztig, Michael, 2000. Predicting the future of the FTAA. *NAFTA: Law and Business Review of the Americas*, 6 (3), 405–420.

Koring, Paul, 2018. Canada should beware the ice dragon. *iPolitics*, February 9.

Lackenbauer, P. Whitney, 2011a. Conclusions: "use it or lose it," history and the fourth surge. In: P. Whitney Lackenbauer, ed. *Calgary papers in military and strategic studies*, Occasional Paper No. 4. Calgary: University of Calgary, Centre for Military and Strategic Studies.

Lackenbauer, P. Whitney, 2011b. Polar race or polar surge? Canada and the circumpolar world. In: James Kraska, ed. *Arctic security in an age of climate change*. Cambridge: Cambridge University Press, 218–243.

Lajeuness, Adam, 2016. *Lock, stock, and icebergs: a history of Canada's Arctic maritime sovereignty*. Vancouver: UBC Press.

Le Mière, Christian, 2013. Arctic doublespeak. *U.S. Naval Institute Proceedings*, 139 (7), 32–37.

Markowitz, Jonathan N., 2014. *When and why states project power*. Doctoral Dissertation. University of California, San Diego, CA.

Martin, Paul, 2008. *Hell or high water: my life in and out of politics*. Toronto: McLelland & Stewart.

Nimijean, Richard, 2006. The politics of branding Canada: the international-domestic nexus and the rethinking of Canada's place in the world. *Revista Mexicana de Estudios Canadienses (Nueva Epoca)*, 11, 67–85.

Nimijean, Richard, 2008. Canadian studies and the Harper foreign policy agenda. *Inroads: The Canadian Journal of Opinion*, 22, 23–27.

Nord, Douglas and Smith, Heather, 2013. Canadian foreign policy. *In*: Mark Kasoff and Patrick James, eds. *Canadian studies in the new millennium*. 2nd ed. Toronto: University of Toronto Press, 346–381.

Parker, Richard D. and Madjd-Sadjadi, Zagros, 2010. Emerging legal concerns in the Arctic: sovereignty, navigation and land claim disputes. *Polar Record*, 46 (4), 336–348.

Pigott, Peter, 2011. *From far and wide: a complete history of Canada's Arctic sovereignty*. Toronto: Dundurn.

Potter, Evan H., 2009. *Branding Canada: projecting Canada's soft power through public diplomacy*. Montreal and Kingston: McGill-Queen's University Press.

Rankin, Pauline L., 2012. Gender and nation branding in "the true north strong and free." *Place Branding and Public Diplomacy*, 8 (4), 257–267.

Ruhl, Jeffrey, 2008a. *Iconification and the nationalized Inukshuk*. MA Thesis, Canadian Studies, Carleton University. August 27.

Ruhl, Jeffrey, 2008b. Inukshuk rising. *Canadian Journal of Globalization*, 1 (1), 25–30.

Saideman, Stephen M., 2016. *Adapting in the dust: lessons learned from Canada's war in Afghanistan*. Toronto: University of Toronto Press.

Shields, Rob, 1992. *Places on the margin: alternative geographies of modernity*. New York: Routledge.

Simpson, Jeffrey, 2014. A long line of procurement failures. *The Globe and Mail*. January 22. Available from: http://www.theglobeandmail.com/globe-debate/a-long-line-of-procurement-failures/article16444421/ [Accessed 23 January 2014].

Smith, Gordon W., 2014. *In*: P. Whitney Lackenbauer, ed. *A historical and legal study of sovereignty in the Canadian north*. Calgary: University of Calgary Press.

Trudeau, Pierre, 2015. *Minister of foreign affairs mandate letter*. Ottawa: Government of Canada.

White, Graham, 2011. Go north, young scholar, go north. *Canadian Journal of Political Science*, 44 (4), 747–768.

# 7 Canada's foreign policy and bureaucratic (un)responsiveness

Public diplomacy in the digital domain

Kai Ostwald and Julian Dierkes

**ABSTRACT**

The Trudeau government's foreign policy seeks to return Canada to its liberal internationalist roots. Executing this agenda falls upon the foreign affairs bureaucracy, particularly the missions and diplomats abroad. Recognizing this, Trudeau "ungagged" bureaucrats, thereby empowering them to engage in public diplomacy that promotes his stated agenda. How responsive have the bureaucratic agents been to the new political directive? We examine available evidence from digital diplomacy to assess whether the new foreign policy agenda and the change in communication policy have altered the public diplomacy of the foreign affairs bureaucracy. Analysis of over 400,000 tweets from the 296 major Twitter accounts associated with Global Affairs Canada points to few signs of a significant shift in levels of engagement, content of diplomatic outreach, independence of missions, or user interaction with tweets. We argue that despite the key policy change and global visibility of Trudeau's professed agenda, institutional stickiness has inhibited a concomitant shift in the bureaucracy, thereby limiting the impact of the political directives.

**RÉSUMÉ**

La politique étrangère du gouvernement Trudeau cherche à ramener le Canada vers ses racines internationalistes libérales. La mise en œuvre de ce plan revient à la bureaucratie des Affaires étrangères, en particulier aux missions et aux diplomates basés à l'étranger. Reconnaissant cette nécessité, Trudeau a « débâillonné » les bureaucrates, leur accordant par-là le pouvoir de s'engager dans la diplomatie publique favorable à son plan. Dans quelle mesure les agents de la bureaucratie ont-ils été réactifs à la nouvelle directive politique ? Nous examinons les données provenant de la diplomatie numérique pour vérifier si le nouveau plan de politique étrangère et le changement de la politique de communication ont modifié la diplomatie publique de la bureaucratie des Affaires étrangères. L'analyse de plus de 400.000 tweets émanant de comptes Twitter majeurs, associés aux Affaires mondiales Canada, révèle un faible nombre d'indicateurs d'un changement important de l'engagement, du contenu de la stratégie diplomatique, de l'indépendance de la mission ou de l'interaction des usagers avec des tweets. Nous soutenons que malgré le changement politique majeur et la visibilité mondiale de la stratégie avouée de Trudeau, la fidélité aux principes institutionnels a inhibé un changement concomitant de la bureaucratie, limitant par-là même l'impact des directives politiques.

## 1. Introduction

Prime Minister Justin Trudeau's vision of Canada differs dramatically from that of his predecessor, Stephen Harper. While Harper's foreign policy focused on a small range of security and economic issues, Trudeau's professed vision of Canada is that of a globally engaged middle power that contributes openly and energetically to a progressive liberal internationalist agenda. It is also a vision of a government that interacts more transparently with the broader public both in Canada and abroad. In short, Canada, under Trudeau, seeks to revive the country's rich global diplomatic traditions through a renewed focus on broad international engagement and open communication.

The Trudeau government has made frequent assertions on the world stage that "Canada is back," underscoring the government's vision of resuming its traditional role in the world. While this message has been articulated by Trudeau and other elected officials in his cabinet, a comprehensive *implementation* of the new policy requires a unified effort by the bureaucratic apparatus tasked with executing Canada's foreign policy; it is the actions of the civil servants within the Ministry of Foreign Affairs, Ministry of Trade, and Ministry of International Development (which collectively comprise Global Affairs Canada – GAC) that are responsible for translating Trudeau's vision into action.

To facilitate this, the Trudeau government has altered the communication policy that governs the organizational relationship between political leaders and the GAC bureaucracy. Under Harper, diplomats had relatively little autonomy in the execution of their tasks, as they were expected to act as delegates of the elected political leadership by limiting their role to the transmission of headquarters (HQ)'s positions. Control was top-down and tight, especially regarding public communication: diplomats were required to secure approval for public appearances and speeches with HQ in Ottawa, which often provided politically sanctioned, detailed talking points from which diplomats were expected not to stray. Trudeau abandoned this policy on the day he took office: As *The Economist* wrote shortly after the new government took power, "Justin Trudeau wastes no time in setting a new tone" by giving an "ungagging order" that provides Canada's diplomats greater discretion and autonomy. A letter Trudeau sent to diplomats reinforced this by noting that "[t]oday begins a new era in Canadian international engagement" in which his government would rely on diplomats "to be engaged energetically in public diplomacy" and use their "judgement, insights, discretion, and work ethic [to advance Canada's] interests."[1]

What has been the practical impact of this new political directive? This article provides an empirical assessment of whether Trudeau's approach to foreign policy has delivered measurable changes in GAC's engagement with the public and with stakeholders. We ask two broad questions: First, has the new directive of greater engagement actually pushed GAC toward more public communication? Second, has the focus and content of engagement changed?

To make these questions more tractable and quantifiable, we limit our focus to Canada's digital diplomacy. Since early 2014 – nearly two years before the end of the Harper government – diplomatic missions have been actively encouraged to maintain a presence on Twitter, and to a lesser extent other social media platforms. The media-savvy Trudeau government has maintained this focus. While Canada is late to this game relative to many countries, the realm of digital diplomacy generates enthusiasm for its potential to upend staid diplomatic communications. As a subject of research, digital diplomacy has the additional advantage that the communications themselves are collected on publicly accessible platforms, which enables systematic and robust quantitative analyses.

Our empirical strategy is straightforward. We analyze over 407,000 tweets made by roughly 300 GAC Twitter accounts. These tweets stretch back well into the late phase of the Harper government, allowing us to directly compare the social media communications patterns of the foreign service under the Harper and Trudeau governments. Since there has been little practical change in the social media policy of the two governments during the period under consideration, we can confidently attribute differences in output to the divergent underlying communication policies themselves.

We find little evidence of an abrupt shift in digital diplomacy following the formation of the Trudeau government. While there is a modest increase in the quantity of Twitter output, it is attributable almost entirely to the trend of new accounts coming online at a consistent rate that extends back into the Harper government. Moreover, the few subtle changes in the content of public diplomacy under Trudeau are smaller in magnitude than the contrasting political visions would suggest. Lastly, we find no evidence of missions becoming more independent from GAC HQ in terms of the focus of content, nor of tweets eliciting substantially greater engagement from followers, both of which the bureaucracy's ungagging had been intended to precipitate.

Why do we see such little change in bureaucratic behavior? While the evidence available to us does not offer a definitive answer, we suggest three potential explanations. First, despite the push for digital engagement by senior GAC officials since early 2014, dedicated resources remain scarce, inhibiting the realization of ambitions. While this explains the generally low quality of engagement, it does not explain the lack of clear divergence between the two governments. This is likely a function, we suggest, of institutional stickiness stemming from two sources, both of which extend beyond the idiosyncrasies of digital diplomacy. First, the longstanding norm of constrained public diplomacy under the Harper government has proven difficult to change. Consequently, diplomats who are inclined to engage openly often proceed with caution, having adapted their behavior to the dictates of the previous government. Second, hiring and promotion patterns at the upper echelons of the public service under the Harper government often rewarded public servants who were generally disinclined to openly engage in public diplomacy; the limited turnover in personnel across governments reinforces institutional stickiness.[2]

Is Canada back? Trudeau's star power and the optimism of his foreign policy vision have raised Canada's profile internationally, thereby increasing its soft power and potentially heralding its return as a middle power. But evidence from the realm of digital diplomacy suggests that this has not been accompanied by an equally substantial about-turn within the bureaucratic apparatus tasked with implementing the vision. While we did not collect evidence from other channels of public diplomacy, the factors inhibiting a clear transition in the realm of digital diplomacy likely exert a similar effect in other areas as well.

## 2. Is Canada back? Intent and execution

For the decade he held power, Stephen Harper sought to redefine the country's place and role in the world by dampening Canada's previous liberal internationalist inclinations.

Harper prioritized economic engagement and sought to limit Canada's engagement in multilateral institutions, due to their perceived inefficiencies in delivering results (Klassen 2014, Schmitz 2014). This orientation was met with some pushback from Canada's diplomatic corps, which Harper perceived suspiciously as having liberal internationalist tendencies. In response, Harper sought to neutralize the corps' agency by restricting its ability to act autonomously, thus reducing its role to that of an executor of political decisions. Multilateral engagement was likewise viewed with some suspicion; consequently, it was pursued cautiously and was strongly guided by its impact on domestic politics (Stoett and Kersten 2014). In short, Harper's decade in power was marked by limited international engagement during which mercantile interests and ideology were privileged over other factors.

Trudeau's political success capitalized on the growing discontent during the tail end of the Harper years among a portion of the electorate, which perceived the country as having gone too far in one direction for too long. Thus, Trudeau's mere utterance of the phrase "Canada is back" – combined with his lineage – were enough to recover the support of the center on many foreign policy issues. Canada was to re-engage with the world and project an image of hope, even if it did not evoke the underlying model of a middle power in public communication. The contrast between Harper and Trudeau on foreign policy has significant nuance that lies beyond the scope of this article (see Chapnick and Kukucha 2016). But even if the two governments were not diametrically opposed on all dimensions, the contrast between their stated foreign policy visions could hardly be clearer in practical terms.

A foreign policy, however, is more than just vision. While elected leaders plot the course, it falls upon the relevant bureaucratic apparatus of the state to implement the vision.[3] As Bloomfield (1982, p. 2) writes about the handoff of directives to the bureaucracy, "[i]t is then that an idea, no matter how morally powerful and however authentically grounded in the national political epistemology, encounters the instruments, the forces, and the fallible (or obstreperous) human beings who implement (or thwart) ... foreign policy programs" (quoted in Drezner 2000). In the case of Canada, that is primarily the three amalgamated ministries that comprise GAC, each of which is led by its own minister. Since most line departments and agencies have specialized international sections, the foreign ministry takes on what is increasingly a coordinating and advisory role.

The most direct linkage between GAC and the foreign entities that are the target of Canada's foreign policy are the overseas missions and their embedded personnel. These act as Canada's representatives abroad, including as the interface between the Canadian and foreign states. The well-established principal–agent framework (Calvert et al. 1989, Downs and Rocke 1994, Miller 2005) brings clarity to the organizational structure and the resultant dynamic of the relevant ministries: The politically elected leadership at GAC HQ in Ottawa has the authority to formulate Canada's foreign policy (at the directive of the Prime Minister) and thus acts as the *principal*; GAC personnel, particularly those in the missions abroad, are the *agents* that implement that policy in the name of the principal.

A key element of the Trudeau government's strategy for implementing its foreign policy vision was to alter the communication policy that governed the principal–agent relationship within GAC's organizational structure. Under Harper, foreign service agents were tightly controlled by the Ottawa-based principal and given little autonomy in the execution of their tasks. Indeed, the Harper government "imposed strict communication controls on its diplomats, including ambassadors and high commissioners, requiring them to clear major public events through the Privy Council Office in Ottawa." It was reported that "bureaucrats at Industry Canada [were required to] run each proposed tweet through a 12-step protocol, and seek approval of the minister's office."[4] Furthermore, diplomats were often provided with detailed talking points from Ottawa, from which they were expected not to stray. In essence, nearly all information meant for public consumption was either disseminated from or directed through HQ, allowing it to maintain substantial control over messaging.

This top-down control created a situation in which foreign service agents, particularly those in missions abroad, acted as delegates of their Ottawa-based principal, which means their actions were to be unaltered reflections of the principal's preferences.[5] As in other places where elected political leaders have sought to "muzzle" the bureaucracy (Lee 2012), this rigid top-down dynamic substantially constrained the ability of GAC agents abroad to engage in effective public diplomacy, since they were unable to fully act upon their natural informational advantages over the Ottawa-based principal. As a result, public diplomacy abroad more strongly reflected the comparatively homogeneous ideological convictions of the principal than the positions of the informationally richer, locally based agents. Facing substantial constraints on communication and resources, many agents resorted to "filler" content that was unlikely to generate backlash or incur transaction costs of repeated revisions.

In several high-profile pronouncements made shortly upon taking office, Trudeau "unmuzzled" GAC agents in a way that fundamentally altered the nature of the principal–agent relationship. As detailed earlier, the directives suggested that GAC personnel were re-empowered to speak openly and were trusted to use their judgment when communicating the policy positions and overall vision of the new government. This does not mean that all controls were removed, but rather that a significant proportion of the bureaucratic processes that were put into place under the Harper government to centralize information and control its dissemination was streamlined. In effect, GAC agents were given substantial autonomy over how they represented the Ottawa-based principal: under the new policy, they went from being *delegates* of Ottawa to being *trustees* of Ottawa, in that they were empowered to use their judgment – grounded in their informational advantages – to decide how to best advance the vision of their elected leadership. The empirical section assesses the responsiveness of the GAC bureaucracy to this change in communication policy.[6] Before we proceed to the data and tests, however, we examine Canada in the digital domain in greater detail.

## 3. Canada's brand in the digital domain

Digital diplomacy has grown in importance for practitioners and policymakers around the world (Bjola and Holmes 2015). Its rise is seen as a natural extension of the digital sphere's transformation of state management (Mergel 2013, Zheng and Zheng 2014). While digital diplomacy has at times been dismissed as nothing more than an avenue through which to cut costs, or criticized for the often banal content it carries (Collins and Bekenova 2018), its unique features give it the potential to fundamentally alter the millennia-old art of diplomacy: In the hands of an adept digitally native user like Justin Trudeau, for example, it enables a *direct person-to-person* engagement that was not possible on a large scale through previous forms of diplomacy. United States president Donald Trump has likewise provided ample evidence of social media's disruptive potential, albeit in a different form.

Digital diplomacy also generates enthusiasm for its capacity to transform how countries leverage their "soft power" abroad. In the context of Canadian diplomacy, digital diplomacy initiatives draw on a longer standing debate and advocacy for public diplomacy as an element in foreign policy that is particularly suited to "middle powers." As Evan Potter wrote in his seminal statement on Canadian public diplomacy, "public diplomacy has been moving rapidly to the forefront of diplomatic practice. ... [I]t is not the techniques of public diplomacy that have changed; rather, it is the environment in which diplomacy takes places that has changed radically" (2009, p. 28). That environment now includes social media, and thus public diplomacy has been extended into the digital realm.

In this context, information technology provides the opportunity to effectively project soft power through targeted campaigning: Rather than a "traditional" advertisement campaign in which a broad branding of a country is uniformly thrust upon a diverse foreign population, digital diplomacy allows countries to disseminate selected elements of their brand to the segments of a target population that are most likely to engage positively. This allows countries to punch above their weight in terms of influencing perceptions abroad, especially in the case of smaller countries that cannot support an extensive physical presence around the world.

A final dimension of digital diplomacy is rooted in the larger shift in understanding of policymaking, which recognizes the increasing need to incorporate the views of stakeholders in policy development, as well as to communicate the outcomes to said stakeholders and the broader community (Johnson 2015). If policymaking is to change from a top-down activity rooted in classical understandings of Weberian bureaucracy to a more open process that sees the citizenry not only as subject to policymaking, but also as active participants, then digital tools can be mobilized to build foreign policy and diplomatic activities on the foundations of ongoing two-way exchanges with stakeholders. Given the ability of digital tools to dramatically reduce transaction costs, this dimension allows diplomacy to become less a purely state-to-state activity, and more an activity that involves a range of stakeholders at home and abroad.

GAC was late to the game of digital diplomacy. Given the previous controls on communications, few missions abroad were willing to take the risk of opening an account without consent from the center. This consent came through the official blessing from the country's former top diplomat, John Baird, in early 2014, following which key offices within GAC HQ and most missions established accounts. While engagement through Twitter has been actively encouraged since Baird's pronouncement, the few dedicated resources available to support digital diplomacy are concentrated primarily in Ottawa. Since social media as a tool of public diplomacy "might involve even more human resources and financial investment than traditional media-based tools [given that] its objective, methods, and operations require a complex digital infrastructure and well-trained staff to carry out the missions" (Bjola and Jiang 2015, p. 75), diplomats abroad – who generally must carve out time from already thinly stretched agendas to promote Canada online – understandably struggle to utilize the platform to its full potential.

## 4. Data and descriptive account

Having been ungagged through Trudeau's reversal of Harper's communication policies, how are diplomats using social media to advance Canadian foreign policy objectives abroad? An initial glance at social media accounts suggests that they are generally used as broadcast platforms to reach a wider audience (Dierkes *et al.* 2016). This section examines the data we rely on to more closely examine communication, while the following section proceeds with the analysis.

We focus our attention on Twitter, given the widespread usage of the platform across GAC and the public nature of the data.[7] We begin the process of identifying active Twitter accounts associated with GAC through a list of accounts on the Canada International government website. We drop accounts that do not relate to foreign affairs, as well as lower level personal accounts that largely duplicate the content of their overarching mission. We also drop inactive accounts. We then search for additional accounts that were not identified in the GAC list, which notably includes many of GAC's vernacular-language accounts. This exercise yielded 296 unique and active accounts, which we believe represents the full spectrum of relevant GAC accounts at the time the list was finalized in May 2016.

The accounts cover the following areas: 18 are associated with GAC HQ in Ottawa; 16 are attached to international organizations, including the United Nations, NATO, and World Trade Organization; 26 are in the United States; 74 in Europe; 56 in the Americas (non-United States); 59 in the Middle East and Africa; and 43 in Asia. Of these accounts, 141 operate in English, with 131 in French and 24 in local vernacular languages. Over half of the accounts (156) were created in 2014; 69 were created in 2013, and 10 each were created in 2012, 2011 and 2010. The earliest account was created in 2009 (Invest_Canada), with the remainder being created after 2014.

To construct our data set, we captured (on 16 November 2016) the most recent 3200 tweets from each of the 296 accounts. This constitutes the entire tweet history of 271 of the accounts. For all but five of the remaining 25 accounts, the most recent 3200 tweets extend back before November 2014, thus covering at least one year under the Harper government and one year under the Trudeau government. The resulting data set has 407,202 tweets, of which 150,056 are retweets. Each observation contains the text of the actual tweet, as well as a range of accompanying information, including account name, a timestamp and location for the tweet, the number of times the tweet was favorited as well as retweeted, and the language of the tweet. We are confident that the data set contains the vast majority of tweets sent by accounts associated with GAC. Collectively, these represent the public diplomacy efforts of GAC on the dominant digital platform used by the foreign ministry. Table 1 presents basic summary statistics of the data.

Several outlier accounts are noteworthy. The Embassy of Canada in France (French language) has roughly 350,000 followers, while the @Canada account has over 200,000 followers. Collectively, those comprise almost half of all GAC Twitter followers. An additional eight accounts have between 10,000 and 30,000 followers: Development Canada (English); the Government of Canada (GoC)'s travel advisory (English); Canada's mission to NATO (English); Canada Trade (English); Canada's foreign policy (English); Canada's foreign policy (French); Canada's trade commissioner service (English); and Invest Canada (English).

The contrast between accounts associated with GAC HQ and the missions is noteworthy: with a median of 7368 followers per account, HQ accounts have on average greater than 10 times the followers of the mission accounts. The HQ accounts are also much more active tweeters (a plurality of them reach our limit of 3200 tweets), though users engage with those tweets at only a marginally higher rate than they do with tweets from the missions. The language dimension is also interesting: while English- and French-language accounts

**Table 1.** Overview of Global Affairs Canada Twitter accounts.

| | Accounts | Tweets | Mean tweets per account | Median tweets per account | Followers | Mean followers | Median followers | Mean engagement (like or retweet) per tweet |
|---|---|---|---|---|---|---|---|---|
| Headquarters | 18 | 46,184 | 2566 | 3200 | 372,102 | 20,672 | 7368 | 32.5 |
| Missions | 278 | 361,018 | 1299 | 1000 | 644,619 | 2319 | 710 | 27.9 |
| Total | 296 | 407,202 | 1376 | 1053 | 1,016,721 | 3435 | 764 | 28.5 |
| International organizations | 16 | 24,075 | 1505 | 790 | 44,809 | 2801 | 1053 | 33.8 |
| United States | 26 | 66,810 | 2570 | 3110 | 35,319 | 1358 | 1215 | 24.2 |
| Europe | 74 | 104,651 | 1414 | 1171 | 418,509 | 5656 | 714 | 39.7 |
| Americas (non-United States) | 56 | 67,246 | 1201 | 812 | 57,464 | 1026 | 654 | 17.3 |
| Middle East and Africa | 59 | 55,190 | 935 | 770 | 38,089 | 646 | 657 | 23.1 |
| Asia | 43 | 41,547 | 966 | 920 | 51,454 | 1197 | 606 | 26.6 |
| English | 141 | 214,571 | 1522 | 1300 | 538,374 | 3818 | 1421 | 44.3 |
| French | 131 | 159,533 | 1218 | 916 | 435,816 | 3327 | 483 | 9.9 |
| Vernacular | 24 | 33,098 | 1379 | 999 | 42,527 | 1772 | 936 | 15.1 |

are active at roughly comparable rates – a reflection of the government's policy of bilingualism in official communication – the median number of followers for English language accounts is roughly three times higher than for French accounts, and the rate of engagement with tweets is more than four times greater.

We suspect that some of the accounts' followers are actually government employees, but we cannot confirm this supposition. For the sake of comparison, Prime Minister Justin Trudeau's own Twitter account has over 2.46 million followers, almost 250 per cent more than all of the GAC accounts combined. But even that figure is overshadowed in the world of diplomacy by the United States' Department of State's Twitter, which has nearly 3.5 million followers.

## 5. Empirical analysis

Our empirical analysis addresses two broad questions. In each case, we focus on whether there are discernible differences in public diplomacy between the Harper and Trudeau governments. We first examine whether there is evidence of increased engagement in the realm of digital diplomacy, specifically Twitter. We do this by measuring the raw output of public communications by both GAC HQ and GAC's missions abroad. Second, we examine whether there has been a change in the content of public communications, focusing on issue areas of substantive importance to both governments. In the case of both tests, the vision of the Trudeau government, in conjunction with the unmuzzling of the foreign affairs bureaucracy, suggests the potential for substantial differences between the governments.

### 5.1. Quantity of output

We begin the analysis by examining the trend over time in raw output of tweets from the 296 accounts associated with GAC. Since we are interested in the effect of the election on public communication, we set the week of the election (4 November 2015) as week zero. Figure 1 is a simple histogram of tweets per week from 24 September 2010 through 16 November 2016.

Several things are noteworthy about the overall trend in Twitter output. The first is that there is a rapid rise beginning roughly two years before the 2015 election, which corresponds with Baird's promotion of social media. Second, there is a sharp decrease in the output of tweets in roughly the three months prior to the election, as the attention of the GoC turns toward the election and the government shifts into caretaker mode. Third and most importantly, while the raw output of tweets is greater following the election, this appears to be largely a continuation of the trend that began roughly two years earlier, rather than a bump in response to the new government.

Two things could be driving this upward trend: increased activity in existing accounts, or new accounts coming online. To distinguish between these two possibilities, we limit the comparison to accounts that were online for at least the one year before and one year after the 2015 election. This allows us to consider only the *within*-account effect of the election. We are left with 209 accounts. Figure 2 illustrates the average number of tweets per account per week for those remaining GAC accounts.

Aside from the drop in output in the 15 weeks prior to the election, there does not appear to be a substantial increase in the average number of tweets per account following the election. This strongly suggests that the upward trend visible in Figure 1 is the result of a steady stream of new accounts coming online – totaling 87 during the year before and after the election – rather than an increase in output from existing accounts. Of those 87 new accounts, 67 were created in Harper's final year of government.

We can estimate the trend of Twitter output over time more precisely through several time series linear regressions. We begin with a simple ordinary least squares (OLS) model

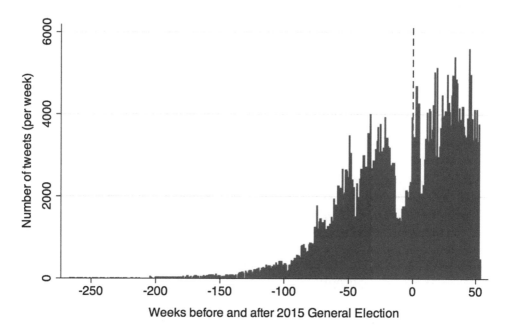

**Figure 1.** Trend in Twitter output (number of tweets per week from all Global Affairs Canada accounts).

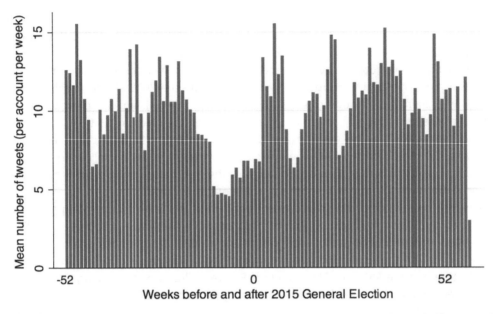

**Figure 2.** Within-account Twitter output (mean tweets per week per established Global Affairs Canada account).

restricted to the year before and the year after the 2015 general election. As before, we also limit the comparison to accounts that were active throughout this period of time. The dependent variable *tweets* is the number of tweets per week per account. *Week* is the time variable. We include a dummy called *caretaker mode* for the 15 weeks before the 2015 election to control for the pre-election lull in Twitter output as the government shifted into caretaker mode. As there is substantial variation in activity across accounts, we use fixed effects at the account level. We also want to distinguish between the output from GAC HQ accounts and missions. Rather than control for the type of account, we run separate models so that interpretation of results remains manageable once we introduce interaction effects in subsequent models. Model 1 aggregates the mission and HQ accounts; Model 2 includes only the mission accounts; and Model 3 includes only the HQ accounts. These models provide us with a simple trend line in Twitter output between November 2014 and November 2016.

Since our primary interest is the effect of the change in government on Twitter output, we run additional linear regressions based on a regression discontinuity design. This allows us to establish whether either the intercept or the slope of the trend line changed following the 2015 General Election. To do this, we include a dummy variable called *post election*, which we code "1" for all 52 weeks after the election ("0" otherwise). This effectively divides the trend line at the election (when *week* equals 0), which allows us to observe a potential discontinuity or "bump" in output from the new government. We also include an interaction term *wk * post elec* to capture any change in the slope of the trend line following the election (Dong 2010). We continue to restrict the comparison to the year before and after the election, as well as to accounts that were online throughout the time period. Like before, we first aggregate the accounts in Model 4, then show mission accounts in Model 5, and finally show the HQ accounts in Model 6. Table 2 displays the results.

**Table 2.** Twitter output over time from Global Affairs Canada accounts.

| Tweets | M1<br>All | M2<br>Missions | M3<br>Headquarters | M4<br>All | M5<br>Missions | M6<br>Headquarters |
|---|---|---|---|---|---|---|
| Week | .001 | −.002 | .105*** | −.023* | −.031** | .190*** |
|  | (.002) | (.002) | (.012) | (.009) | (.010) | (.036) |
| Caretaker mode | −4.833*** | −4.745*** | −7.434*** | −4.117*** | −3.895*** | −9.667*** |
|  | (.138) | (.137) | (1.063) | (.291) | (.296) | (1.532) |
| Post election |  |  |  | 1.146** | 1.127** | −2.101 |
|  |  |  |  | (.374) | (.382) | (1.778) |
| Week * post election |  |  |  | .017 | .024* | −.118* |
|  |  |  |  | (.011) | (.011) | (.053) |
| Constant | 10.79 | 10.45 | 20.24 | 9.89 | 9.39 | 23.13 |
| Observations | 21,985 | 21,203 | 782 | 21,985 | 21,203 | 782 |
| $R^2$ | .382 | .369 | .452 | .383 | .369 | .454 |

Note: Models estimated with fixed effects at account level; *$p < 0.5$; **$p < .01$; ***$p < .001$.

Model 1 examines the change in Twitter output in the year before and after the 2015 general election for all accounts. The trend is flat, aside from a strong decline of nearly half during the pre-election period (*caretaker mode*). Model 2, which is limited to mission accounts, looks substantively identical. By contrast, accounts associated with GAC HQ (Model 3) increased Twitter output by 0.105 tweets per week per account. This amounts to roughly an additional 11 tweets per week per account at the end of the two-year period, which constitutes a doubling of output.

Models 4 through 6 include the *post election* dummy and the *wk * post elec* interaction term to isolate the effect of the election on Twitter output. The interaction term complicates interpretation, since the marginal effect of the independent variables changes depending on the point in time between *week* −52 and 52. Three points, however, are noteworthy. First, there is a statistically significant but substantively small jump in output after the election from mission accounts (Model 5). This is partially offset, however, by a negative slope. In effect, output from missions received a bump from the election, but then trailed off over time, so that mean output from the missions abroad under Trudeau looks very similar to that under Harper. Second, there was no meaningful election bump to Twitter output in the HQ accounts (Model 6). Interestingly, however, HQ accounts' output grew significantly in the final year of the Harper government and then leveled off under Trudeau. Third and most importantly, the increase in $R^2$ from Models 1 through 3 to Models 4 through 6 is very small. This means that the election variables that capture the direct impact of the change in government add very little explanatory power to the models. Simply put, the election mattered to digital engagement in that it depressed the output significantly in the run-up to the election while the government assumed a caretaker role. Once that lull is controlled for, however, the change in government itself had at best a very small impact on the quantity of engagement.

## 5.2. Content of output

Trudeau's vision for Canada calls not only for more foreign engagement, but specifically also for engagement across a substantially broader spectrum of issue areas. The contrast between Trudeau and his predecessor on this front appears stark: Harper advocated for a limited international role for Canada that was constrained largely to narrowly defined security and economic interests, while Trudeau promised to engage the world on issues as diverse as the environment, gender and development.

We test whether there is evidence of a substantive shift in the focus of Canada's digital diplomacy following the change in government. We do this by conducting a content analysis on the full data set of 407,202 tweets. Specifically, we track trends in engagement with substantively important issues, namely in the areas of *economic growth*, *security*, *environment*, *international development* and *gender*. We chose these because the former two represent priority areas for the Harper government, while the latter three are priority areas for the Trudeau government.

We conceive of these categories in the following way: *economic growth* focuses on the economic activities of Canada, including such things as trade, imports and exports. *Security* focuses on traditional "hard" security areas like military engagement and terrorism. *Environment* focuses on a range of areas around environmental protection and sustainability, including air and water quality, climate change, global warming and renewable energy. *International development* focuses on development issues abroad, including poverty reduction, foreign aid and good governance. *Gender* focuses on issues around gender equality.

The analysis is based on a list of both singular and paired key terms in English and French that signal engagement with one of the substantive areas, but are unlikely to be used in engagement with other areas. For example, a tweet that includes the key term "greenhouse" is likely to be about climate change and thus in the *environment* category, as alternative usages are unlikely in tweets from a GAC account. While the term "clean" *or* "energy" might be used in tweets on a range of topics, it is likely that a tweet in which both appear will address energy sustainability, and thus also fall under the *environment* category.

We then compare the key terms against the Twitter data to identify matches, which are categorized into one or more of the respective substantive categories. To account for the general increase in output over the past several years, we standardize our measure by showing the proportion of total tweets in a given week that are positive matches for a substantive category. During the week of the 2015 General Election, for example, 126 tweets were identified as engaging with security-related issues. GAC accounts sent a total of 3924 tweets in that week, so security-related tweets accounted for roughly 3.2 per cent of all tweets. Figure 3 shows the proportion of GAC tweets that engage with the five categories in the three-year period between November 2013 and November 2016, where the y-axis is the proportion of total tweets and the x-axis is weeks before and after the November 2015 election. We opt for a median band line to smooth the visualization. We also display a linear prediction line to provide an estimate of the temporal trends.

The first notable observation is that the substantial contrast in priority areas between the Harper and Trudeau governments does not appear to produce an abrupt and dramatic shift in the content of tweets. In the case of *gender, economic, environment* and *international development* categories, there is clearly some change in focus, but substantial within-government variation makes it difficult to draw clear and definitive conclusions; in any case, there is more continuity across the Harper and Trudeau governments than the high-profile initial public pronouncements would suggest. The second notable observation is that only a small proportion of overall tweets actually engage substantively important areas: when we aggregate all five categories, only about 14 per cent of tweets are flagged in our modeling. There is no clear change in that proportion across the two governments.

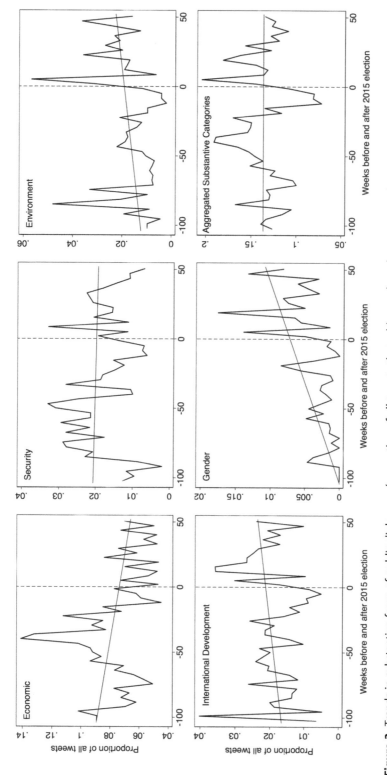

**Figure 3.** Trends in substantive focus of public diplomacy (proportion of all tweets that address selected content areas).

We conduct additional econometric analyses to more precisely estimate the magnitude of change while controlling for the pre-election period and capturing variance in behavior between different segments of GAC. The dependent variable *STweets* is the proportion of total tweets (between 0 and 1) that engage a substantively important area. *Week* is the time variable that ranges from −104 to 52; *caretaker mode* is a dummy that is coded "1" for the 15 weeks prior to the election, when the government shifts into caretaker mode ("0" otherwise). *Post election* is a dummy that is coded "1" for weeks 1 through 52 ("0" otherwise). To understand how Twitter usage varies between HQ and the regional clusters of missions, we create a dummy for each mission area, leaving HQ as the reference category. Model 1 focuses on *economic growth*, Model 2 on *security*, Model 3 on *environment*, Model 4 on *international development* and Model 5 on *gender*, while Model 6 aggregates all substantive categories. We choose to cluster errors at the account level to at least partially account for unobservables. As a maximum likelihood logit regression is difficult to interpret given the model parameters, we opt for a straightforward OLS model. The results are substantively similar. Table 3 reports findings.

The findings can be interpreted as follows: The constant provides the baseline proportion of tweets that engage a given substantive area. Since HQ is the reference category, we can read Model 1 as indicating that roughly 20 per cent of tweets from HQ accounts under Harper dealt with an economic issue. This fell by roughly 3 per cent in the pre-election period. On average, 4 per cent fewer tweets from HQ accounts under Trudeau deal with economic issues (i.e. roughly 16 per cent). Both differences are statistically significant. Roughly 13 per cent fewer tweets from mission accounts (relative to HQ accounts) in Europe deal with economic issues (i.e. roughly 7 per cent).

We can draw three larger conclusions. First, the change between the Harper and Trudeau governments *is* statistically significant in four substantive areas: *economic* (decrease), *environment* (increase), *international development* (increase) and *gender*

**Table 3.** Substantive focus of Global Affairs Canada tweets.

| STweets | M1 Economic | M2 Security | M3 Environment | M4 Development | M5 Gender | M6 All |
|---|---|---|---|---|---|---|
| Week | .000 | −.000*** | −.000 | −.000** | −.000 | −.000 |
|  | (.000) | (.000) | (.000) | (.000) | (000) | (.000) |
| Caretaker mode | −.030** | −.006** | −.005** | −.006** | −.001 | −.047*** |
|  | (.011) | (.002) | (.002) | (.002) | (.001) | (.011) |
| Post election | −.041*** | .005 | .018*** | .010*** | .008*** | −.002 |
|  | (.011) | (.003) | (.003) | (.003) | (.002) | (.012) |
| -International organizations | −.119* | .050* | −.002 | .021 | .013 | −.035 |
|  | (.052) | (.020) | (.004) | (.013) | (.008) | (.047) |
| -United States | −.072 | −.000 | .036*** | .013* | −.002 | −.050 |
|  | (.051) | (.004) | (.004) | (.006) | (.004) | (.047) |
| -Europe | −.131* | .0133* | .004 | −.002 | .001 | −.114* |
|  | (.051) | (.006) | (.003) | (.006) | (.004) | (.046) |
| -Americas | −.147** | −.010* | −.001 | .006 | .002 | −.148** |
|  | (.051) | (.004) | (.003) | (.007) | (.004) | (.046) |
| -Middle East/Africa | −.140** | .006 | −.003 | .015 | .010* | −.113* |
|  | (.050) | (.005) | (.002) | (.008) | (.005) | (.046) |
| -Asia | .108* | −.002 | −.002 | .004 | .012* | −.095* |
|  | (.053) | (.005) | (.003) | (.007) | (.006) | (.048) |
| Constant | .207 | .012 | .005 | .015 | .000 | .233 |
| Observations | 393,735 | 393,735 | 393,735 | 393,735 | 393,735 | 393,735 |
| $R^2$ | .034 | .010 | .011 | .005 | .005 | .020 |

Note: Errors clustered at account level; *$p < 0.5$; **$p < .01$; ***$p < .001$.

(increase). In the area of *security* and in terms of aggregate engagement with substantively important areas, however, the Harper and Trudeau governments are not distinct at conventional levels of significance. Second, we should not conflate statistical significance and substantive significance: The statistical significance is enabled by the very large sample size, which lends considerable statistical power. It is not at all obvious, however, that the magnitude of change across the two governments is especially significant in terms of actual impact: when aggregating HQ and mission accounts, the proportion of tweets that address economic issues decreases from roughly 10 per cent to 7 per cent; with environment the increase is from 1 per cent to 2.5 per cent; with international development, 1.7 per cent to 2.5 per cent; with gender, 0.3 per cent to 1.1 per cent. We do not want to dismiss these changes as irrelevant, but against the backdrop of the dramatic contrast in visions between Harper and Trudeau, as well as the substantial change in communication policy, they appear modest at best.[8] The third notable observation is that with the exception of the economic issue area, there appears to be little variation between HQ and missions, with most of the differences not reaching conventional levels of statistical significance.

The final point raises important questions about Canada's diplomatic efforts abroad. Effective engagement requires being responsive to conditions on the ground, which clearly vary from country to country and region to region. If the "ungagging" of diplomats were successful and GAC personnel abroad were engaging in a meaningful way with issues of local importance – rather than just relaying the political messaging of their Ottawa-based principals at GAC HQ – then we would see a divergence between HQ and missions in terms of the focus of their tweets.

We test the independence of missions by creating a series of variables that track how closely the tweets from missions follow those from HQ in terms of engagement with the five substantively important areas. We create one variable for each region and substance area dyad (for example: Europe – *economic*; Americas – *economic*; Asia – *economic*, etc.). These variables capture the absolute value of the difference (in proportion of tweets that engage a substantive area) between HQ and the respective regions for each substantive area on a weekly basis for the period of time between November 2013 and November 2016. We then aggregate the absolute value of the difference between HQ and each region on a weekly basis, giving us a running trend of how closely mission tweets are following HQ tweets. To facilitate interpretation, the dependent variable *mean divergence* is the mean of the divergence of each of the six regions from HQ. *Week* is the number of weeks before and after the general election. *Caretaker mode* is a dummy that takes the value of "1" for the 15 weeks before the election ("0" otherwise), and *post election* is a dummy that takes the value of "1" for the 52 weeks after the election under the Trudeau government ("0" otherwise). Table 4 reports findings.

In the areas of security, environment, development and gender, the average distance between the missions and HQ has not significantly changed between the Harper and the Trudeau governments. There is, in other words, no clear evidence of a divergence between HQ and the missions following the election and the subsequent "unmuzzling" of the GAC bureaucracy. In fact, in the area of economic activity, HQ and the missions have *converged* under Trudeau relative to Harper.

There is one additional key dimension to consider. Though there is little evidence of an increase in Twitter output or a dramatic shift in the content of tweets, more effective

**Table 4.** Independence of GAC missions in key substantive areas.

| Mean divergence | M1<br>Economic | M2<br>Security | M3<br>Environment | M4<br>Development | M5<br>Gender | M6<br>All |
|---|---|---|---|---|---|---|
| Week | .000 | −.000 | −.000* | −.000 | .000 | .000 |
|  | (.000) | (.000) | (.000) | (.000) | (.000) | (.000) |
| Caretaker mode | .007 | −.004 | −.002 | −.001 | −.002 | .006 |
|  | (.027) | (.003) | (.003) | (.003) | (.002) | (.024) |
| Post election | −.085** | −.000 | .012 | .004 | .003 | −.065* |
|  | (.026) | (.005) | (.005) | (.004) | (.003) | (.023) |
| Constant | .166 | .021 | .009 | .016 | .006 | .140 |
| Observations | 157 | 157 | 157 | 157 | 157 | 157 |
| $R^2$ | .177 | .031 | .097 | .055 | .123 | .179 |

Note: $*p < 0.5$; $**p < .01$; $***p < .001$.

digital diplomacy may also entail higher quality tweets that elicit a greater degree of engagement by followers. On Twitter, "favorites" and "retweets" can serve as a proxy for that kind of engagement. We test for a bump in the quality of tweets in the following way: We take the sum of favorites and retweets for each tweet in our data set. To prevent outliers from exerting excessive leverage in the analysis, we take the natural log of that sum. We then aggregate this figure for every week between November 2013 and November 2016 and divide by the total number of tweets for the respective week, giving us the mean (ln) retweets and favorites for each week. Figure 4 illustrates this.

As Figure 4 shows, engagement with GAC tweets is higher under Trudeau than under Harper. But the increase over time appears linear, perhaps reflecting the expansion of followers rather than an increase in the quality of the tweets. A regression analysis (not shown) supports this supposition: When we control for the pre-election lull (*caretaker mode*) and the

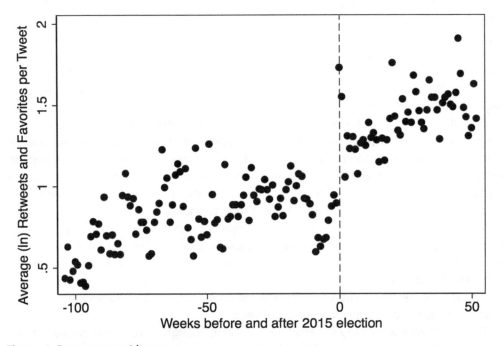

**Figure 4.** Engagement with tweets.

general increase in engagement over time, the difference between the Harper and Trudeau governments does not reach conventional levels of statistical significance. In other words, there is no compelling evidence that the quality of tweets – as measured by follower engagement – has substantially increased under the new government.

## 6. Conclusion

The October 2015 general election appeared to bring a fundamental shift to Canada's foreign policy. Justin Trudeau pledged to "bring Canada back" by re-engaging with the world on a broad range of issues, thus reversing course from the more constrained foreign presence preferred by his predecessor, Stephen Harper. There is little question that Trudeau's star power, together with his liberal internationalist message at a time when many other states have taken an inward turn, has boosted Canada's international profile. But fully executing a foreign policy vision requires more than just pronouncements by elected leaders (Nimijean 2017); it requires the bureaucratic apparatus of the state to translate the vision into practice. Recognizing this, Trudeau "ungagged" Canada's bureaucracy by lifting the public diplomacy restrictions on Canada's diplomats that had muzzled them under Harper. Canada's representatives abroad were empowered to act autonomously and engage the world more openly in accordance with the vision of an open Canada.

This article examines available evidence to assess whether Canada's bureaucracy has changed the patterns of its public diplomacy in line with the elected leadership's vision. To make this assessment more tractable, we focus on digital diplomacy, specifically on roughly 400,000 tweets from 296 core GAC Twitter accounts. Contrary to the dramatic contrast in foreign policy visions, there is little evidence of a fundamental shift in public diplomacy under Trudeau. While the sheer quantity of Twitter output has increased, it is attributable almost exclusively to new accounts coming online at roughly the same rate as under the Harper government. There is a subtle shift in the content of public diplomacy – most notably an increased engagement with gender-related issues – but the magnitude is relatively small. We do not find evidence that missions abroad are acting more independently from GAC HQ in Ottawa, as we would anticipate following the ungagging order. Lastly, there is no evidence of a bump in follower engagement with GAC tweets after the election, which we would normally expect if the quality of tweets had substantially increased. In short, the evidence suggests that the public diplomacy practices of GAC have not experienced a substantial change, at least not in the realm of digital diplomacy.

How can we explain the absence of substantial change in Canada's foreign affairs bureaucracy, given the strong political directives and ostensibly conducive circumstances? Part of the answer is specific to the realm of digital diplomacy. While Twitter engagement has been a priority area for both the Harper and Trudeau governments, few positions are dedicated to digital diplomacy, leaving those tasked with it juggling between competing demands, especially in understaffed missions. There is no question that realizing the full potential of digital diplomacy requires more dedicated and specialized resources that are ultimately difficult to mobilize given other pressing needs within the foreign service.

A substantial portion of the answer, however, goes beyond the idiosyncrasies of digital diplomacy. The Harper government changed Canada's foreign affairs bureaucracy in substantial ways during its nearly 10 years in power. It is clear that institutions and institutional norms, once entrenched, are sticky and difficult to alter. As such, the legacy of the Harper government continues to affect the bureaucracy under Trudeau in ways that constrain public diplomacy. This has two primary manifestations. First, the formal rule changes that grant autonomy in public engagement have not comprehensively altered the Harper-era norm of caution in making public statements: Many diplomats and their staff, despite embracing in principle Trudeau's more activist foreign policy vision, remain hesitant to speak openly on particular issues when they are unsure of Ottawa's position, thus defaulting to "filler" public diplomacy or repeating the politically sanctioned messaging. Second, the bureaucracy itself was substantially reshaped through the hiring and promotion decisions of the Harper years. Though it is by no means universally true, the criteria employed during this period advantaged personnel who were likely to integrate smoothly into the Harper government's engagement priorities and institutional norms. In short, a non-negligible portion of GAC personnel are inherently disinclined toward the type of active public diplomacy suggested by Trudeau's foreign policy vision, despite being empowered – and, indeed, directed from the top – to practice it.

It may be too strong to say that once gagged and gutted, it is difficult to rapidly revive a bureaucracy so that it can effectively implement an ambitious foreign policy agenda. But it is clearly the case that institutions and the policies that comprise them are sticky, and thus that the GAC bureaucracy has not been able to fully execute Trudeau's professed foreign policy vision. We do not exclude that this inertia might be overcome in time, but it would almost certainly require a concerted effort to address the institutional changes that occurred under the Harper government.

This finding has important implications beyond Canada: United States President Donald Trump has signaled intentions to gut and gag the United States federal bureaucracy in a dramatic fashion by "cut[ting] so much your head will spin" and prohibiting several agencies from unauthorized engagement with the media or public.[9] As the scale of Trump's ambitions to bring the bureaucracy in line with his agenda far exceed the more limited and milder nature of the Harper government's actions, this raises serious concerns about long-term damage to capacity in important areas of the United States government. We close, in any case, by returning to Canada and the underlying question of this article. Is Canada back? Simply put: Yes. And no.

## Notes

1. See *The Economist*, "Canada's new government: Ungagging order" (12 November 2015). Excerpts from the letter were reported in *The Star* story entitled "Trudeau tells Canadian diplomats he relies on their judgement" (5 November 2015).
2. See Tsalikis (2017) for a discussion of changes in Canada's foreign service, including under Harper and Trudeau.
3. See Jones (2012) for a comprehensive review of bureaucratic politics.
4. Reported in *The Globe and Mail*, "Canadian diplomats should use social media more, foreign minister says" (7 February 2014). See also Paris (2014).
5. See Urbinati and Warren (2008) for a discussion of representation theory.
6. While extensive research has examined bureaucratic responsiveness (see Bevan 2015, Clinton et al. 2014, Kennedy 2015, Wood and Waterman 1991), we are unaware of work that considers the responsiveness of bureaucratic agents to a fundamental change in their relationship to their principals.
7. See Steinert-Threlkeld (2018) for an extensive guide on using Twitter as data.

8. Here, we acknowledge the limitations of an analysis that relies on keywords, as tweets since Trudeau's election could be talking about the same key topics in a different way. Cursory impressions of tweets, however, do not suggest this as an explanation.
9. See: *The Independent*, "How Trump's first year has decimated the federal bureaucracy" (31 December 2017); *New York Times*, "Federal Agencies Told to Halt External Communications" (25 January 2017).

## Acknowledgements

We would like to thank the editorial team and the anonymous reviewers for their helpful feedback. Robert Bond, Zachary Steinert-Threlkeld, Cesi Cruz, and one further anonymous researcher deserve special thanks for their support. All errors are our own.

## Disclosure statement

No potential conflict of interest was reported by the authors.

## Notes on contributors

*Kai Ostwald* holds a PhD in political science from the University of California, San Diego. He is an assistant professor in the School of Public Policy & Global Affairs and the Department of Political Science at the University of British Columbia. Find him at www.kaiostwald.me or @KaiOstwald.

*Julian Dierkes* was trained as a sociologist at Princeton University. He is an associate professor and Keidanren Chair in Japanese Research at UBC's School of Public Policy and Global Affairs. In addition to Japan and digital diplomacy, much of his research focuses on mining policy and political development in Mongolia.

## ORCID

*Kai Ostwald* http://orcid.org/0000-0002-9876-955X
*Julian Dierkes* https://orcid.org/0000-0003-4322-4699

## References

Bevan, S., 2015. Bureaucratic responsiveness: effects of elected government, public agendas and European attention on the UK bureaucracy. *Public Administration*, 93 (1), 139–158.
Bjola, C. and Holmes, M., eds. 2015. *Digital diplomacy: theory and practice*. Oxon: Routledge.
Bjola, C. and Jiang, L., 2015. Social media and public diplomacy. *In*: C. Bjola and M. Holmes, eds. *Digital diplomacy: theory and practice*. Oxon: Routledge, 71–88.
Bloomfield, L., 1982. From ideology to program to policy: tracking the Carter human rights policy. *Journal of Policy Analysis and Management*, 2, 1–12.
Calvert, R., McCubbins, M., and Weingast, B., 1989. A theory of political control and agency discretion. *American Journal of Political Science*, 33 (3), 588–611.
Chapnick, A. and Kukucha, C., 2016. *The Harper era in Canadian foreign policy: parliament, politics, and Canada's global posture*. Vancouver: UBC Press.
Clinton, J., Lewis, D., and Selin, J., 2014. Influencing the bureaucracy: the irony of congressional oversight. *American Journal of Political Science*, 58 (2), 387–401.
Collins, N., and Bekenova, K., 2018. Digital diplomacy: success at your fingertips. *Place Branding and Public Diplomacy*, First Online, 1–11.

Dierkes, J., et al., 2016. Digital diplomacy: how is the canadian government faring on social media? *OpenCanada.org*. Available from: https://www.opencanada.org/features/digital-diplomacy-how-canadian-government-faring-social-media/ [Accessed 11 February 2016].

Dong, Y., 2010. Jumpy or Kinky? Regression discontinuity without the discontinuity. MPRA Paper No. 25427.

Downs, G. and Rocke, D., 1994. Conflict, agency, and gambling for resurrection: the principal-agent problem goes to war. *American Journal of Political Science*, 38, 362–380.

Drezner, D., 2000. Ideas, bureaucratic politics, and the crafting of foreign policy. *American Journal of Political Science*, 44 (4), 733–749.

Johnson, G. F., 2015. *Democratic illusion. Deliberative democracy in Canadian public policy*. Toronto: University of Toronto Press.

Jones, C., 2012. Bureaucratic politics. *In*: S. Hook and C. Jones, eds. *Routledge handbook of American foreign policy*. New York: Routledge, 118–131.

Kennedy, J., 2015. Do this! do that! and nothing will happen: executive orders and bureaucratic responsiveness. *American Politics Research*, 43 (1), 59–82.

Klassen, J., 2014. *Joining empire: the political economy of the new Canadian foreign policy*. Toronto: University of Toronto Press.

Lee, M., 2012. *Congress vs. the bureaucracy: muzzling agency public relations*. Norman, OK: University of Oklahoma Press.

Mergel, I., 2013. A framework for interpreting social media interactions in the public sector. *Government Information Quarterly*, 30 (4), 327–334.

Miller, G., 2005. The political evolution of principal-agent models. *Annual Review of Political Science*, 8, 203–225.

New York Times. 2017. Federal Agencies Told to Halt External Communications. Available from https://www.nytimes.com/2017/01/25/us/politics/some-agencies-told-to-halt-communications-as-trump-administration-moves-in.html [Accessed 24 April 2018].

Nimijean, R., 2017. A portrait of Justin Trudeau. *The Monitor*, Canadian Centre for Policy Alternatives. Available from: https://www.policyalternatives.ca/publications/monitor/portrait-justin-trudeau [Accessed 24 August 2017].

Paris, R., 2014. Has Canada finally discovered digital diplomacy? *OpenCanada.org*. Available from: https://www.opencanada.org/features/has-canada-finally-discovered-digital-diplomacy/ [Accessed 7 February 2014].

Potter, E., 2009. *Branding Canada – projecting Canada's soft power through public diplomacy*. Montreal: McGill-Queens University Press.

Schmitz, G., 2014. The Harper government and the de-democratization of Canadian foreign policy. *Canadian Foreign Policy Journal*, 20 (2), 224–228.

Steinert-Threlkeld, Z., 2018. *Twitter as data*. Cambridge: Cambridge University Press.

Stoett, P. and Kersten, M. S., 2014. Beyond ideological fixation: ecology, justice, and Canadian foreign policy under Harper. *Canadian Foreign Policy Journal*, 20 (2), 229–232.

The Economist. 2015. Canada's new government: Ungagging order. Available from https://www.economist.com/news/americas/21678266-justin-trudeau-wastes-no-time-setting-new-tone-ungagging-order [Accessed 24 April 2018].

The Globe and Mail. 2014. Canadian diplomats should use social media more, foreign minister says. Available from https://www.theglobeandmail.com/news/politics/canadian-diplomats-should-use-social-media-more-foreign-minister-says/article16758123/ [Accessed 24 April 2018].

The Independent. 2017. How Trump's first year has decimated the federal bureaucracy. Available from https://www.independent.co.uk/news/world/americas/president-donald-trump-white-house-first-year-inauguration-federal-bureaucracy-barack-obama-a8135921.html [Accessed 24 April 2018].

The Star. 2015. Trudeau tells Canadian diplomats he relies on their judgment. Available from https://www.thestar.com/news/canada/2015/11/05/trudeau-tells-canadian-diplomats-he-relies-on-their-judgment.html [Accessed 24 April 2018].

Tsalikis, C., 2017. A foreign service worth fighting for. Published by *OpenCanada.org* [Accessed 26 July 2017].

Urbinati, N. and Warren, M., 2008. The concept of representation in contemporary democratic theory. *Annual Review of Political Science*, 11, 387–412.

Wood, B. D. and Waterman, R., 1991. The dynamics of political control of the bureaucracy. *The American Political Science Review*, 85 (3), 801–828.

Zheng, L. and Zheng, T., 2014. Innovation through social media in the public sector: information and interactions. *Government Information Quarterly*, 31 (1), S106–S117.

# 8 The evolving complementarity of nation-branding and public diplomacy

Projecting the Canada brand through "weibo diplomacy" in China

Evan Potter

**ABSTRACT**

Diplomacy is evolving at a much faster rate today than in the first 70 years of the previous century and diplomats and their foreign ministries have been forced to communicate more with publics at home and abroad. At the heart of this reboot, arguably, is a reconsideration of the value of public diplomacy and nation-branding within diplomatic practice, leading to questions about whether there is convergence of public diplomacy and nation-branding practices in support of international policy goals. The article first examines public diplomacy and nation-branding as concepts and fields of study. It then analyzes the growing complementarity of public diplomacy and nation-branding in Canada's foreign policy due, in large measure, to the growth of digital platforms in international communication. The article concludes by examining how public diplomacy and nation-branding appeared to converge online in Canada's "weibo" diplomacy with China, starting in 2011.

**RÉSUMÉ**

La diplomatie évolue à un rythme beaucoup plus rapide qu'au cours des 70 premières années du siècle précédent et les diplomates et leurs ministères des affaires étrangères ont été contraints de communiquer davantage avec les publics nationaux et étrangers. Au cœur de ce redémarrage, on peut dire que la diplomatie publique et la marque nationale sont reconsidérées dans la pratique diplomatique, ce qui amène à s'interroger sur la convergence de la diplomatie publique et des pratiques nationales pour soutenir les objectifs politiques internationaux. L'article examine d'abord la diplomatie publique et l'image de marque nationale en tant que concepts et domaines d'étude. Il analyse ensuite la complémentarité croissante de la diplomatie publique et de l'image de marque nationale dans la politique étrangère du Canada en raison, dans une large mesure, de la croissance des plateformes numériques dans la communication internationale. Le document conclut en examinant comment la diplomatie publique et l'image de marque nationale ont semblé converger en ligne dans la diplomatie « weibo » du Canada avec la Chine, à compter de 2011.

## Introduction

Diplomacy is evolving at a much faster rate today than in the first 70 years of the previous century, and diplomats and their foreign ministries have been forced to communicate more with publics at home and abroad. Arguably, a reconsideration of the value of public diplomacy and nation-branding within diplomatic practice lies at the heart of these changes. This leads to questions about whether public diplomacy and nation-branding complement each other in support of international policy goals. To further examine this shift toward nation-branding via public diplomacy, Global Affairs Canada's "weibo diplomacy" campaign in China is presented as a case study.

Despite the embrace of public diplomacy by foreign ministries, the ongoing penchant for sophisticated nation-branding campaigns and the latest generation of new communication tools in the form of social media, the central organizing principle of diplomacy remains the same: the projection of the national interest abroad. To put it crudely, governments will engage in public diplomacy and nation-branding when it is in their interest to do so, whether to manage national reputation, increase economic prosperity, promote or defend policies, engineer consent or to listen to and engage foreign publics.

For the first time, governments appear to have developed an appreciation of how nation-branding can complement the public diplomacy efforts by foreign ministries in creating a more robust and resilient national "Master Brand" that supports both national economic and political/security objectives. Nation-branding traditionally has been the purview of national tourism agencies and national investment promotion agencies – a predominantly marketing endeavor. Public diplomacy, by contrast, is predominantly a public relations endeavor. Through this shift toward branding, diplomacy is adapting to the reality of a shrinking and more transparent world in which diplomats have to be seen to be heard. However, as Clay Shirky argues, being seen and "on message" everywhere is simply not enough, and foreign policy outcomes can no longer be fashioned in the absence of genuine public engagement, a form of public diplomacy (Shirky 2011). We would revise Shirky's assessment and aver that the traditional public diplomacy tools of cultural and education diplomacy are evolving into a form of national "Master Brand" management. This can be discerned in digital diplomacy efforts, or Web 2.0 diplomacy, by foreign ministries that combine both public relations and marketing, often in real time, on a single online platform.

The article first examines public diplomacy and nation-branding as concepts. The second section outlines the evolution of Canada's public diplomacy and its nation-branding in a highly networked age. The article then presents the case of Canada's "weibo diplomacy" by its embassy in China in 2011–2012 as one of the first manifestations of the growing complementarity of Canadian public diplomacy and nation-branding. This phenomenon was facilitated by the availability of new social media platforms that allowed the Canadian government, for the first time, to go "over the heads" of official Chinese state media to talk directly to (and thereby exercise influence on) a key middle-class constituency of the Chinese public. This is a public numbering potentially in the tens of millions and with a thirst for information on Canada because the "idea" of Canada was compelling to them. This level of direct communication with a foreign public was unique in the annals of Canadian public diplomacy. The final section draws some preliminary conclusions about what the emerging complementarity of public diplomacy and nation-branding means for contemporary diplomacy.

## Public diplomacy and nation-branding: concept and practice

Public diplomacy functions in three ways: temporally, instrumentally and within a domestic context (Potter 2009).[1] As Figure 1 shows, in practice, public diplomacy reflects short-, medium- and long-term efforts by governmental bodies to shape public opinion. Typically, media relations are the "sharp end": the most highly controlled, short-horizon, process-driven public diplomacy activity measured in hours and days. It is designed to inform and influence public perceptions by embedding key government messages (official positions) or corrections in media coverage through official statements and news releases. Advocacy refers to issue management and lobbying and is often considered the most "strategic" form of public diplomacy because its goal is to achieve specific policy outcomes such as negotiating trade agreements or blunting negative publicity. It can involve the coordination of multiple players in and out of government. Relationship-building develops mutual understanding and is frequently associated with longer term educational and cultural exchanges that may take years or even decades to produce any measurable positive changes to foreign public opinion.

Public diplomacy as a term has received a remarkable level of multidisciplinary study (Gilboa 2008). Moreover, there are a variety of national approaches to understanding it (Potter 2009). It is not surprising, then, that one study refers to 150 definitions of the term, leading some to wonder if there will ever be a consensus (Fitzpatrick 2010). In the interest of concision, a nation's public diplomacy is defined here as the sum of the efforts by the official institutions of one nation (or of a subnational jurisdiction) to influence the elite and/or mass public opinion of another nation for the purpose of turning the policies or views of that target nation to its advantage. Public diplomacy's purpose is to understand, inform and influence foreign publics in order to achieve foreign policy goals broadly defined to include economic, political and security objectives. At its core, public diplomacy is statecraft.

However, public diplomacy is only one slice (and sometimes a very small one) of the sum total of a national or subnational jurisdiction's ability – through the collective

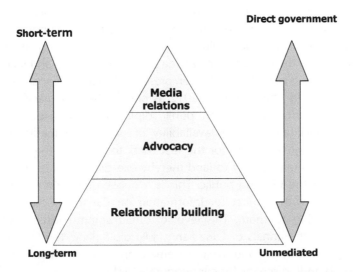

**Figure 1.** The public diplomacy pyramid. Source: Evan H. Potter, Branding Canada, 2009.

contributions of its official institutions, history, people and enterprises – to attract positive attention and voluntary "followership" – soft power – from a foreign audience and its government.[2] In this vein, Anholt (2007) has pioneered the idea of incorporating the concept of public diplomacy into the study of nation-branding. A review of Anholt's hexagon in Figure 2 below demonstrates that, arguably, most liberal democratic governments have a limited ability to affect their "place brand" during a typical multi-year nation-branding campaign. They will likely not be able to change the disposition of their "people" (their citizens' global reputation for competence, openness and friendliness), the attractiveness of "exports" (the foreign public's image of products from a country) or the country's "culture and heritage" (global perceptions of a nation's heritage and appreciation for its contemporary culture). That being said, governments do have control over their "governance" (global public opinion about a government's competency and fairness and its commitment to global issues) and "investment and immigration" (the power to attract people to live, work and study in a country, and how people perceive a country's quality of life). Anholt rightly recognizes that the nation-brand is not only the sum total of the contemporary national experience but is also influenced by a nation's history and cultural heritage. For example, consider the brand advantage accruing to nations such as China, India or the United Kingdom. These countries can draw on the deep wells of their respective histories when they project the national interest abroad.

In this context, public diplomacy and nation-branding are, in fact, complementary and mutually reinforcing elements of a nation's international communication. The most effective management of a country's global image and reputation is when governments carefully control those elements of Anholt's hexagon under their purview. For example, governments can create a just and fair society through impartial laws, implement attractive immigration and business environments and support cultural heritage through public investment in the arts and culture to increase national pride and foreign interest. The nation-brand is then harnessed in support of international priorities through public diplomacy programs and activities. The stronger the national brand, including the pride of citizens (including expatriates) in their country's achievements (both domestic and

**Figure 2.** Nation-brand hexagon. © 2000 Simon Anholt, reproduced with permission.

international), the easier it will be for a foreign ministry or development agency to project this nation-brand abroad through public diplomacy.

In sum, public diplomacy is about nation-branding, but it is not synonymous *with* nation-branding (Singh 2017, p. 12). The advocacy and relationship-building elements of the public diplomacy triangle in Figure 1 are about listening, engagement and dialogue; in its most evolved form, public diplomacy stimulates collaboration between governments and foreign audiences or among foreign audiences. Nation-branding, on the other hand, has largely been about selling and marketing a country's exports, investment attractiveness and tourism. Three fundamental developments served to ensure the greater complementarity between nation-branding and public diplomacy in the Canadian case: the amalgamation of foreign and trade ministries, including development agencies, into single departments of international affairs (as is the case in Canada and Australia), creating the opportunity for a more holistic approach to managing the national brand; the increased diffusion of power on the world stage with more and more actors vying for attention; and the rise of a networked digital world, which has forced foreign ministries like Global Affairs Canada to rethink how they communicate with the world.

## Canadian public diplomacy and nation-branding in a networked age

It is far beyond the scope of this article to attempt a comprehensive review of Canada's digital diplomacy; rather, the purpose of this article is to demonstrate how the rise of a networked world has succeeded in promoting the recognition that nation-branding and public diplomacy are complementary and can no longer be relegated to separate silos in Canada's international communication. The powerful and robust Canadian nation-brand is key to the success of the current Liberal government's efforts to revitalize Canada's public diplomacy, and a large part of this public diplomacy will be executed online.

To start, a historical overview of Canada's approach to public diplomacy and nation-branding is in order. Over the decades, Canadian governments have rarely accepted the premise that culture as a "third pillar" of Canada's foreign policy was the equal of security and trade, nor did they perceive it as a major source of Canadian soft power. Canada has tended to invest more in culture (and more broadly in public diplomacy) in those periods when the threats to national unity are most acute. The Liberal government's International Policy Statement (April 2005) was the first major government statement since the 1995 foreign policy review that articulated a clear role for public diplomacy in Canada's international relations. The rhetoric of public diplomacy was not followed by any major investment in Canada's capacity; a new Conservative government followed in 2006 and eschewed the idea of soft power, preferring instead to focus on trade-driven advocacy campaigns. Starting in 2008, the federal government's role in promoting international cultural relations – a core public diplomacy asset for most countries – became much more diminished, and Canada eventually disbanded most of its signature cultural and academic relations programs (with the notable exception of the Canada–United States Fulbright Program). As noted, the call to "revitalize" Canada's public diplomacy came again with the ascension of the new Liberal government in 2015; the new foreign minister's mandate letter indicated that he was "to increase cultural and educational interaction with the world" (Canada, Prime Minister's Office 2017). Prime Minister Trudeau called on

Canada's ambassadors to communicate (again) with the world. The government's intention to reinvest in arts and culture was evident in Budget 2016, which provided CAD$35 million to this commitment and doubled the budget of the Canada Council or the Arts over five years and also provided renewed funding to key cultural agencies such as The National Film Board and Telefilm Canada. Global Affairs Canada received funding to promote Canada's cultural and creative industries abroad, and, as a nod to the dismantling of Canada's cultural diplomacy capacity over the previous decade, it also received a very modest cultural diplomacy fund (CAD$1.7 million) to be disbursed by Canada's diplomatic network abroad. It is noteworthy that by 2017, the international trade minister's mandate letter called explicitly for a strengthened Canada brand, though it did not link this specifically to the revitalized public diplomacy. As Canada's overall public diplomacy capacity atrophied during the 2006–2015 period, it is somewhat ironic that Global Affairs Canada's Web 2.0 capacity gained momentum, particularly after 2011.

Canada's nation-branding efforts since the mid-1990s did not suffer the same vicissitudes as public diplomacy. The signature Canada branding effort was embodied in the Team Canada trade missions to priority countries such as China, led by Prime Minister Jean Chretien and his trade ministers. Although these trips were criticized at the time for being largely photo opportunities, they nevertheless did (for a period of time) raise Canada's international profile. The Conservative government, while deriding the Liberal government's penchant for these trips, nevertheless sought to promote the importance of Canada's "economic brand" (democratic and safe producer of oil for the American market) by negotiating more free trade agreements culminating in the negotiation of the Canada–European Union Comprehensive Economic and Trade Agreement. As well, the Conservative government used the annual World Economic Forum at Davos and the 2010 Winter Olympics as key platforms for Canada's economic brand. The only other major nation-branding effort during the Conservative government's tenure in office was rolling out an international education strategy to make Canada a top destination for foreign students.

Canada's nation-brand architecture throughout the 2000s could be characterized as diffuse with multiple logos, micro-brand identities, color palettes and approaches to experiential marketing. Government agencies and departments pursued their own branding agendas. There was no storyline that would create a coherent and compelling picture of contemporary Canada. Canada faced a barrage of negative international publicity over its "dirty oil" and annual seal hunt/harvest. That being said, the overall Canada brand – as diffuse as it was and with little public diplomacy support – nevertheless exhibited a surprising resiliency. International surveys consistently placed Canada in the top five country brands, leading some government observers to question whether there was a nation-branding "problem." However, the high ranking masked the persistent problem facing Canada's "economic brand," namely its weaker reputation as a place in which to do business (ranked #27/60 for "best countries to invest in," US News & World Country Rankings, 2016). Unlike its peer competitors, Canada was not investing heavily in brand or reputation management. The United Kingdom's "UK is GREAT" campaign, for example, spent CAD$210.7 million (2012–2015) to showcase Britain's capabilities and to enhance its reputation to the world, which was about 10–15 times more than what was being spent by Ottawa in any given year across the federal government.

In short, Canada was muddling along in the great nation-branding game as its competitors – large and small – launched sophisticated nation-branding campaigns. There was little evidence of any complementarity between Canada's public diplomacy and nation-branding efforts except that Canada had put more stock in its digital or Web 2.0 diplomacy than its competitors. This digital diplomacy would become Canada's "information edge" and allow it to use its very strong international brand as a foundation for advancing its broader foreign policy goals through its public diplomacy (Nye and Owens 1996). In the words of one senior official at Global Affairs Canada, reflecting on the atrophying of Canada's traditional public diplomacy tools, Canada's digital diplomacy was its "default public diplomacy" (personal communication with the author, September 2016).

Between 2011 and 2016, Canada's public diplomacy and large components of its nation-branding were indeed embodied in its Web 2.0 diplomacy. The digital diplomacy context has changed dramatically over the last decade with transition from Web 1.0 to Web 2.0 diplomacy, which has helped to further societize diplomacy (Van Ham 2010). In this networked world, foreign ministries must once again fundamentally rethink how they manage information to ensure that they provide their governments with "information edges." Digital media channels (a foreign ministry's network of online platforms such as embassy homepages and social media sites) have the advantage of scale: they allow diplomats to have more conversations with more people across more spectra, especially if they cannot physically be in a location. For instance, although Canada does not have diplomatic relations with Iran, it still engages in public diplomacy with the Iranian people through its web presence.

Although the transition from a broadcast to a network environment has been widely accepted and adopted by foreign policy practitioners, the shift from a "need-to-know" to a "need-to-share" mindset has been more challenging and raises fundamental questions about the ethos and practice of public diplomacy in the coming years. The first group of questions concerns online intelligence gathering and the purpose of amplifying a country's online presence. Is online diplomacy going to be another form of media monitoring – tracking online debates and noting supporters and critics – or will diplomats insert themselves into online conversations that are open to a global audience? Is the purpose of sharing information online another means of one-way broadcasting of a country's ideals, policy and brand? In other words, is it designed to open a dialogue and create communities of interest in which diplomats and citizens collaborate on shared concerns, or is it primarily another platform through which foreign ministries frame debates and engage in strategic communication? A third question relates to the perennial public diplomacy conundrum of how to measure public diplomacy's longer term effects relative to that of nation-branding. Together, these questions point to a normative question that is implicit in any attempt to understand the complementarity of public diplomacy and nation-branding, and one that has been formulated by Causey and Howard (2013, 145) as: "Are the efforts of diplomats to increase their online and social media presences genuine efforts to engage in a new form of public diplomacy? Or are these efforts merely traditional statecraft wrapped in a new online packing?" In a sense, nation-branding is more transparent than public diplomacy, with the latter always open to the criticism that it is a form of state propaganda under the guise of dialogue. A hint at the answers to the above questions may be found through the experience of how Canada's embassy in China used *weibo* (a Chinese equivalent to Twitter) to reach some 300 million users.

## Convergence of nation-branding and public diplomacy: Canadian "weibo diplomacy"

It would be difficult to imagine that the Canadian embassy and its consulates have the capacity to reach even a fraction of the 1.3 billion people in a country of China's size. However, online platforms offer a convenient, cost-effective way for Canada's diplomatic mission to go directly to an audience that is thirsting for news on Canada. This is not surprising. China is one of the most important source countries for immigrants to Canada, and, with the Canadian government having finally acquired the coveted Approved Destination Status, there has been an explosion of Chinese tourism. And, not to be overlooked is the fact that the number of Chinese students in Canada has grown by more than 300 per cent over the last decade, demonstrating that Canada is viewed favorably as an education market (Canada, 2010).

In June 2011, the Canadian embassy soft launched itself on *weibo* (china.gc.ca), then the most popular microblog in China with 300 million users. Since Twitter, YouTube and Facebook were blocked in China, foreign embassies had little choice but to use *weibo*. It did not take Canada long to break the barrier of 100,000 followers, and by 4 April 2012, it had 186,863, giving it bragging rights as the third most-popular embassy on this site, behind the United States (447,146) and the United Kingdom (224,100) but ahead of France (158,546) and Japan (142,012). This allows significant reach and scale in a country of China's size and diversity. This also permitted Canada's strong nation-brand to be presented alongside so-called "Great Powers."

The benefits are not difficult to discern. The *weibo* platform was used to reach a Chinese audience rather than a Canadian expat audience (a few years later the new and soon very popular WeChat would allow engagement with both domestic Chinese and expatriates). The potential to reach the hard-to-reach in their own language with "thick communication" – messages on Chinese microblog are 140 characters, which is three to four times as much as English-language content on Twitter – cannot be overstated. Perhaps the most significant dimension to Canada's use of *weibo* as a communication platform was that, unlike in the West, microblogging is popular in China because it is considered trustworthy. It is "real news" in a very controlled media environment and is relatively uncensored. This provided the potential for foreign embassies to actually "break" news online and thus to set the public policy agenda on particular issues.

The embassy posted 20–30 messages a week on *weibo*, and, in the words of Mark McDowell, the senior Canadian diplomat who launched Canada's social media presence at the embassy (2011–2012), the watchword was to be "informal, diverse, transparent, interesting" (McDowell, Interview about Sina Weibo, YouTube, January 2013). Yet public sector organizations are not usually known for being exciting; they are associated with dry and staid content. The goal of creating an informal feel to an official government online presence in order to attract and retain users is usually anathema to the "serious tone" and "informational" character of most communication emanating from diplomatic missions. There is also a tendency by government officials to steer away from producing content that could be interpreted by the Canadian media as frivolous or too flashy and therefore as a waste of taxpayers' money.

According to McDowell, knowing what will appeal to an embassy's target audience of Chinese citizens between the ages of 18 and 30 was the key concern of the embassy's staff. *Weibo*'s official Canadian content is all in Chinese and generated by Canada's embassy and its consulates rather than by officials in Ottawa. There were three basic types of content: Canadian events in China (culture and visits); embassy news (the ambassador, open house, activities); and news about Canada (such as festivals, travel, food and the economy). It quickly became apparent that the challenge was to get the right balance between serious topics (e.g. Canada's approach to food safety) that could be deemed an indirect criticism of China's policies and lighter and potentially less controversial topics such profiling a Chinese family's crest showing a panda and a polar bear.

McDowell observed that useful information like visas and exclusive content about the embassy and about life in Canada was much more popular than news about Canadian events in China. De-mystifying the embassy and its people was particularly popular.[3] For instance, photos of the Canadian ambassador's official car – a Toyota Camry hybrid, apparently a modest mode of transportation by official Chinese standards – attracted more than 1100 responses to the Canadian embassy's *weibo* site. As the *Globe and Mail*'s China correspondent Mark McKinnon wrote, "Even the Global Times, a newspaper closely affiliated with the Communist Party, used the online discussion of the official Camry to raise the sensitive topic of government officials and their [high-end] cars" (McKinnon 2012). The surprising end to this story was that the Chinese government apparently changed its regulations on official vehicle sourcing, though no one can prove any causality with the profile of the Canadian ambassador's Camry.

From a strategic communications and Canada nation-branding perspective, the Canadian embassy found that *weibo* was not a platform for messaging in the traditional sense: being preachy or hectoring is death (McDowell 2013). That being said, there was a more implicit ("frivolous"?) way of "selling" Canada as a tourism, education or business destination. Education was perhaps the most useful barometer of the success of social media platforms on multiple fronts. From a public diplomacy perspective, the platforms reach key demographics of the successor generations, who also happen to be the most significant users of social media tools, and who will value the openness of the medium as a means to build mutual understanding. From an economic perspective, moving Chinese students to consider Canada rather than, say, Australia, the United Kingdom or the United States as their first choice for a foreign education contributes directly to Canada's economic bottom line. For this reason, the Canadian embassy took a more active approach to education marketing by live blogging from Chinese education fairs. In the future there would be video testimonials from Chinese students already studying in Canada.

There was also room in social media to get serious and sensitive messages out that could not necessarily be conveyed through official contacts with Chinese media. The case of Lai Changxing, a fugitive from justice who escaped to Canada, was instructive. Canadian authorities extradited him to China in 2011 after extradition negotiations ended with the promise that he would not be executed upon his return. The Canadian embassy posted the court ruling on its website and then used *weibo* to direct people to it. It is a matter of diplomatic convention that embassies do not interfere publicly in domestic politics. But this does not mean that they cannot use social media to affect public opinion. For instance, Canada values transparency and prudence in the expenditure of public money (e.g. the ambassador's car) and the Canadian government does not support the use of capital punishment. These are both important examples of key positive attributes such as "fairness" of the Canada brand, according to international surveys (e.g. GFK 2017).[4] McDowell noted that while *weibo* was not used to send messages to the host government, the messages sent by the embassy resonated with followers, and the host government did become aware that certain topics were eliciting considerable online chatter among its citizens.

Three years after the launch of Canada's presence on *weibo*, Dierkes and Legault (2014) called the "Weibo Experiment" one of the "most sustained and prominent" Canadian experiments with digital diplomacy. They performed a content analysis of Canada's *weibo* posts in January and February 2014 to ascertain the level of engagement with the Chinese audience. By 2014, Canada had nearly 570,000 followers, following three years in which the Embassy had issued almost 4000 posts. Dierkes and Legault noted that Canada's posts in the two months were reposted 78,584 times and commented on 24,937 times, adding up to almost 110,000 actions by followers. The post that received the most interest was that of an announcement for a contest for prizes from Roots Canada, which accounted for two thirds of all the actions taken by users over the two-month period.

Dierkes and Legault concluded that the *weibo* account "certainly seems to have been successful as an alternative way to broadcast information about Canada to a local audience" though they acknowledged that the numbers did hide "ghost accounts" (2014). They also noted that this "channel to engage local stakeholders could easily be activated in the future when deepened engagement is integrated into digital diplomacy aims for Canada" (2014). It would be subsequently revealed that Canada (and presumably other Western nations) had indeed inflated numbers for their followers and that there were potentially tens of thousands of "ghost accounts" (author's personal communication with a senior Canadian official, April 2018). However, according to McDowell's description of his experience with the online engagement with the Chinese, there appeared to be genuine conversations across an array of non-controversial areas that served to deepen understanding of and attachment to Canada (McDowell 2013).

In sum, the management of Canada's *weibo* site produced some unofficial rules for engagement in selecting content: lecterns, ribbon cuttings, boardroom tables, lines of men in suits and "meet-and-greet" photographs – in short, organization-centered content – are to be avoided at all costs, in favor of audience-centered communication. Ensuring that your content is audience centered is the standard premise of any successful marketing or branding effort. The local audience is not interested in what is already in the mainstream media; there has to be an effort to create new content that meets the audience's interest, or to co-create content with the audience through contests and giveaways. For instance, rather than showing the Ambassador shaking hands with a local official, the embassy would show the ambassador in a restaurant tasting local delicacies (author's personal communication with McDowell, 2012). To be sure, the constant pressure to create exclusive, new content creates a burden on resources and staffs since embassies are not newsrooms or advertising agencies. But if the audience of 140,000 followers in the months after Canada's launch on *weibo* can be considered the equivalent to the newspaper circulation of a mid-size city in Canada, then such an effort could be justified.

## Implications for the complementarity of public diplomacy and nation-branding

The *weibo* "campaign" in 2011 was the first Canadian Web 2.0 diplomacy initiative. It was launched without official approval from Ottawa and relied on the good judgment and savvy of Canadian diplomatic personnel at the Beijing embassy. It was undertaken in the face of a number of challenges.

First, the Conservative government was not actively encouraging Canada's diplomatic staff to communicate publicly, much less through social media, raising the specter of sanctions for those who were experimenting with digital diplomacy.

Second, the lack of any baseline information (surveys) on what the Chinese thought of the Canada brand and how their thinking affects their behavior meant that the Canadian embassy was using trial-and-error methods to achieve messages that would resonate with their audiences. Certainly, Destination Canada has the means to find out what the Chinese think of Canada and can adjust their advertising and marketing programs accordingly. In retrospect, this makes Canada's online public diplomacy efforts through the Canadian embassy appear inefficient and somewhat haphazard as a form of strategic communication.

Third, chronic under-investment in Canada's public diplomacy has led to challenges in achieving results, and this has led to problems communicating the value of investing in public diplomacy initiatives. If Canada's embassy in Beijing had petitioned Ottawa for money to launch an online campaign to reach Chinese audiences, it is unlikely that this initiative would have been funded. Compounding this perceptual problem is the fact that building a case for more investment in public diplomacy is difficult if international surveys demonstrate that Canada is near the top in terms of international reputation. The case then has to be made that certain aspects of the Canada brand do not reflect reality and must be updated in the eyes of key foreign audiences (e.g. Canada is not business-friendly; Canada does not have a rich cultural heritage).

Fourth, there was no evidence that any other Canadian government agencies were involved in this effort to reach out to hundreds of millions of middle-class Chinese with an existing, mostly positive perception of Canada. This would be any marketing guru's dream scenario. There was no whole-of-government effort and no master brand to work from.

Fifth, there was no evidence that the large Chinese diaspora in Canada was ever mobilized in support of Canada's online public diplomacy campaign. This would probably have engendered too many questions for what was essentially a pilot initiative that was largely under the radar in official Ottawa.

Despite the challenges, this case does point to the first signs of a new complementarity between public diplomacy and nation-branding as practiced by Canada. Canada could never have enjoyed such influence if it had not already developed a powerful nation-brand. In other words, the public diplomacy efforts online through *weibo* would have fallen on deaf ears if the Chinese audience was not already predisposed to the "idea" of Canada. This "idea" of Canada had organically developed over decades and was mythologized by the Chinese government itself through the virtual deification of Dr. Norman Bethune in Chinese schoolbooks as a result of his heroic service with the Communist Eighth Route Army during the second Sino–Japanese War. To this author's knowledge there was no master brand developed for Canada in China. The public diplomacy as practiced by the Canadian embassy started with an advantage that, for example, Mexico or South Africa or Australia or Poland do not possess in China.

The case also shows that, despite the lack of any concerted effort to develop a master brand for Canada in China, this positive nation-brand was "there" as a function of history, and through the accretion of decades of Canadian government policies that served to create the perception that Canada was an open, fair and just society. Of course, it also helped to have millions of Canadians of Chinese descent who traveled back and forth between the two countries, contributing to a narrative within the community about Canada that was independent of any official Government of Canada narrative.

It is also important to note that there is strong evidence that Canada's Web 2.0 diplomacy in Beijing complemented the nation-brand. Social media skeptic Morozov (2009) argues convincingly that the problem with Web 2.0 diplomacy is that there may be a tendency by governments to generate more "spam" because no one actually wants the "ideas" and "positions" that, for example, are being inserted by a foreign ministry into online conversation threads. In short, there's a demand/supply problem: supply is vast (speeches, statements, news releases) but public demand is very modest. Like Nike and Apple, governments must first create a demand for their "online product" of "good ideas." Morozov proposes that rather than dumping content that no one wants online, governments should expand supply in the one area where there is almost an infinite demand: education. Again, the example of the Canadian embassy in Beijing is instructive. Through its *weibo* platform, the embassy *listened* to the online conversations and determined that the Chinese audience wanted more information on educational opportunities in Canada, prompting the embassy to orient its online content strategically to sources on Canadian education and then live-blog from a local education fair. While Canadian diplomats do not have the same latitude to express themselves online as appears to be the case with their British and American counterparts, Canada's experimentation shows the unique attributes of social media – namely, that they are social and personal.

The hierarchy of communication needs for social media channels – a mixture of so-called frivolous messages and strategic messages[5] that are conveyed in interesting and non-bureaucratic language and indexed to local demand to ensure an online response – implies a *limited interactivity*. Embassies will gladly receive (and respond to) public views on how to improve, for example, collaboration on education and science and technology projects, but it is unlikely that they want to initiate an extended back-and-forth dialogue on contentious issues (e.g. human rights). Unless the government is explicitly launching a public dialogue on contentious issues using social media or crowd-sourcing viewpoints, most users will understand that governments have developed official policies and there is not much point in trying to engineer a debate with public officials online. However, as the *weibo* case shows, Canada's online content succeeded in acting as a catalyst for discussions among the Chinese. Therefore, Web 2.0 diplomacy in more closed societies may initiate local debates about previously taboo topics. Again, I would argue that the Canada brand in Canada helped to move the conversation forward in a way that Mexico, for example, could probably not have moved the conversation on sensitive topics.

Intimately related to questions of content is the very philosophy of evaluating effectiveness, in both its programmatic and normative dimensions, of using social media tools as part of the public diplomacy and nation-branding. How, for example, do you measure and evaluate the success of channels that rely on informality in style and are designed to be two-way flows of information? A traditional means of evaluating diplomatic communication is to perform a content analysis of local media, which, in practice, means that embassies are indexing elite attitudes and attempting to set the local agenda through traditional – primarily print – means. However, in the Information Age, the value of diplomats will be contingent on their ability to interpret "slow pulse" trends, often just below the easily observable surface of societies, that augur more fundamental economic and political shifts. These trends cannot be tracked through a reliance on local media monitoring and regular visits (for consultations or to table démarches) with their equivalently classified civil service colleagues in the capital of the country to which they are accredited. Increasingly, such trends will first appear in the blogosphere where, if the diplomat is to exercise real value, they must be assessed by the embassy *before* they make their way to the offline world of government ministries, think tanks, universities and legislatures. Government auditors, for their part, are accustomed to looking for returns on investment, but this is not easy if foreign ministries are justifying their investment of highly trained diplomats by noting that these officials are in far-flung corners of the world following online discussions and immersing themselves in virtual worlds.

For this reason, the Beijing case is instructive since there is tangible and measurable evidence that the Web 2.0 Canadian public diplomacy as practiced through *weibo* delivered results and enhanced Canada's reputation. Canada's use of *weibo* through public diplomacy *sold* the Canadian brand without *selling* it, a strategy that reflects the distinction that Anholt draws between propaganda and statecraft (Anholt 2010). In fact, if they had chosen to do so, the embassy staff could have developed an evaluation framework to determine the degree to which online discussion of Canada's educational system contributed to increased interest in Canada's nation-brand at educational fairs across China. It bears repeating that the existing Canada brand – even in its unmanaged form – served to facilitate this dialogue.

Finally, we return to the implicit normative question posed in this article about whether Canada's Web 2.0 public diplomacy and nation-branding as undertaken by Canada's embassy in Beijing in 2011–2012 is an example of "authentic" and thus minimally managed government communication that values feedback (i.e. without centrally mandated and approved predetermined messages), or was it just different forms of diplomatic statecraft in which the purpose is to implant key messages while giving the appearance of two-way dialogue. With social media channels, foreign ministries have an opportunity to engage in information gathering, message dissemination, monitoring and surveillance, engagement and evaluation – all at the same time and in real time. Some of this activity will be statecraft (message control) and some of this activity will be more authentic – that is, symmetrical and dialogic, allowing for a negotiation of meaning between diplomats and their audiences.

A nation's brand is the container in which public diplomacy – offline and online – is practiced. The pre-existing predispositions of the target audience to the nation-brand – especially if those views are outdated or wrong – is a key variable determining the success of public diplomacy. Obviously, it is much harder to message and engage an audience that is misinformed about your country. Therefore, it stands to reason that carefully managing the nation-brand serves to facilitate and enhance your public diplomacy. There are multiple dimensions to nation-brand management: creating greater coherence among your sub-brands; highlighting the positive aspects of your overall brand and isolating those areas in which your nation is being misperceived; ensuring that your offline and online brand presence is mutually reinforcing; and developing a master brand narrative.

## Conclusion

This article conjectures that a networked digital world has contributed to a greater complementarity between public diplomacy and nation-branding, two concepts that have often been treated in isolation and two forms of government communication that have, for most of their histories, existed in different organizational silos. The case of Canada's *weibo* diplomacy in China suggests that the unique qualities of the digital world, namely the power of networks, scale and reach, and the value of "sharing," make the nation-brand – whether the highly managed nation master brand or an existing historical nation-brand – a more prominent aspect of the overall success of a nation's public diplomacy.

In Canada's case, its nation-brand has been somewhat under-managed, but the fundamentals of Canadian society and governance as expressed through Anholt's nation-brand framework are so strong that they compensate for the relative lack of attention paid to managing the weaknesses in Canada's nation-brand and the very modest government resources devoted to public diplomacy. Moreover, Canada's successful default to a Web 2.0 public diplomacy in the absence of reinvestment in traditional cultural and educational programs allowed it to project the Canada brand in new ways to a much larger audience. This suggests that Canada began revitalizing its public diplomacy before the ascent of the of the Trudeau government to power in 2015, thus demonstrating some continuity between the Harper and Trudeau governments' promotion of the Canada brand (Nimijean 2017).[6]

## Notes

1. See Potter (2009, chapter 2), who provides a detailed analysis of how public diplomacy can be defined.
2. For a discussion of soft power, see Nye (2001).
3. For instance, the visa and immigration section of the embassy had a weekly column, and the economic section offered economic news three times a week; an "Inside the Embassy" online magazine featured stories about the embassy every Thursday with photographs and videos (the most popular item is food). Saturday's column is by the chef and Sunday's is about the Francophonie (Mark McDowell, personal communication with the author, 2012).
4. According to the 2016 Anholt-GfK Nation Index survey, one of Canada's top attributes as a nation was "Respects the rights of citizens and treats them with fairness."
5. One Canadian diplomat with experience with Canada's social media outreach in China suggests that nine out of 10 pieces of social media content produced by foreign ministries should be soft and not directly related to policy goals.
6. Nimijean (2017) argues that an examination of the Trudeau record suggests that there may be more continuity between the governments of Justin Trudeau (2015–present) and Stephen Harper (2006–2015) than is commonly perceived.

## Disclosure statement

The views expressed in this article are the author's alone, and do not necessarily reflect the views of Global Affairs Canada or the Government of Canada.

## Notes on contributor

*Evan H. Potter* is an associate professor, Department of Communications, University of Ottawa.

## References

Anholt, S., 2007. *Competitive identity: the new brand management for nations, cities, regions*. Basingstoke: Palgrave Macmillan. See also the journal, Place Branding and Public Diplomacy.

Anholt, S., 2010. Nation "branding": propaganda or statecraft? *Public Diplomacy Magazine*, 18 May. Available from: http://www.publicdiplomacymagazine.com/nation-branding-propaganda-or-statecraft/

Canada, Citizenship and Immigration, 2010. *New Release. Canada's immigration minister says doors are open to Chinese to come to Canada*. 15 September.

Canada, Prime Minister's Office, 2017. Available from: https://pm.gc.ca/eng/mandate-letters [Accessed 18 April 2018]

Causey, C. and Howard, P.N., 2013. Delivering digital diplomacy: information technologies and the changing business of diplomacy. In A. Arsenault, R. Zaharna, and A. Fisher, eds. *Options for influence in global politics*. New York, NY: Routledge, 144–156.

Dierkes, J. and Legault, G.F., 2014. Time for a blueprint for canadian digital diplomacy. Available from: https://www.opencanada.org/features/time-for-a-blueprint-for-canadian-digital-diplomacy/

Fitzpatrick, K.R., 2010. *The future of U.S. public diplomacy: an uncertain fate*. Boston: Leiden.

GFK, Press Release, 2017. Canada's global brand ranks fourth in study of 50 nations – ties with Japan, 16 November. Available from: http://www.gfk.com/en-us/insights/press-release/canadas-global-brand-ranks-fourth-in-study-of-50-nations-ties-with-japan/ [Accessed 15 May 2018].

Gilboa, E., 2008. Searching for a theory of public diplomacy. *The ANNALS of the American Academy of Political and Social Science*, 616 (1), 55–77.

McDowell, M., 2013. Interview about Sina Weibo. Available from: https://www.youtube.com/watch?v=yBnqlSZ91NA [Accessed 18 April 2018].

McKinnon, M., 2012. Canada's ambassador to China does a little drive-by diplomacy. *The Globe and Mail*, 31 Jan.

Morozov, E., 2009. The future of public diplomacy 2.0, June 9. Available from: http://neteffect.foreignpolicy.com/posts/2009/06/09/the_future_of_public_diplomacy_20

Nimijean, R., 2017. A portrait of Justin Trudeau. *The Monitor*, September/October. Available from: https://www.policyalternatives.ca/publications/monitor/portrait-justin-trudeau

Nye, J.S. Jr., 2001. *The future of power*. New York: Basic Books.

Nye, J.S. Jr. and Owens, W.A., 1996. America's information edge: the nature of power. *Foreign Affairs*, March/April.

Potter, E.H., 2009. *Branding Canada: projecting Canada's soft power through public diplomacy*. Kingston & Montreal: McGill-Queen's University Press.

Shirky, C., 2011. The political power of social media: Technology, the public sphere, and political change. *Foreign Affairs*, January/February.

Singh, J.P. and Macdonald, S., 2017. *Soft power today: measuring the influences and effects*. Edinburgh: The Institute for International Cultural Relations, The University of Edinburgh.

Van Ham, P., 2010. *Social power in international politics*. New York: Routledge.

# 9 Où donc le Canada est-il de retour dans le monde?

Jocelyn Coulon

**RÉSUMÉ**
Alors dans l'opposition, le Parti libéral de Justin Trudeau a sévèrement critiqué la politique étrangère du gouvernement conservateur de Stephen Harper. Il a décrit cette période comme la décennie noire de la diplomatie canadienne. Pendant la campagne électorale de 2015, Trudeau et son équipe ont proposé aux Canadiens une nouvelle orientation sur les questions internationales afin, disaient-il, de placer le Canada sur le chemin du retour sur la scène mondiale. Trois ans plus tard qu'en est-il exactement? Jocelyn Coulon, ancien conseiller de Trudeau et de Stéphane Dion, livre son témoignage et arrive à la conclusion que la politique étrangère du gouvernement libéral ne crée pas une rupture avec les conservateurs, mais bien une continuité.

**ABSTRACT**
While in opposition, Justin Trudeau's Liberal Party was highly critical of the foreign policy led by the Conservative government of Stephen Harper. It described the period as the dark decade of Canadian diplomacy. During the election campaign of 2015, Trudeau and his team offered Canadians a new direction for international issues in order to, they argued, place Canada on the way back to the world stage. Three years later what exactly has happened? Jocelyn Coulon, former adviser to Trudeau and Stéphane Dion, delivers his testimony and comes to the conclusion that the foreign policy of the Liberal government does not represent a break with the Conservatives, but rather a continuity.

Lors de son élection en octobre 2015, Justin Trudeau avait toute la latitude pour mettre en œuvre le programme de politique étrangère riche et original décrit dans la plate-forme du parti et véhiculé pendant la campagne électorale. Sur le papier, ce programme renouait avec la grande tradition d'activisme diplomatique qui a caractérisé la diplomatie canadienne jusqu'à l'élection des conservateurs en 2006. Trudeau et son équipe avaient d'ailleurs forgé un slogan fort sur la future diplomatie libérale afin de marquer leur différence par rapport aux conservateurs : si les Canadiens élisaient le Parti libéral, « le Canada serait de retour » sur la scène internationale.

Le programme libéral était le fruit des réflexions d'experts réunis au sein du Conseil consultatif en relations internationales mis sur pied par le Parti libéral en 2014 et dont l'objectif était de conseiller Trudeau sur la future politique étrangère d'un gouvernement libéral. J'étais un de ces experts avant de rejoindre le cabinet de l'ex-ministre des affaires étrangères, Stéphane Dion, à titre de conseiller politique. Trudeau et les membres du Conseil ont aussi profité des idées mises de l'avant par Roland Paris, professeur à l'Université d'Ottawa et futur conseiller diplomatique du premier ministre. Paris a cristallisé la dichotomie entre libéraux et conservateurs dans un texte au vitriol sur la politique étrangère de Stephen Harper publié par le *Globe and Mail* un an avant l'élection et intitulé « Canada's decade of diplomatic darkness ».

Le décor était planté, et tout indiquait qu'avec un gouvernement libéral, le soleil allait enfin se lever sur la diplomatie canadienne. Presque trois ans après l'accession de Trudeau au pouvoir, qu'en est-il exactement? La question est d'autant plus pertinente que le même Roland Paris, de retour à l'université, a osé tirer un premier coup de semonce.

Sur son blogue de l'Université d'Ottawa, il s'est demandé à quel moment le premier ministre « convertira sa célébrité mondiale en action » (Paris 2017). Trudeau a aujourd'hui l'occasion d'imprimer sa marque sur la politique internationale, écrit Paris, « d'exercer son influence sur des questions précises, et d'utiliser la réputation dont il jouit dans le monde pour mobiliser l'opinion internationale ». L'expert en relations internationales est bien conscient du caractère éphémère d'une situation donnée. Il faut saisir le moment pendant qu'il passe. « Peu importe la cause que choisit Trudeau, il serait dommage qu'il ne mette pas à profit tout son "capital politique mondial" pendant qu'il en a encore … . D'autres premiers ministres canadiens ont accompli de grandes choses tout en jouissant d'une visibilité internationale beaucoup moins grande. »

En effet, au cours des 50 dernières années, la plupart des premiers ministres ont marqué les relations internationales du Canada par des décisions audacieuses ou controversées, et souvent dès les premières années de leur mandat.

Pierre Elliott Trudeau a reconnu la Chine communiste, s'est rapproché des pays du Sud et s'est lancé dans une campagne pour la réduction des armes nucléaires. Brian Mulroney a négocié le traité de libre-échange avec les États-Unis, animé la campagne mondiale contre l'apartheid en Afrique du Sud et, avec le président français François Mitterrand, créé la Francophonie. Jean Chrétien s'est fait le partisan d'une nouvelle approche en relation internationale – la sécurité humaine – qui a entraîné la signature du Traité d'interdiction des mines antipersonnel et la création de la Cour pénale internationale. Il a dit non à la participation du Canada à la guerre contre l'Irak en 2003. Stephen Harper a militarisé la politique étrangère canadienne, ignoré l'Organisation des Nations unies (ONU) et engagé les négociations sur les traités de libre-échange avec l'Europe et les États de l'Asie-Pacifique, et celles sur l'Accord de Paris sur les changements climatiques.

## Le plan du gouvernement

Le retour du Canada sur la scène internationale préconisé par Justin Trudeau s'inscrivait donc dans la logique adoptée par ces prédécesseurs d'un Canada, puissance moyenne, disposé à intervenir afin d'assurer la paix et la sécurité, et de soutenir l'ordre libéral international. Cette aspiration se retrouve d'ailleurs dans les discussions au Conseil consultatif sur les relations internationales, dans la plate-forme du parti et dans les déclarations de Trudeau et de ses ministres. La « décennie de noirceur » du gouvernement Harper fournissait au gouvernement libéral les raisons d'aller beaucoup plus loin encore dans la promotion et l'affirmation d'une politique fondée sur l'internationalisme libéral.

La plate-forme libérale est à cet égard assez éclairante. Avant d'énumérer les programmes qui redonneront au Canada toute sa place dans le monde, les rédacteurs utilisent à fond le vocabulaire de l'internationalisme libéral : avec les libéraux, le gouvernement « rétablira le leadership » du Canada dans le monde, « rebâtira des ponts » avec les États-Unis et la communauté internationale, « aidera les plus pauvres » dans les pays en développement, « renouvellera son engagement » dans les missions de Casques bleus, « fournira une aide humanitaire » lors de crises et de catastrophes naturelles, et se montrera attentif à la « souffrance » et ouvert « aux réfugiés ». La plate-forme libérale se réalisera à travers des politiques et des programmes empreints « de compassion » et de « bienveillance ». C'est le triomphe de ce que les Américains appellent le « soft power », la puissance douce, sur le « hard power », la puissance dure, si chère aux yeux de Stephen Harper et des conservateurs.

Les engagements contenus dans la plate-forme et dans les discours, et les options développées au gouvernement à l'époque où Stéphane Dion était ministre des Affaires étrangères, reflétaient cette rhétorique : il était envisagé de s'engager sérieusement dans une grande opération de paix de l'ONU en Afrique; d'augmenter l'aide au développement et les dépenses de défense; de renouer le dialogue avec la Russie; de remettre à plat les relations avec la Chine; de revoir les votes pro-Israël du gouvernement conservateur à l'Assemblée générale de l'ONU sur la question israélo–palestinienne afin de respecter les principes du droit international tout en évitant de stigmatiser Israël; de retisser des liens avec l'Afrique; de donner une orientation progressiste et féministe à la politique étrangère en mettant l'accent sur les droits des travailleurs et des femmes dans les accords de commerce et dans les programmes d'aide; enfin, de renouer avec le multilatéralisme avec comme objectif de rejoindre le Conseil de sécurité à titre de membre non permanent. Le *soft power* domine l'agenda libéral, mais le *hard power* garde aussi sa place.

## Où donc le Canada est-il au juste ?

Au moment où cet article était mis sous presse, le Canada accueillait à La Malbaie, au Québec, les leaders des pays du Groupe des Sept (G7). Dans le contexte de ce sommet, le moins qu'on puisse dire est que le gouvernement Trudeau se distingue par le provincialisme de sa politique étrangère. De l'ambitieux programme présenté aux électeurs et développé lors de la première année au pouvoir, il reste peu de réalisations concrètes. On se demande même où trouve-t-on au juste le Canada de Trudeau sur la scène internationale.

Pour le moment, le seul élément positif est la redéfinition et l'approfondissement des relations avec la Chine. Pour la première fois depuis 1987, le gouvernement a entièrement revu et refondé la relation sino–canadienne afin de lui donner un caractère stratégique dans un contexte où la Chine, devenue la deuxième économie du monde, est en passe de dominer la région Asie-Pacifique. Si le rapprochement avec la Chine produit les résultats escomptés dans la stratégie adoptée par le gouvernement, ce sera le plus grand succès de politique étrangère de Trudeau.

On ne peut en dire autant à propos des autres aspects de cette politique. (Je mets ici entre parenthèses la relation avec les États-Unis dont la profondeur et la complexité demanderaient un article à lui tout seul. Il suffit de dire que la renégociation de l'Accord de libre-échange nord-américain (ALENA), quel que soit son avenir, ne découle pas d'une initiative canadienne, mais a été imposée par l'administration Trump.)

En décembre 2016, le premier ministre avait en main un plan visant à assumer le leadership de la Mission de l'ONU au Mali (MINUSMA) au point où l'ONU avait auditionné un général canadien afin qu'il prenne le commandement de la force. Deux ans plus tard, Trudeau a réduit le rôle du Canada à celui de pourvoyeur réticent d'hélicoptères. La politique d'aide au développement a reçu un nouvel emballage – féministe – tout en cachant l'essentiel, c'est-à-dire la chute constante et dramatique des ressources financières consacrées à cette aide si indispensable au développement de certains pays dont la majorité se retrouve en Afrique. Cette Afrique est tout aussi ignorée par le présent gouvernement que par le précédent. Sur le conflit israélo–palestinien, le gouvernement a refusé de changer la politique suivie par les conservateurs. Même constat avec la Russie où, au lieu de faire preuve d'audace et de courage, la ministre des Affaires étrangères, Chrystia Freeland, prend un malin plaisir à répandre de l'huile sur le feu en poussant à l'adoption de nouvelles sanctions et en plaçant sur le même pied les terroristes de Daesh et le régime Poutine. À bien y regarder, la politique du gouvernement libéral ne crée pas une rupture avec les conservateurs, mais bien une continuité.

Cette frilosité, ce repli sur soi diplomatique augure mal pour la campagne du Canada au Conseil de sécurité. À ignorer l'Afrique, à répéter les erreurs de Stephen Harper dans le conflit israélo–palestinien, à refuser le dialogue avec la Russie, le Canada fait preuve d'aveuglement et risque l'isolement. Nous connaîtrons le résultat de cette politique en juin 2020 lorsque les États membres de l'ONU devront départager leurs voix entre le Canada, la Norvège et l'Irlande afin de choisir ceux qui occuperont les deux sièges en compétition de membre non permanent du Conseil de sécurité.

Il est difficile de saisir au juste pourquoi le premier ministre a renié une bonne partie de son programme de politique étrangère et poursuivi celui du précédent gouvernement conservateur. Contrairement à la plupart de ses prédécesseurs depuis son père, Justin Trudeau est arrivé au pouvoir sans aucune véritable expérience et connaissance du monde. Son conseiller diplomatique, Roland Paris, a brusquement « démissionné » sept mois à peine après sa nomination. Quant au ministre Stéphane Dion, il entretenait des relations tendues avec Trudeau et n'a jamais réussi, au cours des 14 mois où il fut aux Affaires étrangères, à rencontrer une seule fois le premier ministre en tête-à-tête pour discuter des orientations de politique internationale du pays.

Qu'un tel dysfonctionnement puisse exister au sein de l'appareil gouvernemental chargé de définir et de mettre en oeuvre la politique étrangère est étonnant. On peut tenter plusieurs explications. L'exercice du pouvoir a visiblement rendu le premier ministre prudent et craintif face à des initiatives (la participation aux opérations de paix, les votes à l'ONU sur le conflit israélo–palestinien, le dialogue avec la Russie) qu'il avait du mal à maîtriser. L'arrivée de Donald Trump à la présidence des États-Unis et la remise en question de l'ALENA ont mobilisé toutes les ressources du gouvernement au détriment des autres dossiers. Trudeau trouvait sans doute Dion trop activiste, trop pressé. Quant à Paris, l'universitaire semble ne jamais avoir été en mesure de s'insérer dans le premier cercle des conseillers du premier ministre où, visiblement, sa conception du Canada dans le monde, telle qu'exprimée dans un important article à la base de la plate-forme libérale, n'a pas réussi à s'imposer (Paris 2014).

Enfin, il est possible que la promotion de Chrystia Freeland aux Affaires étrangères reflète mieux les idées dominantes (pro-américaines et antirusses) chez les conseillers du premier ministre. Il est trop tôt pour développer un argumentaire bien informé sur le comportement du premier ministre et de son équipe. Les historiens et les politologues devront fouiller les archives et interroger les acteurs pour en savoir plus.

Il fut un temps, pas si lointain d'ailleurs, où le Canada était une véritable puissance moyenne avec une politique étrangère originale et créative. Sa présence au G7 signifiait quelque chose. Ses initiatives – les Casques bleus, la Cour pénale internationale, le traité antimines, la création du Groupe des Vingt (G20), la campagne contre l'apartheid, l'aide au développement – lui donnaient une voix au chapitre. Aujourd'hui, le Canada n'est plus la septième économie du monde (elle est la dixième et sera remplacée en 2019 par la Corée du Sud) et son statut dans le système international ne cesse de décliner. Le monde se reconfigure autour des grandes puissances traditionnelles et des nouvelles émergentes, et le Canada est de plus en plus relégué aux marges.

Peut-être, après tout, le Canada n'est-il qu'une puissance parmi tant d'autres dont le représentant, Justin Trudeau, est l'astre qui lui permet encore de briller pour quelque temps encore.

## Disclosure statement

No potential conflict of interest was reported by the author.

## Notes on contributor

*Jocelyn Coulon* est chercheur au Centre d'études et de recherches internationales de l'Université de Montréal (CÉRIUM) et fellow au Canadian Global Affairs Institute (CGAI). Il a été membre du Conseil consultatif sur les affaires internationales de Justin Trudeau, en 2014–2015, et conseiller politique principal de l'ex-ministre des Affaires étrangères Stéphane Dion, en 2016–2017. Il vient de publier Un selfie avec Justin Trudeau. Regard critique sur la diplomatie du premier ministre, chez Québec Amérique (2018).

## Référence

Paris, Roland, 2014. Are Canadians still liberal internationalists? Foreign policy and public opinion in the Harper era. *International Journal*, 69 (3), 274–307.

Paris, Roland, 2017. When and How Will Trudeau Convert His Global Celebrity into Action? 5 août 2017, traduction de l'anglais.

## 10 "Canada's back" – can the Trudeau government resuscitate Canadian diplomacy?

Daryl Copeland

**ABSTRACT**
Canadian Prime Minister Justin Trudeau and his ministers have been fond of emphasizing that "Canada is back" on the global stage. Defense and development reviews have been completed, but, with the exception of Foreign Minister Freeland's brief parliamentary address in June 2017, little is known of the government's intentions regarding international policy, diplomacy or grand strategy. This analysis reviews key developments during the transition from the Cold War to the globalization age, examines Canada's evolving place in the post-war world, and assesses that the performance of the government through to mid-term has been, at best, mixed. To improve results, the author sketches an ambitious five-point plan for fundamental diplomatic, institutional and international policy transformation.

**RÉSUMÉ**
Le Premier ministre canadien, Justin Trudeau, et ses ministres, se plaisent à souligner que « le Canada est de retour » sur la scène mondiale. Un examen de la défense et du développement a été effectué mais, à l'exception du bref discours de Mme Freeland, Ministre des Affaires étrangères, au Parlement en juin 2017, on connaît mal les intentions du gouvernement en matière de politique internationale, de diplomatie ou de grande stratégie. Cette analyse passe en revue les développement clés correspondant à la période de la Guerre froide à celle de la mondialisation, examine la position en évolution du Canada dans le monde d'après-guerre, et vérifie que la performance du gouvernement, à moyen terme, a été, au mieux, mitigée. Dans une perspective d'amélioration des résultats, l'auteur esquisse, en cinq points, un plan ambitieux de transformation fondamentale de la diplomatie, des institutions et de la politique internationale.

### Cold War Comfort – the way we were

In the wake of a series of disturbing events that have left many fearing a generalized descent into chaos, and a growing sense of uncertainty, if not unease, with the continuing drift of Canadian foreign policy, it all seems so long ago and far away. Yet surviving baby boomers and most Gen-Xers will remember the elegant simplicity and terrifying symmetry of the Cold War years, 1947–1991. Best understood as a binary construction, the Cold War featured a planet divided neatly between the Free (First) and the Communist (Second) Worlds, each with their respective client states and spheres of influence (in the Third World). Competing blocs were led by a metropolitan center – the United States of America or the Union of Soviet Socialist Republics – and the world atlas of the day was dominated by large swathes of red and blue. In a rather white-bread, middle-of-the-road, middle-class consensus, most Canadians seemed content with their country's place in the wider world.

With its purges, parades, multifarious back channels and powerful, iconic imagery, the Cold War occupied vast tracts of the collective imagination. There were air raid sirens, basement and backyard bomb shelters, "duck and cover" exercises in public schools and regular headlines warning us of the ubiquitous Communist threat. Rabid finger-pointing reached an apogee during the McCarthy hearings, and fearmongering attained levels not to be seen again until after 9/11.

Beneath the gleaming surface of missiles, warheads, and intercontinental bombers on 24-hour standby, deterrence, containment and Mutually Assured Destruction ensured that the "Red Menace" and the "Capitalist Imperialists" remained at bay, albeit with daggers drawn. First strike, throw weight, launch on warning ... power was measured in the kilo-tonnage of warheads, and influence calibrated in numbers of hardened silos and submarine-launched ballistic missiles. Terrifying prospects – ranging from urban incineration to radioactive clouds and black rain, to endless nuclear winter – made it difficult for most people to "stop worrying and love the bomb."

Ironically, although the brink was sometimes approached, that heavily armed peace provided the basis for almost a half-century of Cold War comfort. The apocalypse was averted. International relations, if dumbed down and punctuated by proxy wars and occasional near catastrophes such as the Berlin Blockade or Cuban Missile Crisis, were for the most part stable and orderly, patterned and predictable. Then as now, military establishments thrived, demonstrating convincingly that they work best when not used.

Still, a hoard of treasure was squandered and plenty of blood was spilled. Death squads and rebel groups were armed and trained. Nasty regimes were propped up – plus ça change – elected ones subverted, and whole generations deprived of their most basic rights. But many of these events seemed part of a script. Checkpoint Charlie, the crossing point between East and West Berlin, was made famous in spy novels and films. The capture of a US Navy vessel, the USS *Pueblo*, during an intelligence mission off the North Korean coast, and the alleged attacks by the North Vietnamese against US destroyers, which led to the Gulf of Tonkin Resolution and the ill-fated American military intervention across Southeast Asia, seemed to come right out of central casting. And all of it was chronicled in the *Pentagon Papers*. From time to time, sparks flew around the perimeter and conflicts – in Korea, Cuba or Vietnam – threatened to escalate into something larger and more dangerous. In the end, however, most of the confrontations abated and the lid was screwed back on.

Subtle, it was not. Yet the bipolar world order model set out the agreed strategic geography, and rules came to be easily enough understood. As the Cold War ebbed and flowed, with periods of détente interspersed with moments of intense drama, there developed a certain degree of familiarity, continuity, even predictability.

That was the way we were, and at minimum the long superpower standoff did offer some scope for diplomacy. Canadian officials rarely failed to step up to the plate.

As a helpful fixer, honest broker and pioneering peacekeeper, Canada played an oversized international role in the second half of the twentieth century. From the fashioning of post-war multilateral institutions to Suez, from North–South relations to the Earth Summit (United Nations Conference on Environment and Development, UNCED) to the Human Security Agenda, Canadian diplomatic activism was palpable.

That all changed, however, under the Harper Conservatives. During that period the revolving-door foreign ministry endured seven mainly indifferent, and sometimes antagonistic, ministers. Over the course of a decade of retrogression and retreat, the Boy Scout morphed into a warrior nation wannabe, and Canada's once widely respected brand was spoiled.

And now? Amidst the anxiety and uncertainty of present times, at Davos, in the United Nations (UN), and elsewhere, Prime Minister (PM) Trudeau has placed the international community on notice that "Canada's back." Although many analysts seem prepared to extend the benefit of the doubt, evidence of substantial delivery on that pledge is in fact scarce. While there have been changes in tone (the UN), approach (listening and lingering rather than lecturing and leaving) and content (climate change), we have not yet seen much heavy lifting. Calling upon the UN General Assembly to discuss the conflict in Syria may make headlines, but it is not likely to bring peace. And, from dithering over Columbia to flying blind into Mali, we have certainly underdelivered on peacekeeping promises. Instead, decisions such as approving the sale of light armored vehicles to Saudi Arabia, and continued dissembling on the treatment of Afghan detainees, all echo Harper-era positions and send contradictory, even subversive signals.

If this country is to resume the kind of diplomatic initiative for which it was once renown, including success in its current G7 Presidency and bid for a seat on the UN Security Council in 2021, full account will have to be taken of the three fundamental features of the transformed operating environment. These attributes will condition, if not determine the success or failure of future Canadian forays. And in terms of a detailed assessment of the government's performance at mid-term, the judgement is certainly mixed.

In important respects, there is no way to go but up.

## Globalization, power shift and heteropolarity: the way things are

We have seen that during the Cold War period, whatever its many hazards, Canadians were able to find ample room for diplomatic maneuver, and, occasionally, to lead.

Are accessible openings still available today?

Perhaps, and some have recently been seized, but clearly, navigation is difficult. World order has given way to a *whirled* order, with many of the old distinctions and assumptions, as if placed in a blender, either blurred or erased. There is less political or ideological conviction, and more volatility, uncertainty, complexity and ambiguity. In the 25 years since the Soviet Union imploded and the icy grip of Cold War constraint melted away, much has changed. The Great Thaw has transformed the operating environment, freeing up virulent strains of ethno-nationalism, nourishing political violence and religious extremism, and – much more significantly – gestating a new threat set.

Defining features?

(1) ***Intensified globalization.*** With ever-increasing levels of trade, investment, travel and migration, globalization accelerates time while compressing and deterritorializing

political space. Paradoxical, totalizing and highly asymmetrical, it both integrates and fragments, connects and differentiates. Driven by the revolution in information and communication technologies, it is the defining historical process of our times. Resilient and complex, the globalization age came fully into its own at the end of the Cold War, and has survived the Asian economic crisis of 1997–1998, the bursting of the tech bubble in 2001, the passing of the US unipolar moment, and the Great Recession of 2008–2009. Amidst the raging debate, it remains with us still.

Globalization's flagship is the Internet, and its transnational tides have eroded sovereignty and reduced the importance of borders. That said, neo-liberal globalization is not a neutral force. It is inextricably linked to deregulation, privatization, free trade and austerity, all parts of a laissez-faire package intended to reduce the size and scope of government and enlarge the role of the private sector. Globalization creates wealth, but not for all. Its tendency toward the socialization of costs and privatization of gains exacerbates inequality and heightens distributive injustice. By relying on highly complex technologies and centralized systems, communications in the globalization age are highly prone to manipulation and vulnerable to disruption. By polarizing at all levels, globalization creates deeper divides, sharper edges, winners and losers. Whatever its virtues – not least the efficient allocation of productive resources – the greater connectivity that is a hallmark of globalization has also, paradoxically, engendered mass anxiety, resentment and alienation.

Science and technology (S&T) drive globalization, but function as a two-edged sword, providing solutions to the problems of poverty and suffering, but simultaneously degrading, eroding, and supplying the tools that contribute to conflict and exploitation. On globalization's underside – in the world's banlieues, barrios and export-processing zones – underdevelopment and insecurity flourish. The erstwhile global village looks increasingly like a modern-day Dickensian dystopia, a smattering of gated "green zones" engulfed by a seething sea of shantytowns. Brexit, Trump, populism, plutocracy … cosmopolitan, but unrepresentative elites most everywhere are closing ranks and circling the wagons as the tribes rise and the demons multiply.

(2) **Power shift.** Since leaving behind the comparative stability of the Cold War, power at all levels is now very much on the move. Much has been made of the emergence of BRICS (Brazil, Russia, India, China, South Africa) and migration of the global political economy's center of gravity from the North Atlantic to the Asia Pacific. Of equal significance is the end of state-centricity in international relations and the concomitant emergence of new actors. Foreign ministries, for their part, have lost a good deal of their turf to cabinet offices, executive bodies and other government departments and levels of government. Power is always restless, and is once again on the move, shifting up (to central agencies and supra-national institutions), out (to multinational corporations, non-governmental organizations (NGOs), private philanthropic foundations,) and down (to sub-national players such as states, provinces, cities, and even wealthy celebrities).

Both rising and declining power require careful handling and management. Given the stakes associated with the proliferation of weapons of mass destruction, we must do a better job of managing the shift than was the case during the twentieth or previous centuries, when war served as the ultimate arbiter. In this very fluid environment, traditional methods and tools will need to be supplemented by less conventional, more innovative approaches to diplomatic practice and representation.

(3) **Heteropolis rising.** Received wisdom regarding a return to multipolarity notwithstanding, the model of world order currently under construction is better described as *heteropolar*. During the multi- and bi-polar eras that marked the past few centuries, the sources and vectors of power and influence among countries at broadly analogous levels of development were for the most part similar and easy to measure and calibrate – military might, population size, national wealth, territorial extent, number of colonial possessions, and so forth. Today those sources and vectors are characterized by difference (heterogeneity) rather than similarity (homogeneity), and hence are much more difficult to compare or balance.

Great statesmen with longstanding interpersonal familiarity – think Metternich, Castlereagh and Talleyrand – each with a slightly different hand but playing from the same deck, no longer gather regularly to negotiate over green felt tables. Unlike the clubby days of the Congress of Vienna and Concert of Europe, in the twenty-first century the United States, China, Russia, India, Brazil, Turkey, Indonesia and Japan have little in common. Moreover, many poles are not states – they may be multinational corporations, groups of states (Association of Southeast Asian Nations (ASEAN), the European Union), NGOs (Medecins sans Frontières, Amnesty International), or certain individuals (Bill Gates, Bono). In the emerging *heteropolis*, the pursuit of any kind of equilibrium has become more complex and difficult. This world order in the making will be diverse and dynamic, but messy, complicated and highly competitive.

The effective management of global issues, of conflicting interests, and of the planetary commons which must be shared, will above all require evidence-based policy- and decision-making, and knowledge-based, technologically enabled problem-solving. As there are no military solutions to the most pressing challenges facing humanity, these functions will of necessity depend primarily upon diplomacy rather than defense.

## Looking back is no substitute for being back

What, then, does a world in ceaseless transformation mean for Canadian diplomacy and international policy?

Since the last burst of Canadian international activism under the direction of Foreign Minister Lloyd Axworthy 1996–2000, the operating environment for diplomacy has continued to evolve. Moreover, it has been a long time since Canadian leadership helped bring to fruition the Land Mine Ban Treaty, the International Criminal Court, the Kimberly Process to curb trafficking in "blood diamonds," and efforts to regulate the trade in small arms and address the problem of children in conflict. The Canadian-convened International Commission on Intervention and State Sovereignty produced its influential Responsibility to Protect report in 2001, but in subsequent years this country has been largely absent from the world stage. With the exception of the Harper government's controversial foray into maternal, newborn and child health and participation in ill-starred military interventions in Afghanistan and Libya, Canada's once-ubiquitous presence in the international arena became spectral, and our democracy deeply corroded.

Worse yet, far too many of those who actively shaped Canadian policy at that time, and, by defending it, helped to legitimize those disastrous military misadventures, have seen their unquestioning dedication to folly richly rewarded. Instead of being called to account publicly, a veritable hive of both civilian and military officials, as well as politicians – including everyone from the ticket punchers to the architects and cheerleaders – have prospered, undisturbed, individually and privately.

That unacceptable situation, in conjunction with the likely violations of international humanitarian law related to Canadian treatment of Afghan detainees, represents unfinished business of the first order. If left untreated, it will continue to fester like an open sore on the bosom of the body politic. Although neither excised nor even cauterized, the fact is that all of Canada's major political parties, despite the mountains of evidence and every good reason to the contrary, supported the move from the UN's peacekeeping and democratic development mission in Kabul in favor of signing on to Operation Enduring Freedom and war-fighting in Kandahar, bought into the dubious Manley Report, and approved extensions of the counterinsurgency combat operation.

That there is blood on so many hands has to date effectively obviated any willingness to undertake the sort of rigorous public enquiry required (i.e. one equipped with full powers to investigate and subpoena). The constant stonewalling by both this and the previous government has concurrently dampened any vestigial political enthusiasm for launching a searching re-examination of the events and their causes, or, and even less so, inviting the judicial intercession of the International Criminal Court.

For the sake of the Canadian brand – and not to mention a whole host of even more compelling reasons – the *status quo* must not be allowed to stand. Absent the necessary surgical remedies, the rot will inevitably spread.

The Trudeau government has been fond of proclaiming that "Canada's back," and has taken some steps, both symbolic and substantive, to modify this country's international engagement. Set against raised expectations and a decade of foreign policy retrogression, however, overall performance has been underwhelming. The Canada to which the PM refers has been a long time gone. The erstwhile honest broker, helpful fixer, compassionate aid donor, pioneer of creative policy ideas and purveyor of good offices morphed during the Harper years into the Colossal Fossil, an obstruction to environmental progress, a pariah to be avoided. The ongoing effort to reconnect with a storied internationalist past won't in itself be enough.

While in some respects different in tone, content and overall direction, several aspects of the new government's record to date – mixed signals on climate change, a lack of significant reinvestment in international policy institutions and an absence of global initiative – suggest real cause for concern. The endless charm offensive in Washington and upping of Canada's ground game elsewhere in the United States have yet to show much in terms of results. Moreover, the unnecessary intervention in Syria/Iraq, provocative deployments to the Baltic states, and an incoherent approach to arms exports and non-proliferation have raised some disturbing questions. Spending on official development assistance remains below 2011 levels, and more far-reaching and enlightened changes in policy direction have yet to begin. This gathering of dark clouds and the lack of a coherent international policy strategy and objectives may test PM Trudeau's ability to credibly project his trademark "sunny ways" into the future.

As a point of departure, it will be incumbent upon Canadian policymakers to recognize that in the globalizing *heteropolis*, security is no longer a martial art. Instead, it is a function of long-term, equitable and sustainable development – an imperative by no means limited to what was once referred to as the Third World. Security and development have become indivisible, two sides of the same coin, with the welfare of the human person, rather than the state or alliance, as the central referent. Think the elimination of fear and want, and the meeting of basic needs in the absence of violence and unreasonable obstacles. Responsibility for advancing security and development, like the challenge of balancing asymmetrical power, must fall upon diplomacy rather than defense. The military is both too sharp and too dull an instrument with which to address complex global issues.

Someone should tell Minister Freeland, who seems enthralled, and in large part blinded by hard power.

Ditto for the PM, who despite the adulation from the once-adoring international media seems way out of his depth when it comes to diplomacy and international affairs, as seen in his widely-panned 2018 trip to India.

Today, the most profound threats to mankind's survival – as well as the possible solutions – are intimately related to S&T. Climate change, diminishing biodiversity, urbanization, environmental collapse, pandemic disease ... these "wicked" transnational challenges that together constitute the new threat set require the application of knowledge-based, technologically enabled problem solving. Canada, however, is woefully unprepared to respond, and it is by no means clear that performance is set to improve – just search, by way of example, for any evidence of innovative international policy thinking emanating from the charred remains of Global Affairs Canada (GAC). Far too many of those inside have swilled the Kool-Aid and became corporate clones, while others – an entire cadre of senior officials – have emerged at work's-end only to fast-fade into genteel oblivion, diminished and unrecognizable after the long passage.

As Lord Acton long ago so poignantly observed: There is no worse heresy than that high office sanctifies the holders of it.

Acton captured a hallmark of the culture that has permeated Canada's foreign ministry and infected its staff. With its rigid, labyrinthine and top-down structure, adherence to vaguely authoritarian social norms, and a distinct tendency toward groupthink and running with the herd, today's GAC is a study in public maladministration. Ideas are judged by their provenance rather than their quality. Snickering opprobrium is directed at the unorthodox. Risk is averted rather than managed. Many, and especially among the younger members of GAC's not infrequently talented workforce, have found their potential frustrated, their profession marginalized and sidelined, their job satisfaction undermined by the toxic working environment, and their motivation blunted by dumbed-down taskings typically more transactional than substantive or analytical.

In short, there is a yawning disconnect between the international policy, diplomacy and foreign ministry that we've got, and the remedial mega-project that we need.

## And onward rode the six hundred

What, then, to do?

(1) Launch a comprehensive international policy assessment, rolling in the recent defense and development reviews, and include politics, commerce and immigration. The 2005 International Policy Statement, despatched with extreme prejudice by the Conservatives following their election in 2006, provides a useful model. Roll out the impressive line-up of female cabinet ministers (plus the new Chief Scientist) who have direct international policy responsibilities – talk about *girl power* – to promote their portfolios and put some flesh on the bones of the otherwise emaciated "feminist foreign policy." Engage Canadians in national conversation about grand strategy and the Canadian brand, identifying areas of both capability and constraint in the quest to chart where we are going and how we will get there. In the meantime, keep up the close ground game and charm offensive in the United States, and, in terms of strategic and geopolitical assessment, take closer account of China, India and Russia, all of whom have ambitious game plans and increasing capability.

(2) Re-invest in diplomacy, development and all international policy institutions – Canada is not paying its share, and is seriously underperforming as a contributor to collective efforts. Bring Canada's world view into alignment with the government's domestic vision, and reverse the counterproductive plunder of our diplomatic crown jewels. As the globalization nation, target inequality and polarization by assisting with governance, public administration, the rule of law, democratic institution-building and human rights support. Multilaterally, focus on the achievement of the UN sustainable development goals through the provision of tangible political and material support. Get back into public diplomacy, education promotion, international peacekeeping training, and active participation in peace support operations. To resume diplomatic leadership, initiate the negotiation of an international convention governing the management and stewardship of freshwater resources. Or the Arctic ecosystem. Or managing the impact of climate change. *Something*.

(3) Recast the mandate, mission and structure of GAC to create a central agency for the management of globalization and integration of international policy across government. Functioning at a higher level will require some fundamental re-engineering, legislative action, and a more sophisticated approach to the use of social and digital media. To better generate intelligence and to take full advantage of the vital connection to place, the reform package should feature a more flexible approach toward overseas representation, and an enlarged role for missions abroad. Prerequisites include a revolution in bureaucratic culture and the empowerment of bold, new bureaucratic leadership; and a willingness to speak truth to power, to treat failure as a learning experience, and to offer fearless policy advice. Putting an end to the practice of elevating obsequious apple polishers – ambitious careerists who prefer kissing up and kicking down to actual diplomatic practice, and specialize in making their bosses look good in order to get ahead – is a *sine qua non*. To eliminate the legions of chronically poor performers and create space for new and aspiring entrants, make the demonstrated ability to function at a high level in another organization (public or private sector, NGO, university, think tank, whatever makes sense) a prerequisite to promotion into the Executive Group or assignment abroad as Head of Mission.

(4) Re-build and reinforce relationships in Asia Pacific, which is rapidly re-emerging as the dynamic center of the global economy. Canada's connection to this vital region was severely mismanaged and run down by the Conservatives, not only with giants China and India, but also with the promising ASEAN countries. Jump-start the reconnection by making better use of Canada's large Asian diaspora communities. The Asia Pacific Foundation of Canada has produced some useful new thinking on future Canadian strategy, and Trudeau's visit to China and decision to join both the Asian Infrastructure Investment Bank and Trans Pacific Partnership will help to anchor a larger regional reset. The ride so far has been uneven. Learn from mistakes.

(5) Champion international S&T. Today, the planet's most pressing perils are rooted in science and driven by technology, and have little to do with ideological rivalry, territorial ambition, religious extremism or political violence. These *wicked* problems are immune to the application of armed force. Although subject to occasional revolutions that can overturn the reigning orthodoxy, science remains civilization's best bet for achieving progress. The Trudeau government has finally acted to restore science advice in senior decision-making. Still, little is known about its commitment to science diplomacy, which should be the centerpiece in any resumption of progressive diplomatic activity, and GAC is flying blind, bereft of anything even approaching the requisite S&T policy and analytical capacity.

Much was lost during the decade of darkness, and the unexpected accession of Donald Trump to the American Presidency has undoubtedly complicated the initiation of any rigorous process of reform. That said, for Canada to come back meaningfully on the world stage, our diplomacy and international policy will under any circumstances need a radical, comprehensive and intensive revamp, which is to say the antithesis of most of that which has been demonstrated since November 2015.

It is long past time to put our money where our mouth is. Rhetoric, posturing and a still-adoring global media are no substitute for credible action directed toward the achievement of concrete results. The fiasco of the PM's visit to India visit in February 2018 should be understood as a bellwether, an indelible case in point.

Yet in adversity lies opportunity. To move convincingly beyond the obscurity of former Foreign Minister Stephane Dion's stillborn doctrine of "Responsible Conviction" will require attention to fundamental issues of coherence, capacity and content.

Evidence of that commitment remains to be convincingly registered.

The triumphant declaration that "Canada's back" is morphing rapidly into the more widely held conviction that on the matters that count internationally, Canada isn't even here.

Or there.

Or anywhere.

With an election fast approaching and public sentiment heading decidedly south, time for the government to act with sufficient imagination and deliberation would appear to be running out.

## Disclosure statement

No potential conflict of interest was reported by the author.

## Notes on contributor

Former diplomat *Daryl Copeland* is a research fellow at the Canadian Global Affairs Institute, a policy fellow at the University of Montreal's Centre for International Studies (*CERIUM*), and Senior Advisor, Science Diplomacy at the International Institute for Applied Systems Analysis (IIASA) in Laxenburg, Austria. He recently completed terms as a visiting professor at the Diplomatic Academy of Vienna and the Academy of Diplomacy and International Governance (UK).

# 11 Conclusion

Don't look back: they might be gaining on you

David Carment and Richard Nimijean

In an era of instability, upheaval and change, Canada's place in the world remains uncertain. Under the circumstances, a study of foreign policy branding might seem superfluous, perhaps even trivial. This is, after all, an era of significant geopolitical shifts, unrelenting violent confrontation, nationalism and identity politics. As a result, the institutions in which Canada and its allies have invested significant capital, such as trade, political, and security organizations, are being tested and stretched to the limit. This demonstrates the value of critically examining foreign policy branding. The European Union, for example, faces challenges from within as its member states confront a changing political landscape in the United Kingdom, a European state desperate to break free of the shared values that made a peaceful continent possible. At the same time, EU member countries such as Hungary and Poland stand accused of backsliding and illiberal behaviour as their leaders engage in populist policies that pit them against the values of their EU partners. In so doing, populist politicians are challenging the power of the EU's brand, which offered central and east European member states an immediate boost in image and status produced by adhering to EU values surrounding democracy, human rights and security following the collapse of the Soviet empire (van Ham 2001, 2005).

Closer to home, Canada confronts a distinctly different kind of disruptive politics embodied in the presidency of the United States, whose goals and motivations of putting America "first" are widely shared across a broad political and economic spectrum. The unexpected election of President Donald Trump in 2016 severely disrupted the governing Liberal Party's momentum towards realizing a progressive trade agenda, causing the Trudeau government to shift their focus and prioritize the North American trade relationship above all other interests, especially with regards to potential opportunities with China.

In its unrelenting confrontation with China, for example, the US has shown that it sees that country as a clear rival to American hegemony, an idea that resonates within Congress and among voters of different political stripes. For example, Canada's recently completed trade negotiations with the US and Mexico demonstrate quite clearly that the US has shifted its political and economic priorities to challenging China on the trade front. In turn, Canada's commitments to multilateralism are constantly tested as the US signals its dissatisfaction with current arrangements, whether that be on the trade front through the WTO, climate change or the United Nations. In essence, Canada's fate and future are structurally contingent on its relationship with the United States, a relationship that paradoxically is key to enhancing Canadian sovereignty while at the same time having the potential to reduce it.

In all these cases, democracy itself has provided the fertile ground from which these inward-looking nationalist policies have grown. The rise of populist nationalism may be unanticipated to some, but the possibility has always been embedded in liberal democracies. This is especially true in an era of globalization, with its clear cut economic "winners". But there are also the "losers", whose need for dignity and voice is acutely felt around the world. The economic and political grievances of today, whether real or perceived, have been framed by leaders like Donald Trump as an affront to their dignity.

Not surprisingly, when liberal democracies seek to protect individual dignity and rights, they often do so at the expense of a collective identity that is necessary to unite society, or they engage in a revisionist reframing of historical identities that appeal to a nation's sense of nostalgia. In the absence of a shared identity, further fragmentation and division will continue. Nowhere is this more true than Canada, a country which struggles to define and perhaps even brand itself as distinct, more often than not, in juxtaposition to the United States.

After years of struggling with the question of Canada's place in the world, we now know that Canada's path forward remains undefined. The election of Stephen Harper, for example, not only demonstrated significant dissatisfaction with "large L" Liberal Party policies; it showed that the public was ambivalent toward "small l" liberal political ideology. This so-called "big shift" has had some lasting effects despite the election of Justin Trudeau. In more ways than one can imagine, the current Liberal government under Justin Trudeau has embraced much of the Harper government's Conservative agenda, whether that be on the trade front, defence, development or security.

What is less clear is whether this shift has become embedded in public opinion, post-Harper. In the Canadian context, one clear transformation is the creeping incursion of political marketing strategies to micro target individual voters. In a sense, individual interests are being satisfied by policies that appeal to particular constituencies. The upshot is a political branding process to build support for the Liberal Party – a state of constant electioneering endemic to the era of the permanent campaign (Giasson, Marland, and Lennox Esselment, 2017) – rather than the development and implementation of "good" or "sound" public policy. For example, the Liberal Party's pursuit of a seat on the United Nations Security Council is designed to attract voters to whom that policy appeals, not simply or primarily because it is in Canada's interest. Instead, Canada appeals to a nostalgic vision of Canada as a constructive middle power as a rationale for Canada deserving the seat. This is a necessary strategy, given that Canada's poor record in development assistance will hurt Canada's chances.

A key player in this process is the unelected policy advisor, whose job it is to build political support for the party though specific policy initiatives, often using social media and digital policy to engage ordinary Canadians. This kind of branding through marketing has become a cornerstone of Canadian politics. This suggests that Canada is in desperate need of a strategic vision for its place in the world. Statecraft emanates from building stability through linking domestic opportunities (e.g. a strong economy) with international constraints (finding reliable trade partners).

The continuities from government to government don't stop there. Just like Harper's similar claim a decade earlier, Justin Trudeau signalled that his government would operate according to politically defined Canadian values. Trudeau wanted Canadian politics to be less partisan, yet he portrayed Conservative voters as less than Canadian when he said that

Canada was back. His government increasingly references Harper – and not Conservative Leader Andrew Scheer – to remind voters that his government's values are distinct from his opponents.

In this volume, we find that Liberal branding is often a ploy to differentiate between governments that are at best only superficially different. As Stephen Brown's critique of Trudeau's foreign aid shows, the government's signature policies, such as its new feminist international assistance policy and its progressive trade agenda, are identity politics designed to mobilize support from domestic constituencies.

Following a decade of decline, and challenged on both the left and right, the Liberals recast their brand to pull votes from the Conservatives and especially the NDP. Yet, in power, many of the left-of-centre "values" have been abandoned or severely watered down. Think peacekeeping, a commitment to United Nations reform, a balanced approach to the Middle East, the environment, and climate change. Moves intended to appeal to right-of-centre voters include increased defence spending, strengthening NATO, taking on Russia, and the pursuit of free trade deals, especially the single-minded focus on renegotiating NAFTA.

This ongoing politicization of the Canadian identity shows how rhetorical constructs framed around values are used to distinguish leaders and their parties from one another as their party platforms, especially economically, become less distinct in an era of globalization. This is the essence of domestic brand politics. Emotions and values, more so than policy, are the means and basis for electoral competition. In foreign policy, parties reduce complex issues to "feel good" rhetoric that connects with voters, giving them hope for a better future. This was the case of the response to the 2015 Syrian refugee crisis.[1]

Ultimately, however, the gap between rhetoric and reality, as seen in the Trudeau government's management of the refugee file, is so yawning that a government's inevitable shortcomings nourish the already entrenched sense of cynicism and disappointment with government. The cycle begins anew. Since Louis St. Laurent, prime ministers regularly project politically defined "Canadian values" abroad, not just as signals to global partners, but to Canadian citizens. Today, Trudeau does this with statements on diversity and gender equality. But despite all the window dressing and rhetorical differences across governments, Canadians have seen relative continuity in policies. Economic policies continue to be neoliberal, minimizing the role of government, and they continue to promote free trade.

Indeed, a less engaged Canada is the new normal. Trudeau often speaks of Pearsonian values, yet the pursuit of economic interests – which increases the odds of electoral success – over the promotion of so-called "Canadian values" dominates. His government is on pace to become the least generous aid donor since Pearson. He pays only lip service to the global institutions in which we had a founding role, reflecting ex-Liberal foreign policy aide Jocelyn Coulon's claim (2018) that Trudeau was not overly interested in foreign affairs when he won his party's leadership. His 2017 speech to the UN General Assembly that focused on an apology to Canada's Indigenous peoples, despite a year earlier claiming that Canada was "here to help", shows that domestic politics are always top of mind. While the Trump administration clearly wishes to challenge China on *fair* trade, Canada continues to pursue *free* trade with China despite its opposition to Canada's progressive trade agenda. While the Canadian public has shown an overwhelming desire to curb military equipment sales to Saudi Arabia following the murder of the journalist Jamal Khashoggi (Angus Reid Institute, 2018), the Canadian government is reluctant at best to consider this option.

Polls and pundits reveal increasing fatigue with Trudeau hypocrisy. The government seems long on rhetoric and short on action, providing new opportunities for the opposition. But can they offer something different? Not likely. The battle is to control and redefine the centre as the major parties seek to distinguish themselves by politically redefining Canada's identity and its rhetorical role in the world, even though the broad trajectory of foreign policy is unlikely to change.

The idea that Canadian foreign policy is mostly a branding exercise raises some uncomfortable and perhaps irreconcilable questions, such as "what is Canada?" Perhaps we are not mature enough as a nation and our democracy is too fragile to deal with uncomfortable truths, such as the Afghan detainee scandal, our relationship with Saudi Arabia and Omar Khadr's mistreatment at the hands of CSIS. More pointedly, given that China is the focal point of US policy, Canada has not dealt very well with that shift in strategic orientation. The repeated call for trade diversification, for example, is often made but rarely heeded, and little thought is given to developing alternative economic strategies that lessen Canada's trade dependence on economic powers that subject Canada to their political agendas. If anything, Canada is now more tightly bound to the continent even as it expresses a desire to weaken these ties. This demonstrates the significance of political branding for thinking of Canada as a global actor.

The question is whether those transcendent values that one might describe as "historically" if not "uniquely" Canadian can continue to shape and inform discourse on Canadian foreign policy in an era of disruption and instability. The current Liberal government would have us believe they can and still do. Indeed, the 2015 election platform upon which the Liberals staked their political future was premised on a set of propositions about those values that define Canada's place in the world: its commitment to multilateralism, its respect for human rights, its long-standing support for the rule of law and its position in the world as a middle power with influence and pride of place.

These values not only served the Liberals well in distancing themselves from the previous Harper government; they served as the platform upon which the government has chosen to build its reputation abroad and define itself against the Trump presidency and the concomitant rise of American parochialism. For example, in her speech to parliament in the spring of 2017, Foreign Minister Chrystia Freeland spoke of these values as the means to confront a changing world order beset by revisionism, nationalism and illiberalism. Yet it is clear that this speech, as well as those given by Prime Minster Trudeau since then, are far more about the past than they are about confronting the future. This is problematic. The merit of such rhetoric is constantly challenged on empirical grounds, whether that be Trudeau's palpably contradictory position on climate change and pipelines, selling military equipment to human rights violators like Saudi Arabia, or the government's failure to uphold the International Criminal Court (an entity that Canada was instrumental in creating).

In coming to grips with the increasing gap between rhetoric and reality, we see that the Liberals are at times inconsistent and even at times self-defeating. This volume shows how big these gaps are and in so doing, demonstrates the extent to which the expression of core Canadian values is more of a rhetorical exercise reflecting a branding strategy than a basket of transcendent overarching principles of Canadian foreign policy making. The stakes are high, since such rhetoric is less directed towards making a difference abroad and appears more concerned about the Trudeau government's electoral prospects. This casts doubt about the government's suitability for recalibrating Canada's position in a turbulent world. The 2015 federal election featured a leaders' debate on foreign policy – much welcomed – that should have led to a focused discussion of alternative visions of what Canada stands for – or could – in a world where traditional norms of state conduct are continuously challenged. Instead, we have seen that rhetorical posturing more often than not dominates public debate.

Consider as an example the Liberal government's decision to uphold the Harper government's contract to build and sell LAVs to Saudi Arabia. On the one hand, the decision is consistent with the history of Canadian arms deals and was undertaken with a very specific political and economic calculus. On the other hand, the Liberal decision to uphold the contract – justified through the convoluted doctrine of "responsible conviction" or on the grounds that Canada must live up to its word – is at odds with its public message that Canada wants to be "back" on the world stage to protect and promote human rights.

A subtler contradiction is evident in the "virtue signalling" in Trudeau's speeches abroad, reflecting a self-congratulatory tone that lays claim to being both principled and core to the Canadian identity and that such values can be embodied in a leader. If there is cause for concern, it is simply that political power in Canada is deeply concentrated at the federal level. The Prime Minister is arguably the most powerful actor in Canadian foreign policy. Taken together, the concentration of power and the idea that the PM is himself the repository of core Canadian values is to discount the important role of diverse influences such as the provinces, civil society, cities and ordinary citizens on foreign policy. There are many interests and values instrumental in the making and implementation of foreign policy.

A third example is Canada's wavering commitment to liberal internationalism, a body of values central to how Trudeau brands Canada as a global actor. Despite repeated claims that Canada is a fully engaged multilateral player in diplomacy and trade, the record is rather weak. If Canada has become economically strong, it is largely due to the success of the US market and the expansion of Canada's resource and manufacturing sectors in which our trading relationship with the US is paramount. Successive governments failed to build ties with emerging markets which are now Canada's chief economic competitors. As a result, Canada has fallen behind in market competitiveness. Indeed, our multilateral engagement has mostly focused on the dominance of established powers and the institutions they uphold rather than those institutions that are not dominated by the established powers. Today, Canada's role as a traditional middle power, buttressed by membership in the G-7, is challenged by a changing global economy featuring emerging middle powers and rising economic powerhouses. Canada's relative economic and political decline globally might explain why traditional middle powers seek to preserve the status quo and why leaders seek to convince audiences abroad and at home of their importance.

Canada's leadership on Indigenous issues exemplifies how past policy is ill-suited to projecting Canadian values abroad. On the Arctic Council, we can point to Trudeau's unilateral move to pass the US–Canada Joint Leaders Statement, which drew substantial criticism. The Liberals thus far have implemented very little in UNDRIP and took months to give their support to Bill C-262, legislation to harmonize the declaration within Canadian law. While some may believe Canada is still a leading nation with regards to Indigenous rights, Canada is constantly reprimanded across international human rights forums for its treatment of Indigenous peoples. The Canadian Human Rights Commission, the UN Human Rights Committee, and Amnesty International regularly issue reports condemning Canada's poor performance with respect to Indigenous rights.

Finally, we come to the question of whether the past is a good platform for building Canada's future. In dealing with the Liberal government's core marketing slogan of "Canada is back", we must ask if pursuing a status quo ante strategy merits the attention it has been given. Cognitively, such a proposition is appealing because it implies – and there is some truth to this – that a return to "old style" diplomacy would return us to the glory days of Canada's golden era of diplomacy. But to date there are few indications that such an approach has traction, in so far as inconsistent international conduct impacts international perception of Canada as a country in decline.

Indeed, since the end of the Cold War, Canada's commitment to and involvement in multilateralism and international institutions have shifted due to changes in the global political economy. Today, the multilateralism that Canada helped develop and which was initially beneficial for Canada as a middle power works differently. Canada increasingly must engage with states with different value systems, yet it has not figured out how to make compromises in shaping a new international order. A case in point is Canada's official development assistance. Despite their rhetorical differences, the Trudeau Liberals have not changed much about the way Canada does foreign aid compared to the Conservative practices, except for the slogans they use to promote it. The growing distance of Canadian foreign aid policy and practice from the real needs of developing countries, not to mention the rhetoric the Liberals articulate, demonstrates that foreign aid policies under the more self-consciously internationalist Trudeau government, have, to a certain degree, been characterized by mixed motives. "Canada is back" has proven to be a useful political slogan for Conservatives and Liberals alike. However, as contributors to this volume have demonstrated, "being back" requires action reflecting the values Canadian governments claim they believe in.

The value of foreign policy branding has been demonstrated in a number of the chapters here, and the hazards of choosing rhetoric over tough answers confirmed in others. The path forward for Canada depends on leaders who can transcend parochial electioneering in favour of long-term interests. This volume provides a basis for understanding how that might happen even after Justin Trudeau has left politics and all his selfies behind him.

**Note**

1 See Carment, David, and Richard Nimijean. 2018. "On foreign policy, Trudeau's Liberals are long on rhetoric, short on action." *Hill Times*, June 28.

**References**

Angus Reid Institute. 2018. "Nine-in-ten Canadians say 'no' to future arms deals with Saudi Arabia; divided over cancelling current one." Accessed November 27, 2018. http://angusreid.org/saudi-arabia-canada-khashoggi/.
Carment, David, and Richard Nimijean. 2018. "On foreign policy, Trudeau's Liberals are long on rhetoric, short on action." *Hill Times*, June 28.
Coulon, Jocelyn. 2018. *Un selfie avec Justin Trudeau: regard critique sur la diplomatie du premier ministre*. Montréal: Québec Amérique.

Giasson, Thierry, Alexander J. Marland, and Anna Lennox Esselment. 2017. *Permanent Campaigning in Canada*. Vancouver; Toronto: UBC Press.
van Ham, Peter. 2001. "The Rise of the Brand State: The postmodern politics of image and reputation." *Foreign Affairs* 80(5):2–6.
van Ham, Peter. 2005. "Branding European Power." *Place Branding* 1(2):122–126.

# Index

*Note*: Page numbers in **bold** refer to tables.

@Canada (Twitter account) 89

abortion 24–25
l'Accord de libre-échange nord-américain *see* ALENA
accountability 30, 42
Acton, Lord 130
Afghanistan 15, 31, 66, 129
AFN (Assembly of First Nations) 49, 57–58
Africa 27–28, 32; *see also* South Africa
African Union 55
*Agence québécoise de solidarité internationale* 26
Aglukkaq, L. 53
Akin, D. 4, 50
Alaska 51, 54, 71
Alaska Native Land Claims Settlement 51
ALENA (l'Accord de libre-échange nord-américain) 122
Ames, H. 48
Angus Reid Institute 17
Anholt, S. 3, 5, 107, 116
Anti-Personnel Mine Ban Convention 120
APF (Arctic Policy Framework) 54, 59
Arctic, the 63–78; Canada's brand and 77–78; environmental protection of 51, 52–53, 67, 68, 69–70, 74, **76**, 78; exclusive economic zones (EEZ) 69–72, **73**, 75, **76**, 78; fishing rights 70–71, 74; forecasting 66–78; Indigenous peoples 50–54, 59; offshore extraction 54; North West Passage (NWP) 66, 69–72, **73**, 74–76, 78; seabed resources 71, 74; search and rescue 69, 73–74, **76**, 78; sovereignty 64–69, 75, 77–78
Arctic Council 47, 51–53, 59, 66, 69, **70**, 73, 138
Arctic Environmental Protection Strategy 52
Arctic Peoples' Conference, Copenhagen 51
Arctic Policy Framework *see* APF
Arctic Search and Rescue Agreement 69
Arctic Waters Pollution Prevention Act *see* AWPPA
arts *see* culture
ASEAN (Association of Southeast Asian Nations) 132

Asia Pacific Foundation of Canada 132
Asian Infrastructure Investment Bank 132
Assembly of First Nations *see* AFN
Association of Southeast Asian Nations *see* ASEAN
Atlantic Charter 50
Atlantic provinces 23
Atwal, J. 6
Audet, F. *et al.* (2013) 26
Australia 16, 49, 55, 56, 58
AWPPA (Arctic Waters Pollution Prevention Act) 69
Axworthy, L. 128

Babb, G. 48–49
Baird, J. 88, 91
Bangladesh 29
Beaufort Sea 69
Belanger, Y. 48
Bellegarde, P. 57
Benin 27
Bennett, C. 57
Berger, C. 64
Berger Inquiry 51
Berthiaume, L. 30
Bethune, N. 114
Bibeau, M.-C. 24, 25, 40
Bill C-45 49
Bill C-262 58, 138
Bjola, C. 88
Black, D. 28
Blanchfield, M. 3, 15, 31
Bloomfield, L. 86
Brexit 134
bribery 30
BRICS (Brazil, Russia, India, China, South Africa) 127
Bronskill, J. 2
Bueno de Mesquita, B. 67, 72
Burkina Faso 27
Bush, G.W. 15
Byers, M. 79n5

Campagna, P.F. *et al.* (2013) 65
Campbell, K. **21**
Canada 150 celebrations 59
Canada Council for the Arts 109
Canada–European Union Comprehensive Economic and Trade Agreement 109
Canadian Alliance 22
Canadian Charter of Rights and Freedoms 2, 14
Canadian Coast Guard *see* CCG
Canadian Council for International Co-operation 25
Canadian Environmental Protection Act 49
Canadian Forces *see* CF
Canadian International Development Agency (CIDA) 42
Canadian International Development Platform 7
*Canadian Journal of Development Studies* 26
Cannon, L. 24
Carment, D. *et al.* (2018) 6
Castro, F. 16
Catholicism 24
Causey, C. 110
Central Intelligence Agency 67
CCG (Canadian Coast Guard) 69, **70**, 73
CF (Canadian Forces) 44n2, 65–66
Charlottetown Accord 51
Chartier, C. 57
Chicago World Fair 48
China: and the Arctic 65, 66; foreign policy and 121, 131, 134, 136–137; Trudeau and 16, 132; US and 136; "weibo diplomacy" 104–117
Chrétien, J. 3, **21**, 22, 109, 120
Churchill, W. 50
CIDA *see* Canadian International Development Agency
civil society organizations *see* CSOs
climate change 4, 14, 23, 29, 67, 137
Clinton, H. 24
Coates, K. 55–56, 58
Cold War 124–125
colonialism 14, 47, 59
Come, M.C. 49
Commonwealth 48
Compton, C. 49
Conservative Party: electoral base 20, 22–23, 24, 26–27, 29–30, 32; faith-based organizations and humanitarian assistance 28–29; foreign aid 21–23, 26, 30–31; foreign policy 1, 15, 126, 128–129; gender equality 40; geographic priorities foreign aid 27; Indigenous issues 49, 56–57; International Development and Humanitarian Assistance Civil Society Partnership Policy 26–27; International Policy Statement 131; military sales to Saudi Arabia 138; prioritization of domestic policy 15; public diplomacy 108; social media 114; socially conservative base 24; and women in development 23–24
contraception 24–25, 32

Cooper, A. 47–48
Coulon, J. 136
CSOs (civil society organizations) 41–42
culture 107–109
Curry Jansen, S. 3

Daesh 122
*Daily Mail* 5
decolonization 50
defense 30, 33, 66
DeGeneres, E. 15
Denmark 52, 66, 71
Deskaheh (Levi General) 48
Development Finance Institute *see* FinDev Canada
diasporas 6, 22, 28, 114, 132
Diefenbaker, J. 48
Dierkes, J. 113
Dion, S. 120, 121, 122, 132
diversity 5, 58, 59, 64
domestic challenges 9n2
Drezner, D. 86

economic growth 29, 94, 96
*The Economist* 47, 84
Elsie Initiative 39
emissions targets 4
Emmerson, C. 69
Engle, K. 55
English, J. 50, 52
environmental protection: the Arctic and 51, 52–53, 67, 68, 69–70, 74, **76**, 78; diplomacy and social media 94, 96–97, **98**; Harper and 3; and Indigenous peoples 5; Trudeau and 2, 4, 14
Epcot Center, Florida 64
ethnonationalism 3
EU (European Union) 28, 109, 134
evangelical Christianity 22, 23, 24, 26
extractive industry 25, 27, 51, 54, 109

faith-based organizations 26, 28–29
Fantino, J. 30
Favel, B. 55–56
federal elections *see* general elections
female empowerment 6, 24, 25, 40, 42
feminism: cabinet composition 15; and development 27, 29, 31–33, 34n3, 122; and foreign policy 4, 121, 131; and humanitarian assistance 25; supporters of 25; Trudeau and 15, 23, 39–44; *see also* gender equality
FIAP (Feminist International Assistance Policy) 23, 25, 27, 28, 29, 31–32, 34n3, 39–44
FinDev Canada (Development Finance Institute) 31
Finland 66
First Nations Financial Transparency Act 49
First Nations people 49, 50, 54, 56, 57, 59

Fisheries Act 49
Fonda, J. 5
forecasting 66–78; data and analysis 72–77; model 67–68
foreign aid 19–33; budgets 29–32; effectiveness 30–31, 33; francophone African countries 27–28; geographic priorities 27–28; ODA/GNI ratio 21–22, 29–30, 32; political ideology and 21–22; and trade agenda 27
foreign policy 3–7, 83–100; and the Arctic 54, 64, 68, 77; Conservative Party and 1–2, 7, 15, 84, 85, 86–87, 93, 120–122, 126, 128–129; culture and 108; Liberal Party and 2, 4, 6, 94, 119–123, 137; and neoliberalism 3; principal–agent framework 86–87; privatization and 3; rhetoric and 136; *see also* GAC (Global Affairs Canada); social media and public diplomacy
foreign students 109
France, Embassy of Canada 89
Francis, D. 64, 65, 79n1
Freeland, C. 40, 122, 123, 137
Fuchs, A. *et al.* (2014) 21
Fulbright Program 108
FutureBrand Country Brand Index 14

G7 (Group of Seven) 42, 121, 123, 138
G8 (Group of Eight) 23
GAC (Global Affairs Canada): on the Arctic 53; current 130; on human rights 4; on feminism 25, 27, 42; on foreign aid 30; and foreign policy 84, 85–100; future goals 131–132; and Trudeau 5, 15
gas pipelines 4, 5, 51
gender equality: and social media 94, 96, 97, **98**, 99; Trudeau on 2; women in development 23–25; *see also* female empowerment; feminism; FIAP (Feminist International Assistance Policy)
general elections (federal elections) 2, 6, 22, 26, 27, 92–94, 99, 138
Germany 21, 66
Global Affairs Canada *see* GAC
'global South' and feminism 43
*Global Times*, the 112
globalization 126–127, 131, 135, 136
*The Globe and Mail* 4, 112, 120
gold rush 79n1
Gorbachev, M., Murmansk Speech 51
Greenhill, R. 30
Greenland 51, 66
Grégoire Trudeau, S. 15
Griffith (2011) 78
Griffiths, F. 51, 67
Griffiths, F. *et al.* (2011) 64
Group of Eight *see* G8
Group of Seven *see* G7

Haiti 28, 32
Hale, G. 79n16

van Ham, P. 2
hard power 121
Harper, S.: on the Arctic 64; on colonialism 47; diplomacy 126; election 134; electoral base 20, 22–24, 26–27, 29–30, 32; on the environment 3; faith-based organizations and humanitarian assistance 28–29; foreign aid 20, **21**, 27, 30–31, 32; foreign policy 1–2, 7, 15, 84, 85, 86–87, 93, 120–122, 126, 128–129; and gender equality 40; Indigenous issues 49, 53, 56–57; Israel-Palestine conflict 122; Liberal references to 136; maternal, newborn and child health (MNCH) initiative 23–24; popularity level 17; prioritization of domestic policy 15; reputation 59
heteropolarity, post Cold War 128, 130
homophobia 26
Hopson, E. 51
Howard, P.N. 110
Huebert, R. 65, 67, 78
human rights: Trudeau and 4; and gender equality 40, 44; and Indigenous peoples 48, 55, 56, 57, 139
humanitarian assistance 28–29, 30, 41
humanitarian law, violations of 129

iAffairs 6
IAR *see* international assistance review
Ibbitson, J. 7
ICC (Inuit Circumpolar Conference (now Council)) 51, 52, 57
Ice Exercise 2016 (ICEX) 66, 71
Iceland 66
ICJ *see* International Court of Justice
Idle No More movement 49, 56
ILO *see* International Labour Organization
IMO (International Maritime Organization) 72
INAC (Indigenous and Northern Affairs Canada) 51, 54, 56, 57
independence, national 50
India 6, 16–17, 131
Indian Act 49, 58
Indigenous and Northern Affairs Canada *see* INAC
Indigenous issues 46–60; early 48; environmental issues 5; franchise 48; mental health and suicide 53; Missing and Murdered Indigenous Women and Girls (MMIWG) 49, 50; myth and 64; political empowerment 50–54; self-determination 50, 54, 55, 59; traditional knowledge 53; Trudeau and 49–50, 58–59, 136, 138–139; welfare state 50; *see also* Arctic, the; UNDRIP (United Nations Declaration on the Rights of Indigenous People)
International Assistance Innovation Program 31
international assistance review (IAR) 41
International Commission on Intervention and State Sovereignty, Responsibility to Protect report 128

International Court of Justice (ICJ) 71
International Criminal Court 120
International Decades of the World's Indigenous People 55
international development 39, 94, 96, 97
International Labour Organization (ILO) 54–55
International Maritime Organization see IMO
International Policy Statement 108, 131
International Work Groups for Indigenous Affairs (IWGIA) 50
internationalism 20, 23, 25, 28, 41, 120–121
Inuit Circumpolar Conference (now Council) see ICC
Inuit people 50–51, 52, 54, 56, 59
Inuit Tapiriit Kanatami 51
inuksuks 59
"Investing in Canada" 3
Iraq war 120
Ireland 122
Israel 15, 121
Israel-Palestine conflict 121–122
IWGIA see International Work Groups for Indigenous Affairs

James, P. 68, 79n6
James Bay and Northern Quebec Agreement (JBNQA) 50–51
Jiang, L. 88
Johnston, D. 30
Jones, R.J. 79n6

Kelowna Accord 49
Keskitalo, C. 52
Khashoggi, J. 136
Kuptana, R. 51

Lackenbauer, P.W. 47–48, 66, 67, 78
Lai Changxing 112
*The Lancet* 24
Law of the Sea Conference see LOSC
League of Nations 48
Legault, G.F. 113
LGBTQ issues 15
liberal internationalism 2, 29, 84, 85–86, 99, 120, 138
Liberal Party: and Arctic Policy framework (APF) 54; electoral base 15, 20, 22–23, 25–26, 28–29, 31–33; faith-based non-governmental organizations (NGOs) 26; Feminist International Assistance Policy (FIAP) 23, 25, 27, 28, 29, 31–32, 34n3, 39–44; foreign aid 20, **21**, 23, 27–28, 30–33; foreign policy 2, 4, 6, 94, 119–123, 137; humanitarian assistance 29; Indigenous issues 49–50; public diplomacy 108; and Saudi Arabia 138; Truth and Reconciliation Commission 55; United Nations Security Council 134; and urban elite 15; and women in development 24–25
LOSC (Law of the Sea Conference) 69, 71

Lusztig, M. 68

MacCharles, T. 30
MacKay, P. 4
Mackenzie King, W.L. 48
Mackenzie River Valley 51
Mackey, E. 49
Makivik Corporation 50–51
Mali, UN mission to see MINUSMA
Marland, A. 24, 25
Martin, D. 6, 16
Martin, P. **21**, 22, 27, 29
"Master Brand" 105
McDowell, Mark 111–113
McGill University 2
McKinnon, M. 112
McNee, J. 55–56
Mercredi, O. 48
Métis people 54, 56, 57, 59
Mexico 134
Mikkelsen, C. 50
Miliband, D. 24
MINUSMA (UN Mission in Mali) 4, 122
Missing and Murdered Indigenous Women and Girls (MMIWG) 49, 50
Mitterrand, F. 120
Montreal 28
Morneau, B. 7, 30
Morozov, E. 115
Mulcair, T. 2
Mulroney, B. **21**, 22, 48, 52, 120
Mulroney, D. 6
Muskoka Initiative for MNCH (maternal, newborn and child health) 23–25, 32

Nakimayak, H. 57
nation-brand hexagon 107
national identity 3–4, 39, 41, 42, 43, 64–65, 136–138
*The National Post* 50
Nault, R. 49
Navigable Water Protection Act 49
NDP see New Democratic Party
negative international publicity 109
neoconservativism 22
neoliberalism 2, 3, 136
New Democratic Party (NDP) 2, 22, 29, 32, 58, 136
*The New York Times* 58
New York University 5
New Zealand 16, 48, 49, 55, 56, 58
Newhouse, D. 48
Newman, D. 58
NGOs (non-governmental organizations) 20, 24, 25–28, 32, 41, 67
Niezen, R. 48
Nimijean, R. 3, 14, 65, 77, 78, 117n6
non-governmental organizations see NGOs
Nordic Sami Council 52

Norway 66, 122
Nossal, K.R. 23
Nunavut 51

Obama, B. 14, 16, 53
Oda, B. 24, 30
ODA (official development assistance) 21, 28, 29, 30, 31
ODA/GNI (gross national income) ratio 21–22, 29–30, 32
OECD (Organisation for Economic Co-operation and Development) 21, 30; DAC (Development Assistance Committee) 42
official development assistance *see* ODA
oil resources 14, 54, 109
Ontario 22–23
Organisation for Economic Co-operation and Development *see* OECD

Palestine 25, 121–122
Paris Climate Accord 120
Paris, R. 2, 120, 122
Parkin, D. 5
peacekeeping 4, 5, 15, 23, 39, 126, 129
Pearson, L.B. 23, 136
Peguis First Nation 48
Percival, V. 6
Pettigrew, P. 47
Philippines 27
Potter, E. 64, 88
Prentice, J. 55
privatization 3, 31, 32, 127
Progressive Conservative Party **21**
public diplomacy 83–100, 104–117; social media and 87–100, 105; "weibo diplomacy" 111–117
public diplomacy pyramid *106*
public opinion surveys 16
Putin, V. 122

Quebec 23, 26–28

RAIPON (Russian Association of Indigenous Peoples of the North) 52
Rangers 66
Rankin, P.L. 65
rational choice models 68
Reform Party 22
refugees 5, 15, 29
Reputation Institute 58
Residential School Apology 56
Rohingya refugees 29
*The Rolling Stone* 15, 58
Roosevelt, F. 50
Ruhl, J. 64, 77
Russia 52, 66, 76, 121, 122, 128, 131
Russian Association of Indigenous Peoples of the North *see* RAIPON
Ruth, N. 24

S&T (science and technology) 127, 130, 132
Saganash, R. 58
Sami people 49, 51, 52
Saudi Arabia, military sales to 4, 5, 44, 126, 136, 138
science and technology *see* S&T
Scrivener, D. 52
seal hunts 109
security 6, 51, 94, 96, 97, **98**, 130
Segal, H. 64
sexual and reproductive health and rights (SRSH) 25
Shared Arctic Leadership Model 54
Shields, R. 64
Shirky, C. 105
Simon, M. 51, 52, 54
Six Nations 48
Smith, D. 47, 54
social media and public diplomacy 87–100, 105; foreign policy and 110; policy advisors and 135; Trudeau and 5, 14–15, 84–85, 87–99; Trump and 87; "weibo diplomacy" 111–117
soft power 88, 107, 108, 121
South Africa 48–49, 120
South Korea 123
Sovereign Loans Program 31
Spence, T. 57
SRSH *see* sexual and reproductive health and rights
Staples, L. 52
stereotypes 14, 64
Stevenson, L. 48–49
*Strong, Secure, Engaged* report 44n2
Sustainable Development Working Group 52
Sweden 42, 66
Swiss, L. 34n3
Syria 2, 5, 15, 29, 136

Team Canada trade missions 3, 109
trade 23, 27, 42, 89, 108–109, 134, 136–137
Trans-Pacific Partnership 6, 132
Trudeau, J. 1–7; and Arctic affairs 53–54; "Canada's back" 2, 4, 124–132; and diplomacy 124–132; electoral base 15, 20, 22–23, 25–26, 28–29, 31–33; feminism 23, 39–44; foreign aid **21**, 27–28, 30–33; foreign policy 2, 4, 6, 94, 119–123, 137; humanitarian assistance 29; and Indigenous issues 49–50, 58–59, 136, 138–139; international brand image 13–17; on maternal, newborn and child health (MNCH) 24–25; politically defined values 135–136; popularity level 17; public diplomacy 108–109; and social media 5, 14–15, 84–100; United Nations Declaration on the Rights of Indigenous People (UNDRIP) 56–58; virtue signaling 28; visit to China 132; visit to India 6, 16, 17

Trudeau, P. 14, 16, 27–28, 120
Trump, D.: and l'Accord de libre-échange nord-américain (ALENA) 122; branding of 43; on bureaucracy 100; and China 136; impact of 132, 134; Trudeau and 5, 15, 16, 17, 58, 137; use of social media 87
Truth and Reconciliation Commission 47, 50, 55, 56, 57

Ukraine 15, 28, 32
"Understanding Canada" program 3
UNDRIP (United Nations Declaration on the Rights of Indigenous People) 47, 50, 54–58, 138
UNESCO (United Nations Economic and Social Council), Working Group on Indigenous Populations 55
United Kingdom 21, 109, 134
United Nations 15, 23, **70**, 71, 120, 121, 131; Declaration 1942 50
United Nations Commission on Human Rights 55
United Nations Commission on the Continental Shelf 70–71
United Nations Declaration on the Rights of Indigenous Peoples *see* UNDRIP
United Nations Economic and Social Council *see* UNESCO
United Nations Mission in Mali *see* MINUSMA
United Nations Permanent Forum on Indigenous Issues 57
United Nations Security Council 4, 20, 42, 122
United States: and the Arctic 66, 69, 70–71; and China 134; civil rights movement 50; Indigenous issues 49; Mulroney and 120; and North West Passage (NWP) 71, 72; relationship with 42, 129; United Nations Declaration on the Rights of Indigenous Peoples (UNDRIP) 55

"United States–Canada Joint Arctic Leaders' Statement" 53–54
United States Coast Guard Cutters *see* USCGC
University of Ottawa 120
USCGC (United States Coast Guard Cutters) 72, 75

value-signalling 40
Vancouver Olympics 59
Vander Zaag, R. 26
Victoria Island 57
Vinding, D. 50
virtue signaling 28
*Vogue* 14, 58
voter targetting 15, 20, 23, 41–43, 135

Watt, C. 51
Watt-Cloutier, S. 51
WeChat 111
"weibo diplomacy" 111–117
Wells, P. 4
Western Canada 22, 26, 27
White, G. 77
WID *see* Women in Development
Willis, M. 53
Wilson-Raybould, J. 57–58
Winter Olympics 2010 109
women: in development 23–25; empowerment of 6, 24; humanitarian aid and 29; voter targeting 23; *see also* feminism; FIAP (Feminist International Assistance Policy); gender equality
Women in Development (WID) 41
World Conference Against Racism, Durban 49
World Economic Forum Summit, Davos 16, 109

Yemen 5